WOMEN
ON A
MISSION

WOMEN
ON A
MISSION

The role of women in the church
from Bible times up to and including
a history of
the Lutheran Women's Missionary League
during its first twenty-five years

RUTH FRITZ MEYER

Dedicated to Mrs. Oscar E. Feucht
for twenty years of faithful service to
the Lutheran Women's Missionary League

Contents

2 67 87

Foreword

ON JULY 7 AND 8, 1942, at St. Stephen's Lutheran Church, Chicago, Ill., the Lutheran Women's Missionary League came into being.

Several *Facts and Figures* booklets recording the history and growth of the League were published at intervals of about 5 years. Another such booklet would normally have appeared in 1965. But since the 25th anniversary of the formation of the League would occur in 1967, the Executive Committee decided not to publish another *Facts and Figures* but instead to have a detailed 25-year history of the organization prepared.

Mrs. Ruth Fritz Meyer, wife of Rev. Adolph R. Meyer, Warrensburg, Mo., was commissioned to do the work. Undergirded by extensive research, Mrs. Meyer's history is an unusually solid achievement. Included in her presentation is a background chapter on the attitudes of the Lutheran Church toward women's church activities, particularly on the factors that influenced these attitudes. There is also a chapter each on women's work in other denominations and in other Lutheran church bodies. These chapters precede the seven that tell of the preliminary attempts to organize, the eventual success in forming an organization, and the historical development up to the present time. The appendix offers several tables of "facts and figures" of both international and District historical interest.

Therefore, in observance of the silver anniversary of the founding of this fine organization, I as President am happy to present this book.

The history of the past can be a persuasive teacher for those who work in the present. Our fervent hope and prayer is that those who read this book will be inspired by the untiring efforts of those who have worked in the past and will thus be led to do even greater work for our Lord in the future.

EULA I. HANKEL, *President*

Preface

TO HAVE BEEN CHOSEN by the Executive Committee of the Lutheran Women's Missionary League from its membership of over 200,000 to write this volume as part of its 25th-anniversary is an honor undeserved by the author. The assignment was accepted with gratitude and executed with humility.

The pressure of time and the limitations of space had to be reckoned with constantly and are responsible for the exclusion of some material which would have proven informative as well as interesting. The role of women in the church from Bible times, its development through the centuries, including the foundations laid in The Lutheran Church — Missouri Synod for a century prior to the organization of the Lutheran Women's Missionary League, all contributed to making the present position of women in the church possible. Without them the picture is incomplete. Their inclusion therefore was deemed necessary to achieve a better understanding of the history of the League.

The fact that a history of the Lutheran Women's Missionary League and its predecessor organizations had not been written in detail previously necessitated a great deal of probing. We therefore acknowledge with gratitude the assistance given by numerous individuals. Our special thanks go to Mrs. J. H. Deckman, Mrs. Henry Heitner, Mrs. W. A. Maier, Mrs. L. Meyer, Mrs. R. H. C. Meyer, and Mrs. Albert Schulz for making available materials which would otherwise have been inaccessible.

In addition, we are grateful to those who read the manuscript either in part or in its entirety and offered valuable suggestions for its improvement. They include Mrs. F. A. Baepler, Miss Marie Ehle, Dr. O. E. Feucht, Mrs. M. Franzmann, Mrs. Arthur Greenwood, Miss Marie Louise Gebhardt, Mrs. Gilbert Hankel, Mrs. Walter N. Hoppe, Mrs. Roy Jorgensen, Mrs. R. H. C. Meyer, Mrs. W. C. Nieman, Mrs. Arthur Preisinger, Miss Ruby Rutkowsky, Mrs. A. E. Swanson, Mrs. Jack Taege, and Mrs. Henry Tuchenhagen.

We are also indebted to Rev. Luther Poellot for his assistance in translating some of the German source materials for us. Dr. Walter C. Birkner, Rev. Walter Gerken, Mrs. R. C. Jahn, and Mrs. Frederick Schuermann also supplied important information.

The section dealing with women's organizations in other denominations and other Lutheran synods was enhanced by the assistance given by the following: Miss Margaret Mealey, executive director of the National Council of Catholic Women, from whose manuscript history of the NCCW we quoted extensively; also Mrs. Paul Reid, Dr. Dorothy E. Haas, Miss Dorothy Marple, Miss Margery Nelson, Mrs. George Ammon, Mrs. Richard Innes, Mrs. Albert Hawn, Mrs. Clyde Miller, Mrs. Harry Wilkey, Rev. Robert Wiederaenders, and Rev. Joel Lundeen.

The cooperation of former District LWML presidents as well as past officers and committee members of the international LWML, also Counselors, both past and present, is likewise acknowledged. We are indebted further to Mrs. O. E. Feucht, Mrs. William Eisenhauer, and Mrs. Paul Hedden in the headquarters office of the LWML, whose cooperation in supplying a great deal of material was vital. Mrs. Feucht also assisted with the final typing of the manuscript and compiled the Appendix.

The cover design is the work of Mr. Frederic N. Feucht.

A special debt of gratitude is owed Rev. August R. Suelflow, Director of Concordia Historical Institute, who not only spent many hours reading the manuscript but also gave generously of his time in making suggestions for its improvement. The staff of Concordia Historical Institute is also to be commended for its cooperation and assistance. Miss Sandy Turner deserves special mention, as do also Mrs. Herbert Dorn, Steve Carter, and Merle Kitzmann.

Finally, I am deeply indebted to my husband, Rev. Adolph R. Meyer, who, in addition to reading the manuscript, permitted me, for the sake of the Kingdom, to be away from home for 7 months so that the manuscript could be completed and the book ready in time for the 25th-anniversary convention of the LWML.

We hope this volume will not only preserve the record of the past but also help in a small way to light the path for the future.

February 1967   RUTH F. MEYER

I
Woman's Role in the Church

Nazis Report Capturing Key Rail City Beyond Don,[1] **British, Rommel Spar in Egypt,**[2] **Three Enemy Ships Sunk in Aleutians** [3] — these were the headlines early in July 1942 that gave an index to conditions of worldwide interest. On the home front the newspapers reported the loss of 500,000 Federal Aid or Depression Jobs as a result of the abolition of the Civilian Conservation Corps (CCC). They also reported a sharp curtailment in the Works Progress Administration (WPA) and the National Youth Administration (NYA).[4] These depression-born Federal agencies had cost the government more than 17 million dollars. Nevertheless, "the rising boom of defense and war production already has witnessed the eclipse of the Public Works Administration, which during the depression lent and granted more than six billion dollars to create jobs." [5]

The same issue of the St. Louis *Post-Dispatch* carried a review of the book *Arms and the People,* by Alden Stevens, a contributor to leading periodicals. Stevens had spent over a year traveling around the country to see firsthand what effect the war effort had on the country. The reviewer, Selma G. Kallis, says: "It is by now only too obvious that the war emergency has entered the lives of all of us. Although to many it still means little more than rubber shortage and sugar rationing, the lives of millions of others, both in and out of the armed services, have been revolutionized." [6] Stevens observed the building up of America's first large peacetime army, the building of the necessary camps and factories to implement the war effort, and saw the country become "not only the arsenal of democracy, but its granary. It is the greatest boom this country has ever known." [7]

By contrast, at the same time, on July 7 and 8, 1942, a small group of women met in St. Stephen's Lutheran Church on Chicago's south side to witness the culmination of a "war" effort they had been waging for many years. Their struggle was carried on more quietly (and more cheaply) than the great World War II which was ravaging large areas of the world. Their purpose was development rather than destruction, their strategy perhaps more subtle, but their leaders were equally determined to "win the war." This gathering marked the organization of a national federation of women of The Evangelical Lutheran Synod of Missouri, Ohio, and Other States (which later changed its name to The Lutheran Church — Missouri Synod). Many of the women present at that historic meeting had hoped and worked and prayed for this day for many, many years. Details of the organization meeting and the steps which led to it will be treated subsequently. Suffice it now to say that the Lutheran Women's Missionary League, which was organized on those eventful days in Chicago in 1942, was the result of the changing role of women in society through the centuries. This in turn brought about a reevaluation by the church of the practical application of its doctrine to the role of women in the church.

Women in the Bible

That women have a role in the kingdom of God is clear; Scripture itself speaks of the various roles played by many women throughout both Old and New Testaments. In the course of time, however, women's role became beclouded, and even today there is disagreement among churchmen of all faiths as to just what the role of women ought to be. There have been those in the past, as well as the present, who have been convinced that women should play a very limited role in the work of the Kingdom, restricted largely to the influence that they exert in the church through the home. They will cite various Scripture passages to prove their argument. On the other hand, there are also those who hold that because Paul says, "There is neither Jew nor Greek, there is neither bond nor free, there is neither male nor female; for ye are all one in Christ Jesus" (Gal. 3:28), there should be no distinction between what men and women are permitted (or commanded) to do in the church.

While it is not the purpose of this writer to attempt an evaluation of the theological issues involved in the role of women in the
church, we believe it will be helpful for a better understanding of
this role in the church today if we trace its historical development.

The role of women in the Old Testament is discussed by Rev.
Paul Lindemann, a far-sighted leader in The Lutheran Church — Mis-
souri Synod, one of the founders of the American Lutheran Publicity
Bureau and editor of the *American Lutheran* for many years. Pastor
Lindemann says, in part:

"Note the freedom and importance of woman in private and social life in ancient Israel. The early Hebrew wife and mother held
much control over her household (cf. Prov. 14, 1; 31, 10-31), and
even invited guests to her dwelling and hospitalities . . . the Shunamite
woman [invited] Elisha to her home. . . . In Job's day women attended feasts with their brothers (Job 1, 4). . . . Note the freedom
and activity of Hebrew women in public and religious affairs. Miriam
led the women of Israel in public rejoicings over the nation's deliver-
ance at the Red Sea (Ex. 15, 20. 21); Jephthah's daughter went out
publicly to congratulate her father on his triumphal return from battle
(Judges 11, 34). . . . Deborah was a judge, prophetess, and sacred
poetess in Israel, and of high distinction in public service (Judges
4, 6. 14; 5, 7). Hannah offered a remarkable prophetic song in the
house of the Lord (1 Sam. 2, 1-10); and the public office of inspired
prophetess was held in the earlier day, at least, by the four: Miriam,
Deborah, Huldah (2 Kings 22, 14), and Noadiah (Neh. 6, 14).
Women took part in the ancient worship (Ex. 15, 20. 21; 48, 8;
1 Sam. 2, 22); also in the choir (1 Chron. 25, 5. 6; Neh. 7, 67).
They were required to attend the reading of the Law (Deut. 31, 12;
Josh. 8, 35)." [8]

In the New Testament St. Luke refers to Anna, the prophetess,
who was present at the presentation of Jesus and "spake of Him to
all them that looked for redemption in Jerusalem" (Luke 2:38 b).
Luke also refers to "certain women [who] ministered unto Him [Jesus]
with their substance" (Luke 8:2-3). Of special note is the role
played by women at the time of Jesus' crucifixion, death, and resur-
rection. Matthew (27:55—28:7) describes how many women followed Jesus to the cross "beholding afar off," how they anointed the

body of Jesus when it was taken from the cross, how after His body had been anointed they sat over against the sepulcher, and finally how, early on Easter morning, they appeared at the sepulcher. They were there, in fact, when the angel of the Lord came and rolled the stone away from the door of the sepulcher and at the earthquake which accompanied his coming. Most important, they were the first to hear the good news, "He is risen!" and to receive the directive from the angel to "go, tell" the disciples, who were cowering in fear behind closed doors.

The New Testament also records the vital role played by other women in the work of the church. Romans 16 has been referred to as the "roll of honor" of Christian women. Paul speaks first of "Phoebe, our sister, which is a servant of the church which is at Cenchrea" (v. 1). The word used here for "servant" is the masculine *diakonos* (deacon). "At that time the feminine form of the noun was evidently not yet in use," says Paul E. Kretzmann, pastor, Concordia Seminary professor, and author, whose works include *The Christian Woman as a Social Worker* (1929) and *Glimpses of the Lives of Great Missionary Women* (1930). "But less than a decade later he [Paul] describes the work of such deaconesses, for 1 Tim. 3, 11 gives their qualifications: gravity, sobriety, and faithfulness." [9] Others included in this chapter of Romans are Priscilla, the wife of Aquila, to both of whom Paul refers as "my helpers in Christ Jesus, who have for my life laid down their own necks" (Rom. 16:3-4), and Mary, "who bestowed much labor on us." (Rom. 16:6)

Kretzmann points out that, while the sphere of Christian women in the apostolic church was not nearly as limited as some would have us believe, the chief activity of woman remained "as it had been of old, the home, and her chief function and glory was that of a wife and mother." [10] This, Dr. Kretzmann pointed out, is the highest role to which woman may aspire. However, if the Lord does not make it possible for her to assume this role, she can find an outlet for her ambitions in other ways which do not conflict with Scriptural principles, such as teaching (provided it does not involve lordship or leadership of men), charitable endeavors, and serving the Lord through her financial ability. In this connection Kretzmann calls attention to Dorcas, of whom Paul says: "This woman was full of good works and almsdeeds which she did" (Acts 9:36); and to Phoebe, the deaconess.[11]

"By the fourth century, deaconesses were to be found throughout the Eastern church and to a lesser degree in the West. Several pieces of canonical legislation and other records remaining attest to their existence. Just as prominent as their appearance, however, is the obvious fact of their demise, so that references to the female diaconate become obscure after a few centuries. Obviously, the place for women in the church shifted from the diaconate to the monastery — a transition which was accompanied by a change in the nature and theological understanding of the work these women did." [12]

Woman "Dethroned"

During the Dark Ages preceding the Reformation the status of woman degenerated to the point where she was considered little more than a brute who had no soul. "As early as the sixth century a council at Macon (585), fifty-nine bishops taking part, devoted its time to a discussion of this question, 'Does woman possess a soul?' Fortunately the decision allowed Christian women to remain human beings in the eyes of the clergy. . . . At an early date woman was forbidden to receive the Eucharist into her naked hand on account of her impurity (decree of the Council of Auxerre, 578) or to sing in church. To such an extent was this opposition carried that the Church of the Middle Ages did not hesitate to provide itself with the eunuchs in order to supply cathedral choirs with the necessary sopranos. One of the charges against the Huguenots was that they permitted the women to sing in church, using their voices in praise of God contrary to the express command of St. Paul, Catherine de Medici reproaching them for this great sin. The *History of Music* says that when part-singing was first introduced into the United States, great objection was made to the taking of the soprano or leading part by women, which, by virtue of his superiority, it was declared, belonged to man. Therefore woman was relegated to the bass or tenor. But nature proved too powerful, and man was eventually compelled to take bass or tenor as his part, while woman carried the soprano." [13]

While in the West the place of women in the church shifted to the monastery, in the Eastern Orthodox Church the diaconate continued to flourish. "Two compilations of church regulations provide the clearest pictures of the structure of the early diaconate. The Syrian Didascalia (a third century work) and the Apostolic Constitutions (likely somewhat later and also from the Syrian church) provide for the selection and ordination of women by the imposition of hands and the use of a prayer which is still widely used in liturgies for the consecration of deaconesses. The responsibilities of these women were largely in ministry to their own sex, anointing and preparing them for baptism (which was by immersion in the Eastern church), accompanying them before a bishop or a deacon, tending the women's entrance of the church. They ranked somehow within or very close to the clergy, but sweeping prohibitions against women also pertain to them. . . . Deaconesses also visited and nursed the sick women at their homes. They were unmarried, attached to a congregation, and entered the office at the age of forty. It is more accurate to describe the early deaconesses as assistants to the church hierarchy than as the holders of a special ministry for the practice of mercy." [14]

The female diaconate was not accepted in the West, partly because baptism was not by immersion, partly because the closeness of the deaconesses to clergy status was not tenable. As adult baptisms diminished in the East, the need for deaconesses decreased, and ultimately they disappeared entirely. The last reference to a deaconess, so far as is known, is one dated in the 12th century.[15]

Though Luther did not reestablish the female diaconate, he did favor it and paved the way for the reestablishment of such an office through the Reformation. Luther also encouraged the teaching role of women. This is evidenced by a letter which he wrote to one Else von Kanitz, inviting her to come to live with him and his family and to begin instructing young girls. He hoped, he said, that in so doing she would be an example to others.[16]

New Era for Women

From the time of the Reformation until the middle of the 19th century, however, women had as small a part in the life of the church as they had ever had. There was one exception, however, the Society of Friends (Quakers), who from their earliest beginnings not only permitted but expected the women members of their group to share every responsibility (and every danger) faced by the men.[17] However, despite the limited sphere of woman in the church during this period, it was a time in which woman exerted a tremendous influence, nevertheless, through the home, which produced a "quiet growth in spiritual power among ordinary people and it was from them and not from the accredited leaders of the Churches that new life returned to the Church and with that new life a great upsurge of activity among women." [18]

The 19th century, with its Industrial Revolution, which brought about sweeping changes through scientific discoveries and the emergence of the machine age, also brought about changes in the population. Not only did the population increase at a more rapid rate, but it shifted from the rural to the urban centers of Europe, and from Europe to both North and South America, and even to Australia. It was during this period, too, that while "the Churches . . . never succeeded in making the Gospel a living power in the lives of the new city proletariats," the church nevertheless became the center of community life.[19]

In the early part of the 19th century there are isolated instances of women workers, known as deaconesses, in several parts of Europe. Yet it was not until Pastor Theodore Fliedner (1800—64) established his hospital at Kaiserwerth, Germany, on Oct. 13, 1836, that the deaconess movement was revived. Pastor Fliedner's work, known as "The Institution of Protestant Deaconesses," had a motherhouse and hospital, a center for prisoners who were to be rehabilitated, a training school for teachers, a girls' high school and laboratory, kindergarten, orphan home, a home for female Protestant lunatics, a home for lonely and invalid women, and a preparatory school for deaconesses. In addition, it operated a farm for its own needs.[20]

Florence Nightingale received the only systematic nurse's training she had at Kaiserwerth. She had written to Dean Stanley, a close friend, in 1852, telling him of her reaction to the rebuff she had received from her own church, the Church of England. She said: "I would have given her [the church] my head, my hand, my heart. She would not have them. She did not know what to do with them. She told me to go back and do crochet in my mother's drawing-room. 'You may go to Sunday School if you like,' she said. But she gave me no training even for that. She gave me neither work to do for her, nor education for it." [21] Through Florence Nightingale the nursing profession was raised to heights it had not known before, and the work of Kaiserwerth spread to England and America.

The work of Pastor Fliedner's deaconesses was, in a measure, also responsible for the emancipation of women. "The German proverb that women's place is with *Kinder, Kirche, und Kueche* — children, church, kitchen — was altered when women were accepted in highly placed professions through the diaconate." [22]

With the upsurge and change in population during the 19th century there also came into being a broader program of the church through the printed page, as a complement to the preaching of the Gospel. This period also saw the establishment of educational facilities and a program of social welfare. "How was all this done? The Church drew upon its untapped resources, its laity and very specially upon the women among them. . . . In all Churches women's activity was a response of the Church to sweeping social change which affected all Churches alike. . . . There are, first, the great voluntary organizations of women in most of the Churches. The majority of these movements have branches in local congregations which are more or less closely connected with regional and national committees." [23] The development of the organizations of women in the church will be dealt with subsequently.

Role of Women Today

The role of women in the church, as such, today, in the year 1967, is still not crystal clear. There are still those who would have women sit back quietly and do nothing in the church, citing 1 Cor. 14:34-35: "Let your women keep silence in the churches, for it is not permitted unto them to speak; but they are commanded to be under obedience, as also saith the Law. And if they will learn anything, let them ask their husbands at home; for it is a shame for women to speak in the church." In fact, some pastors still carry out this principle to such an extent that they will not even permit the women in their congregation to sit down with a small group of other women for a study of the Bible without pastoral attendance and supervision. On the other hand, there are those who point out that "in this rapidly changing era, women have demonstrated abilities in the arts, professions, business, and government. Where do such women fit into our churches?" [24] The dogmatic recitation of this Scripture passage, they say, will not "reach them," because "many of them don't even have husbands!" [25] They raise other questions, for example: If it is permissible for women to teach children, at what point does a teen-age boy become a man? Is it permissible for a woman to teach a mixed college-age class? Another practical problem which confronts the church today in connection with the role of women is whether a woman who is a trained accountant must, of necessity, be deprived of serving as the church treasurer despite the fact that none of the male members of the church are as well qualified.[26]

Amid all the confusion which surrounds the role of woman in the church, Paul's admonition to "glorify God in your body and in your spirit" (1 Cor. 6:20) was intended also for woman and is as compelling now as ever. Both the physical and the mental faculties of woman, like those of man, ought to be employed in the Kingdom to the fullest extent for the glory of God and in the framework of the society in which she lives. In America particularly, woman today enjoys a place in the church, both in the local congregation and in the church at large, such as she has never enjoyed before. Woman's role in the church in the future, as in the past, will be determined both by the society in which she lives and by its reflection on the practice of the church. "The question for the future is how the immense achievement of the work of women for women and with women can be made fruitful in the life of the whole Church. This is not a women's question, it is a Church question." [27]

Notes

I

1. St. Louis *Post-Dispatch,* July 7, 1942, p. 1.

2. Ibid., July 8, 1942, p. 1.

3. Ibid., July 7, 1942, p. 1.

4. Ibid., July 1, 1942, p. 5 B.

5. Ibid.

6. Selma G. Kallis, "War on America's Home Front and New Problems It Creates" (a review of Alden Stevens' *Arms and the People,* New York, Harper & Brothers, 1942), St. Louis *Post-Dispatch,* July 7, 1942, p. 2 C.

7. Ibid.

8. Paul Lindemann, "The Woman in the Church," *Theological Quarterly,* XXIV (Jan. 1920), 35—36.

9. Paul E. Kretzmann, "The Position of the Christian Woman, Especially as Worker in the Church," *Concordia Theological Monthly,* I (May 1930), 357.

10. Ibid., pp. 358—359.

11. Ibid., p. 359.

12. Frederick S. Weiser, *Love's Responses: A Story of Lutheran Deaconesses in America* (Philadelphia: The Board of Publications of the United Lutheran Church in America, 1962), p. 17.

13. Lindemann, p. 38.

14. Weiser, p. 19.

15. Ibid.

16. *D. Martin Luthers Werke, Briefwechsel* 4 (Weimar: Hermann Böhlaus Nachfolger, 1933), p. 236.

17. Kathleen Bliss, *The Service and Status of Women in the Churches* (London: SCM Press Ltd., 1952), p. 22.

18. Ibid., p. 26.

19. Ibid., p. 27.

20. Weiser, p. 40.

21. Bliss, p. 14.

22. Weiser, p. 42.

23. Bliss, p. 28.

24. Letha Scanzoni, "Woman's Place: Silence or Service," *Eternity,* XVII (Feb. 1966), 16.

25. Ibid.

26. Ibid.

27. Bliss, p. 31.

II
Beginnings in Other Denominations

THE SHIFTING AND EXPANDING POPULATION which came as a result of the Industrial Revolution, and more specifically, the migration of Europeans to other continents, had a profound effect, as we have already indicated, on the role of women both in and out of the church. The characteristics which made women willing to leave the security of their homelands and face the hardships and uncertain way of life awaiting them in the New World were apparent also in their new environment, including also their church life.

Neither time nor space permits an exhaustive study of the role of women in their respective churches as these churches expanded and their programs changed to meet the challenges which confronted them. However, a brief glimpse at the development of the role of women in a few other denominations will, we believe, help to a better understanding of their role in The Lutheran Church — Missouri Synod as it sprung to life and grew. We cite the following brief account of the beginnings of women's organizations in other denominations (1) to show that in some cases women were active in the work of their respective denominations even before the founders of The Lutheran Church — Missouri Synod arrived in this country and (2) to point out that many of the efforts to organize women's groups in other denominations met with the same problems that the women who pioneered in such efforts in The Lutheran Church — Missouri Synod encountered.

New Frontiers

Mary Webb, a Baptist, together with other Baptist and Congregational women, formed the first women's missionary society in the world in Boston in 1800, known as "The Boston Female Society for Missionary Purposes." [1] A spark which it was hoped would further ignite the flame of enthusiasm for such work was the personal appeal of Luther Rice, a Baptist. Upon his return as a missionary from India he championed the cause of an organization of Baptists in America for missions, but his plea failed.[2]

In the Presbyterian Church, U. S. (the southern branch of the Presbyterian Church) "the women were engaged in missionary activities before the Church had approved Foreign Missions and were organizing *female societies* for helping ministerial students, Bible societies and missionary societies before 1817 within the bounds of our own denomination." [3]

The first missionary society for women only in the Methodist Episcopal Church (the northern branch of Methodism) was organized in 1832 as "The Female Missionary Society of Lynchburg and Auxiliary Missionary Society of the Methodist Episcopal Church." [4] "It would be a mistake," says Stella Wyatt Brummitt, "for any one to conclude that at last woman had decided to assert herself and therefore organize just for the sake of organizing. It should be rather realized that such counter forces were at work in America as compelled women who called themselves Christian to help stay the onrush of these forces.

"It is said that 'all movements which are worth while and are of permanent value to society involve the heroic, untiring and faithful service of noble, intelligent, broadminded and philanthropic men and women, who suffered much to make the public take interest and see the significance of the early beginnings.' " [5]

After the slavery question divided the Presbyterian Church into the Northern and Southern Groups in 1861, the conservative spirit seemed to grow stronger in the Southern group because "the women of the churches in the North were then not only organizing women's Boards but also collecting and disbursing their own missionary funds, independent of the sessions. There were from the very beginning a large number of conservative ministers who opposed *any organization* of women in the Presbyterian Church, U. S., fearing it would lead to usurpation of authority in the affairs of the Church and to activity 'unbecoming pious females.' " [6]

Expanding Horizons

A breakthrough in the slow but steady stream of events which was going on in various denominations in regard to women's organizations came in 1868, when the Board of Missions of the Episcopal Church asked the bishops to form auxiliaries of men and women. Though there was no immediate response, two auxiliaries ultimately resulted, one being the auxiliary which "was composed of men who represented every interest of the Board of Missions." The other auxiliary, which was authorized by the General Convention in 1871, was the Woman's Auxiliary to the Board of Missions.[7] This came about as the result of repeated urging on the part of a layman, Mr. Welsh, in behalf of the role of women. Through his friend and neighbor, Rev. J. A. Harris of St. Paul's Church, Chestnut Hill, Philadelphia, a motion was made to appoint a committee on the organized service of women as "most important in missionary work" at a meeting of the Board of Missions in 1869.[8]

In June of the following year (1870) *The Spirit of Missions* commented on "the general activity among the women of the land," citing the work of the Woman's Union Missionary Society, which had been at work for 9 years, and "urged that our women could do more, if better organized." [9] As a result, the work of organizing women's work "in aid of the Board of Missions" was entrusted to the secretaries of the Mission Board then serving, with power to act immediately.[10] In addition to the Woman's Union Missionary Society, there were already Women's Boards in the Congregational, Methodist Episcopal, Baptist, and Presbyterian Churches.[11]

Things were happening in the Methodist Church at about the same time which were to have a profound effect on the program of women's work in that denomination. Mrs. Jennie C. Hartzell went to New Orleans in 1870 as the bride of a young pastor who was later to become a world figure. Mrs. Hartzell was soon found going from door to door on errands of mercy among the Negroes. Despite the fact that in time she became a mother and her social duties were numerous, she always found time to do good among the black people. "This 'work' was a tireless visiting, without a plan, collecting and disbursing money given for the purpose, and a 'mission school started and taught by white missionaries at Wesley Chapel in the winter of

1877—78.' " Mrs. Hartzell says of this understaking, "I became responsible for the regular salaries and for the rent and furnishings of the house." [12]

Yellow fever drove Mrs. Hartzell and her children north, but letters from Negroes in Louisiana followed her, assuring her of their prayers in her behalf that she might be able to bring back missionaries and teachers for their daughters. Mrs. Hartzell did take such help back with her.[13]

When the tremendous load Mrs. Hartzell carried became too much for her, she appealed to the General Conference for help. The rush of business, however, prevented her request from being considered. Nevertheless, through the efforts of Drs. A. B. Leonard and J. N. Irwin a meeting was arranged for June 8, 1880.[14]

"The meeting was held, and the epoch-making motion 'to form a Woman's Home Missionary Society with recommendation for special attention to the Southern field' prevailed." [15] Thus was born the organization which was to serve so well in the future. (The Women's *Foreign* Missionary Society had been organized in 1870.) [16]

The first president of the Woman's Home Missionary Society was none other than Mrs. Rutherford B. Hayes, wife of the President of the United States.[17]

Progress was noted in the Baptist Church during this time, too. A plan was suggested in 1877 to inaugurate a woman's society in every church. The Southern Baptist Convention viewed with trepidation this movement for action on the part of women. A. T. Spalding, chairman of the Committee on Woman's Work for the Foreign Mission Board, expressed this concern. However, he added: "We have yet been slow to recognize and employ their power. And now, in no mere spirit of gallantry, but with abiding gratitude to God, we would record our appreciative testimony to the efficiency, fidelity and success of those noble women who have labored with us in the gospel. . . . The time may be at hand when it will be advisable that they shall appoint a Central Committee to combine their efforts, to stimulate the work, and to give permanent record to their success." [18] This, it seems, was the first vague suggestion to coordinate the women's work throughout the entire country.

Just a few years later a successful meeting in Georgia was reported which represented the first open meeting of women. This is of particular significance in view of the fact that it was in that state that reports of women's work sent to the state convention had been ignored; in fact the Committee on Women's Work had asked to be discharged without reporting, "fearing to tread on ground in such dispute." [19]

This did not mean, however, that opposition did not exist elsewhere. "Pastors in Kentucky 'sat in stony silence' when asked for names of women in their churches who would be interested in organizing. The breakthrough to women in that state can be attributed to the cooperation of postmasters who supplied names." [20]

The seed which had been sown was slowly springing to life, and little by little, women all over the South were becoming more and more interested in a general organization. At a meeting in Baltimore in 1884 another step in the direction of such an organization was effected when it was voted "that societies here represented make the Union meeting permanent, to meet annually during the sessions of the Southern Baptist Convention, the Central Committee of the state in which the Convention is held having charge of the meeting in that year." [21]

In the Episcopal Church the subject of the general organization of the Auxiliary was presented in a report to the Board of Missions by the Board of Managers in 1886. It asked that the Board recommend the adoption of a constitution for the Auxiliary, "accurately defining the relations between itself and this Board, mapping out with tolerable precision the field of labor proper to such an organization, and providing for the annual and triennial election of officers." It recommended further that "should the Auxiliary at this time desire to organize itself in the manner indicated in the previous resolution, this Board will gladly do anything in its power to facilitate the process." [22]

These resolutions were presented to the Board of Missions, together with reports from the secretary and honorary secretary of the Woman's Auxiliary. The board then presented a detailed plan calling for the "training and systematized service of women in the work of the Church." [23] After it had heard various suggestions, the Board of Missions adopted a resolution which read as follows:

"Whereas, There appears to be no evidence at present of a general desire on the part of the various branches of the Woman's Auxiliary for any further organization of their work, therefore

"Resolved, That this Board, without considering the question of organization, desires to place on record its entire approval of the purposes of the Woman's Auxiliaries, not only to assist the Board in making its regular appropriations, but also to aid all missionary work of the Church, in any direction and in any way that may be recommended by this Board or endorsed by the several Bishops." [24]

The women of the Northern Presbyterian group did not, it seems, organize immediately after the division. Three Women's Foreign Missionary Societies organized in Philadelphia in 1870, and a few years later (1878) the "Woman's Mission Executive Committee" was organized. It was not until 10 years later (1888), however, that the "Women's General Missionary Society of the United Presbyterian Church of North America" got its charter.[25]

Hallie Paxson Winsborough, in her book *Yesteryears,* bemoans the fact that in 1911 "the Presbyterian Church, U. S. [the Southern branch] was the only evangelical denomination in America with no department of woman's work; with no systematic promotion of the missionary program of the Church among the women." [26] However, the following year (1912), despite the prejudices which prevailed, "The Woman's Auxiliary of the Presbyterian Church, U. S." was organized at Montreat, N. C.[27]

"Here at Montreat was launched our plan of work for the women of our Church. With strong and influential opposition on one side; with the Synodical presidents and most of the Presbyterial presidents in its favor, as well as many leading ministers of the Church; with no financial backing except what might be gathered from the then existing societies in the Church; and guided by officials inexperienced in such service — the new organization began its work, confident of ultimate success." [28]

When the Assemblies of the three branches of Presbyterianism met in Atlanta in 1913 for the purpose of promoting unity, the Women's Missionary Board of the United Presbyterian Church (one of the northern bodies) expressed its alarm lest a real organic union be effected. "A telegram was sent . . . to the Moderator of the United Presbyterian Assembly, asking that they not consider union with the Southern Presbyterian Church because of the *auxiliary* type of *organization* the *women of that Church had adopted — not an independent Board!*

"Yet, in spite of this criticism from our Presbyterian sisters of the North because of our *auxiliary character* and our *lack of authority* in our own denomination, this same Auxiliary was still receiving *drastic criticism* and *outspoken opposition* because of *our liberal tendencies* and the fear of our violation of *the official ruling of our denomination in regard to woman's place in the Church.* Truly, we seemed destined for criticism from both the liberals and the conservatives." [29]

The rigid control which the church maintained over the women, despite their accomplishments, is evidenced by the fact that it was not until 1928 that the Secretary of Woman's Work was permitted to make her own report to the Assembly in Atlanta.[30]

Purposes

Without exception, the organizations in other denominations which we have discussed have been "missionary" in purpose. We have already indicated that the Woman's Home Missionary Society of the Methodist Church came into being as the result of a specific need: to assist with the work among the Negroes in the South. The purposes of some of the other denominational groups were not so clearly defined at the beginning, but, without exception, they soon found many avenues of service open to them, and in time their programs were enlarged to include "missionary" work in its all-inclusive meaning.

Some aspects of the various groups seem to be shared by virtually all of them. For example: "The missionary imperative which brought Woman's Missionary Union [Baptist] into existence has not changed," says Alma Hunt. "Methods may change. Terminology appropriate to the twentieth century must be used to speak to the modern day. But these changes do not touch the eternal New Testament message or alter the basic purpose of Woman's Missionary Union." [31]

The motivation for the work of the United Presbyterian Women, which is the result of mergers of previous groups, is expressed in its motto: "The task ahead of us is never as great as the Power behind us." [32] This task is likewise missionary.

The Woman's Auxiliary of the Episcopal Church became the Episcopal Church Women in 1958, but its missionary purpose has not changed.

The present organization in the Methodist Church, The Woman's Society of Christian Service and the Wesleyan Service Guild, also the outgrowth of mergers, celebrated its 25th anniversary recently. In announcing the observance of this anniversary, a call to Methodist women was issued which said in part:

"Along with new revelations in science have come new involvements in human relations.

"These changes call for a new kind of commitment to God's mission in His world: new understanding of new needs, new plans for new programs and new support for newly trained personnel. Every Christian is called to creative witness and enlarged service through all channels of church and society." [33]

We record briefly a few aspects of the programs of the women's groups in other denominations early in their history which have a counterpart in the program of the Lutheran Women's Missionary League.

Mites

The Woman's Mission to Woman (Baptist) sent out its first circular letter in 1871 encouraging women to raise funds for missions through a mite box in each home, to which all the members of the family were urged to contribute. "It was a small garnet-colored paper box with an opening in its top and with the words 'Woman's Mission to Woman' in shining gold letters on the side." [34]

The idea of the mite box was introduced to the Foreign Mission Board as a means of increasing gifts for the work of the Board by a Mrs. Graves. "The *Foreign Mission Journal,* March, 1878, published the plan for using the boxes: 'we would beg those who have these boxes to use them regularly, and deposit according to constitution commonly adopted by our Mite Box Societies — two cents per family every Lord's day, and not wait until the end of the month or quarter and then deposit the whole amount. The training is as valuable as money.' " [35]

Almost from the beginning of the Woman's Home Missionary Society of the Methodist Episcopal Church the mite box has not only been used but has "been a definite power in the organized work." From a beginning of $247 collected in mite boxes in 1888, the amount climbed to $198,608 by 1929, just before the 50th anniversary of the organization.[36]

Long before either of the above, however, there were at the beginning of the 19th century various "cent" or "mite" societies that raised money for missions. One of the earliest was in Boston in the early 1800s and was concerned particularly with work among the Indians, who were considered "foreign" missions.[37]

The object of the Female Missionary Society of Lynchburg and Auxiliary Missionary Society of the Methodist Episcopal Church is set forth in the preamble as follows:

"Being deeply sensible of the unmerited goodness of our Heavenly Father in having cast our lots in a land of light and liberty, having bestowed upon us the invaluable privileges of the gospel, we deem it our duty to put our mites into the treasury of the Lord to aid in sending the good news of salvation to those who know not a Savior." [38]

Mite boxes have not been the sole source of funds for missionary purposes, however. Earlier we referred to the fact that in the northern branch of the Presbyterian Church women were "collecting and disbursing their own missionary funds, independent of the sessions," about 1861.[39] If not then, at least later, they adopted the practice of having a United Offering, which is still carried out today.

Literature Program

At a time when there were no means of mass communication such as radio and television and even the printed page was not what it is today, women were alert to the important role which literature of one sort or another could play in promoting their cause.

The first publication of the Methodist women's group, *Woman's Home Missions,* began Nov. 23, 1884, as an 8-page monthly with a subscription price of 25 cents a year. The following year it was enlarged to 16 pages and in 1897 to 20 pages, with the subscription price increasing to 35 cents.[40]

The Department of Literature was formed in 1917, followed by the issuance of the first mission study book and later by study courses, leaflets with collateral reading, and various other leaflets.[41]

In 1922 General Publications was moved from New York to Cincinnati, at which time its duties were placed in the hands of the Editor and Publisher, putting all the Society's publications under the control of these officers.[42]

The first Prayer Card was distributed by the Baptist Mission Rooms in 1887 (a venture of the Baltimore, Md., Baptist women).[43]

At the request of the Executive Committee in May 1906, the Maryland Literature Department provided funds to establish a Literature Department as part of the Woman's Missionary Union (Baptist). July 1, 1906, was set as the date on which it would be officially opened for business.[44]

Hospice Work

The Methodist women were offered a resolution as part of the Annual Report, 1884—85, asking that careful consideration be given to supplying a missionary for Castle Garden, the port of New York, where all immigrants arrived. The result was not only the beginning of such work in New York, with the opening of a home there in 1891, but similar homes on the Pacific Coast, in Philadelphia, and in Boston.[45]

Catholic Women

The story of the role of women in other denominations would not be complete without inclusion of the work which Catholic women are doing. Though it came into existence much later than the foregoing groups, the National Council of Catholic Women has developed a program which is more far-reaching than any of the others. Since the structure of the Catholic Church is quite different than that which prevails in most Protestant churches, its program is also different. We are grateful to Miss Margaret Mealey, executive director of the National Council of Catholic Women, for supplying us with the following information about this group.

"The National Council of Catholic Women (NCCW) is a federation of Catholic organizations of women throughout the United States and on American military bases overseas. It is composed of more than 14,000 national, state, diocesan and parish organizations which number about 10 million women in their combined membership. An individual woman cannot be a member of the NCCW directly; she is a part of the federation by virtue of her membership in an organization affiliated with it.

"NCCW was established in 1920 by the bishops of the United States as an integral part of the National Catholic Welfare Conference (NCWC). The Conference had been organized the year before as a voluntary union of American bishops, whose purpose was to insure that the Catholic Church in the United States might always be involved and concerned with the life of the nation as a whole. To achieve this purpose, NCWC established various departments and bureaus. One of these was the Department of Lay Organizations, composed of two branches: the National Council of Catholic Women; and the National Council of Catholic Men. Other departments such as Education, Press, Immigration, Social Action, and Youth provide information and material in specialized areas for the use of NCWC and for the Councils of men and women. This material is channeled to Catholic groups, by NCCW and NCCM, affiliated in the federations. These above federations frequently represent the laity in national and international movements and conferences.

"The stated purpose of the National Council of Catholic Women, a service organization, is: (1) to unite Catholic organizations of women in purpose, direction, and action in religious, social, educational and economic fields; (2) to channel information from NCCW departments and bureaus to all affiliated organizations; (3) to assist these affiliates through publications, field services, correspondence, leadership training institutes, and biennial conventions; and (4) to provide national and international voice for Catholic women in the United States.

"Nationally, the NCCW encourages member organizations to greater activity in civic and community activities and encourages their work with other organizations of similar purposes. NCCW is one of four member organizations of Women in Community Service, an inter-faith, inter-racial group incorporated to assist in the Job Corps phase of the War on Poverty.

"On the international level, NCCW operates as one of the 105 affiliates of the World Union of Catholic Women's Organizations (WUCWO). Founded in 1911, WUCWO, like NCCW, is a federation and unites women's organizations in all parts of the world — sixty countries on five continents. Its purpose is to study the religious, family, cultural, social and civic problems of the world; to coordinate the contributions of Catholic women in international life; and to represent them at movements and conferences of international concern. Through WUCWO, the National Council of Catholic Women reaches the ever broadening horizons of today's world and provides a medium of exchange between American Catholic women and Catholic women throughout the world.

"NCCW is governed by a board of directors elected by delegates from the affiliated organizations. . . . The headquarters offices of NCCW are located in Washington, D. C., where a professional staff under the direction of an executive director (Margaret Mealey), responsible to the president, coordinates and directs the programming and planning of the affiliates' activities.

"Standing midway between the national office and the local or parish groups, are the archdiocesan or diocesan councils (A/DCCW). They serve the local organizations directly, channeling down the information and direction from the national headquarters. . . .

"Various means have been developed to pursue the stated objectives of NCCW. One is a system of committees, at present numbering eighteen, in which national committees work with their counterparts on the archdiocesan and diocesan level. . . . Each committee has both national and diocesan chairmen who cooperate with the staff at national headquarters in disseminating information and instruction, training and education.

"Other services offered by the national office include field services, film strips, the publication of pamphlets, brochures, and handbooks outlining areas of action and suggesting ways and means of organizing and following through in these areas. Ten times yearly the national office publishes WORD, a magazine offering in-depth coverage of all that the affiliates should know of plans, programs, and achievement. Each officer and chairman in the entire national structure receives a subscription of WORD by virtue of her office.

"When the National Council of Catholic Women was brought into existence in 1920, it was established by the American bishops to give Catholic women of the country a common voice and an instrument for united action; it projected an extended role for Catholic women in parish, local community, national and international affairs. Two hundred sixty-four organizations joined the new federation.

.   .   .   .

"Over the years the federation grew in scope and purpose until it is now one of the major organizations of the country. Its function as contained in its Charter is 'that of uniting in purpose, act and direction the Catholic women of the United States in organized efforts, in all useful fields of educational, social, religious and economic work, for the betterment and happiness of the people.' " [46]

Summary

Since that first women's missionary society was organized by Mary Webb in 1800, many changes have taken place: in the organization themselves; in the churches, through division in some cases, but more frequently through mergers; and in the world in which both organizations and church bodies exist. Despite all this, the women of all the denominations, Protestant and Catholic alike, continue to represent the church in mission, the all-inclusive mission of serving their fellowman through the preaching of the Gospel and the practical application of that Gospel.

Notes

II

1. Alma Hunt, *History of Woman's Missionary Union* (Nashville: Convention Press, 1964), p. viii.

2. Ibid.

3. Hallie Paxson Winsborough, *Yesteryears* (Atlanta: Committee on Woman's Work, Presbyterian Church, U. S., 1937), p. 59.

4. Stella Wyatt Brummitt, *Looking Backward – Thinking Forward* (Cincinnati, 1930), p. 11.

5. Ibid.

6. Winsborough, p. 59.

7. Julia C. Emery, *A Century of Endeavor* (New York: Church Missions House, 1921), p. 183.

8. Ibid., p. 184.

9. Ibid., p. 185.

10. Ibid.

11. Ibid.

12. Brummitt, p. 16.

13. Ibid., p. 17.

14. Ibid.

15. Ibid., p. 18.

16. Ibid., p. 11.

17. Ibid., p. 18.

18. Hunt, p. 16.

19. Ibid., p. 20.

20. Ibid.

21. Ibid.

22. Emery, p. 211.

23. Ibid.

24. Ibid., p. 212.

25. *United Presbyterian Women* (Handbook), UPW Library, No. 1, p. 7.

26. Winsborough, p. 20.

27. Ibid., pp. 42—46.

28. Ibid., p. 46.

29. Ibid., p. 54.

30. Ibid., pp. 72—73.

31. Hunt, p. 190.

32. *United Presbyterian Women,* p. 8.

33. *The Methodist Woman,* XXV (Jan. 1964), center spread.

34. Hunt, p. 12.

35. Ibid., p. 13.

36. Brummitt, p. 241.

37. Kathleen Bliss, *The Service and Status of Women in the Churches* (London: SCM Press Ltd., 1952), p. 34.

38. Brummitt, p. 11.

39. Winsborough, p. 59.

40. Brummitt, p. 32.

41. Ibid., p. 34.

42. Ibid., p. 35.

43. Hunt, p. 47.

44. Ibid., pp. 48—49.

45. Brummitt, pp. 86, 88—90, 92—93.

46. Margaret Mealey, "History and Purpose of the National Council of Catholic Women," unprinted manuscript, pp. 1—4.

III
Lutheran Women at Work

Beginnings

THE INTEREST OF CHRISTIAN WOMEN in using their God-given talents
in the service of the Kingdom is not, of course, limited to women of
other denominations. Lutheran women, too, have played a role in
the church, some for a much longer period of time than others, some
to a greater extent than others, but in all branches of Lutheranism
women have contributed to the total picture of the work of women
in the Kingdom. Again, it will be possible to give only a brief summary of women's organizations in other Lutheran bodies, but we
cite them as a prelude to the development of the role of women in
The Lutheran Church — Missouri Synod. We shall likewise limit
ourselves to groups affiliated with the Lutheran Church in America
and the American Lutheran Church (and their antecedents), which
together with The Lutheran Church — Missouri Synod comprise the
vast majority of Lutherans in this country.

One of the earliest, if not the earliest, accounts of the role of
women in the Lutheran Church is about a group which ultimately
became a part of the United Lutheran Church, the largest of the member bodies of the present Lutheran Church in America. In 1837,
some 40 years before any general organization of women was formed,
the foundations for such an organization were laid.

"Walter Gunn, of Carlisle, Pennsylvania, had made a solemn
promise that if the Lord would open the way, he would go out to
preach the gospel to the heathen. His pastor, knowing that Mr. Gunn

had no funds for an education, made his hopes known to the Hartwick Synod which met at Cobleskill, New York that year" [1837].[1] It was not the Synod which took action, however. The wives of some of the pastors spent an afternoon in the home of one Mrs. Shaffer, the wife of Colonel Shaffer. "After a period of prayer, one of the number proposed that they educate Mr. Gunn for the work of a missionary. The proposition met with unanimous approval and work was begun immediately. Each pledged herself a definite sum and determined upon her return home to endeavor to interest others of her congregation in the objective. The spirit of this meeting, out of which grew the 'Female Association of Hartwick Synod for the Education of Foreign Missionaries,' proved the leaven which extended its influence beyond the Hartwick Synod into other parts of the church." [2]

Missionary Gunn was not only the first missionary sent out by this particular branch of Lutheranism (June 18, 1844), but he was supported by the women's association during his entire service. The association continued until about 1910.[3]

The Movement Spreads

The first written record of organized women's work in the Evangelical Lutheran Church, a part of the present American Lutheran Church, "comes to us from Ascension Lutheran Church in Milwaukee, Wis. They worked for funds to build a church long before the church became a reality." [4] Prior to this, there had been a sewing circle in Decorah, Iowa, begun in 1862, its function being to sew and sell articles to the stores to help pay the debt on the new college there.[5]

An exception to the usual pattern of women's work was the case of the Aid at St. Ansgar, Iowa, whose work is described as follows:

"These women worked for missions and as we read, we learn what real mission work can be like. They bought two boys out of slavery in the Schreuder Mission in Madagascar in the year 1862. A sum of money was sent annually to keep them in school. One became an ordained minister, doing home mission work, the other became an instructor in the Lutheran Mission School." [6]

A little later work was initiated by Mrs. Diderikke Brandt, the wife of Pastor Nils Brandt, who went to Luther College at Decorah, Iowa, as a teacher in 1865. Mrs. Brandt served as "mother" to the students, inviting them into her home, teaching them the niceties expected of theological students, etc. She was assisted by women of the congregation who organized and met regularly in the homes of the members, mending clothes for students. "For years Mrs. Brandt was the only one to sew, launder and set the fluted ministers' collars. The charge for ironing a collar, which took about two hours, was fifty cents." [7]

In two other groups which form a part of the present American Lutheran Church, pastors' and professors' wives also played an important role. In the one case, the pastors' and professors' wives organized a society which met simultaneously with the annual meeting of their Synod. Later they adopted the name "Mission Dove" for the organization and enlarged the sphere of their activity and also their membership. "Turning their interest to China, this organization made possible a Bible School for Women. At a cost of $6000 they built and equipped a home in St. Paul for missionaries on furlough in this country. They financed a hospital for the students at The Red Wing Seminary, and aided in financing one at Jewell, Iowa." [8]

In the other case, the pastors' wives centered their activities around Luther College at the beginning and later enlarged their interest to include Christian education and mission work.[9]

United Lutheran Church

Though the association which sponsored Missionary Gunn was organized early in the 19th century, it was not until much later that a general organization of women became a reality in the United Lutheran Church. In 1875, at a meeting of the Synod, a letter was read from Rev. W. E. Parson, at that time a professor at the University of Tokyo, Japan. He said that he had observed how helpful women's organizations were in other denominations in promoting the work in Japan, and he inquired why there could not be such an organization of Lutheran women. "The matter was discussed and commended in the *Lutheran Observer* a few weeks later, but no immediate action was taken." [10] Later that year three pastors who were motivated by what they heard and read about the work of other denominations "became the promoters of an organization for women in the Iowa Synod" (of the United Lutheran Church).[11]

A similar movement was taking place almost simultaneously in Ohio. Mrs. J. H. W. Stuckenberg, whose husband was on the Wittenberg College faculty at Springfield, was interested in a women's missionary society but had been unable to find any literature on missions. She learned from regular church papers about two young women who had offered their services as missionaries but had been turned down because of lack of funds.[12]

Mrs. Stuckenberg was sufficiently aroused by the inability to send these two women into the mission field because of a lack of "a little systematic and united effort" that she on her own initiative visited churches in the East and Middle West to inform and enthuse the people, especially the women, for the cause of missions. As a result, when the general church body, through a committee headed by Dr. Stuckenberg, called a meeting in Canton, Ohio, in June 1879 for the purpose of organizing a society, the number who responded to the invitation totaled 116.[13]

The resolution passed at this meeting read as follows:

"Resolved, that we hail the organization of this General Woman's Home and Foreign Missionary Society of the General Synod as the dawning of a new era in the history of women's work in the Lutheran Church, and will not rest until there is an auxiliary society in every congregation connected with the General Synod." [14]

In the Scandinavian segment of the present Lutheran Church in America there is a record of the idea of organizing a Woman's Home and Foreign Missionary Society originating during the convention of that particular church body in June 1891 at Chisago Lake, Minn., when the subject was discussed by some of the women who were present. They were motivated by what they saw and heard about the work the women in other denominations and other Lutheran groups were doing. As a result they decided to take the initiative in the matter of organizing such a society when the next synodical convention took place.[15]

The following year, 1892, in June, 50 women from various parts of the synod met during the synodical convention at the home of Dr. and Mrs. C. A. Swenson in Lindsborg, Kans., and organized a missionary society.[16] A resolution was drawn up recommending the support of the pastors and congregations for this new venture. "After the aim and purpose of the Society had been made clear the Synod accepted the resolution and thereby sanctioned the movement." [17]

The resolution of the synod recognized that "missions is the greatest and most important activity of the Church of Christ." It also realized that the church had an obligation to utilize all its resources for the cause of missions, also through the women of the church. It therefore gave its undivided approval to the establishment of the Evangelical Lutheran Woman's Society and encouraged its pastors and congregations to support it.[18]

"The women were deeply moved and overjoyed. With hearts aglow they gathered for a season of prayer and thanksgiving! Then they set about to make plans for their program of service. The opportunity was now theirs to apply themselves to a vital cause." [19]

At the first annual convention, held in Rock Island and Moline, Ill., in 1893, the president, Mrs. Emmy Evald, gave the first of a record-breaking series of 43 successive annual reports. Various appeals for the cause of missions were presented to the women at this convention. Among them was an appeal for a hospital for women and children in India. This met with wholehearted response on the part of the women. The president made her two daughters life members. These funds were applied to the cause, and the Hospital Fund was founded. "The Society thereby joined with other groups in the campaign for 'oppressed womanhood and childhood' in India where hospitals were for men only until Christianity entered in." [20]

Though the Woman's Home and Foreign Missionary Society of one Scandinavian segment of the Lutheran Church in America had been organized, as we have previously indicated, in 1893, and the work of this organization had progressed, it had not increased numerically to the degree that had been hoped. This was due, in large part, to the fact that, because of long distances and economic conditions, only relatively small numbers could attend the synodical conventions. Therefore in 1899, during the business sessions, it was decided to organize conference societies, or branches, through the appointed vice-presidents, six in number — one in each conference — who had been appointed at the organization meeting.[21]

Awakening in the South

In the South women began to organize congregational societies in 1885, but it was not until 1906 that three synodical societies united to form the Woman's Missionary Conference of the United Synod in the South. This was ultimately absorbed by the United Lutheran Church and is now a part of the Lutheran Church in America. In another group, the General Council, likewise a part of the present LCA, congregational groups are among the oldest societies of women, but the first conference group was organized in Allentown, Pa., in 1885. Another was organized in 1895, but it was 1911 before the Women's Missionary Society of the General Council was organized by 300 women at Lancaster, Pa. These three ultimately merged in November 1918, immediately following the organization of the United Lutheran Church in America, in New York City.[22]

The purpose of this organization has always been missionary. The constitution adopted in 1919, which was essentially the same in 1959, states the objectives as being (1) to fulfill the great commission (Matt. 28:19-20); (2) to promote and stimulate churchwide interest in missions; (3) to disseminate missionary information, promote missionary education, and provide financial assistance in the missionary operations of the church; and (4) to coordinate and unite the work of synodical societies.[23]

In addition to assistance which the organization gave to the Mission Board, it also gave assistance for many years to the boards of American Missions, Foreign Missions, Social Missions, Higher Education, Parish Education, Deaconess, and Pensions. Many special gifts were given in addition to the annual grants.[24] "Women missionaries have been recommended and supported in connection with the work of all boards, excepting the Board of Pensions. Women staff members have been provided and supported also.

"The purpose of the organization has, therefore, been churchwide, and the term 'mission' is interpreted in its all-inclusive meaning.

"The primary purpose, that of missionary education, likewise includes education with regard to all phases of Christian work in our own church and interdenominationally, as well as programs to cultivate the spiritual life individually and corporately." [25]

Ohio Synod

The idea of organizing a women's organization in the Ohio Synod, a component part of the American Lutheran Church, originated during a convention of the Men's Missionary Conference in February 1913. One of the women who was in attendance, while observing the men in action at the convention, wondered why such an organization could not become a reality for women in the church. She mentioned the idea to her husband and, after discussing it at length, it was mentioned to the resolutions committee.[26] When the resolutions were presented toward the end of the convention, one of them proposed: "That the women of our Synod be encouraged to form a Conference of their own." Though there was some opposition, the motion carried, and the Fremont Local Conference was instructed to prepare suggestions with this purpose in mind.[27]

Collection Devices

The mite box and its counterpart, the Dime Book, played a part in at least some, if not all, of the women's organizations in the various Lutheran synods. During the convention of the United Norwegian Church (subsequently merged into the present American Lutheran Church) mission boxes were given to pastors' wives to distribute as early as 1903, although permission was not granted for the women to organize until 1911.[28]

In 1917, when three Norwegian synods merged, the women met on June 12 and dissolved their separate organizations in order to form a single organization. Its goal was to unite, if possible, all women's organizations in the Norwegian Lutheran Church to promote the cause of missions.[29] At the first convention, held in June 1918, the president in her address proposed the idea that "Mission boxes should be distributed in every home within the church and a fund created for the work of missions." The motion was unanimously adopted.[30]

About the same time in the Augustana Synod, now a part of the Lutheran Church in America, the Women's Missionary Society in 1911 "sent out five thousand Dime Books [in 1911] to our members for the purpose of raising funds for the hospital in [Rajahmundry] India, as well as that of paying Dr. Betty Nilsson's salary. . . .

"In the beginning Dime Books were sent out to the members and friends of missions by members of the executive committee. In 1913 Mrs. C. A. Erickson was appointed to arrange and have charge of a card system in which record was kept of 14,000 Dime Books sent out." [31]

Women of other Lutheran bodies have not limited their contributions for the work of their women's missionary societies to the "dime books" or "mite boxes" but have supplemented these with other offerings. The use of thankoffering boxes, which came from the organizations which merged to form the United Lutheran Church in America in 1918, was not discontinued. This offering was used for home missions and was promoted by the Department Chairman of Home Missions. The chairman of the department in 1917, Mrs. George A. Schnur, wrote about it as follows:

" 'The Thank Offering box has become a fact. The Board of Home Missions provided for the cost of the boxes. They were sent last fall to all societies, literature explaining their purpose accompanying them. The contents are to be turned in at an annual Thank Offering meeting in November each year. . . .

" 'The Thank Offering box does not in any way interfere with any other mite box. It has a place distinctively its own. It is to be used only when one has *special* cause for thankfulness. It is to be opened at the Thanksgiving season, and is devoted to the Field Missionary Fund alone. It is not compulsory upon anyone, and those who have no cause for thankfulness ought not encumber themselves with one. On the contrary, if you find as did one woman that "you never knew you were thankful so often before," you will need two boxes in your home.'

.   .   .   .

"More than half of the budget of United Lutheran Church Women today [1959] is from Thank Offering." [32]

Literature

The value of the printed page was noted in Lutheranism, too, but apparently not as early as in some of the other denominations. The Women's Missionary Society of the Augustana Church (now a Lutheran Church in America affiliate), realizing the importance of promoting the cause of missions through literature, passed a resolution in 1905 to publish a small missionary paper. The first issue of the publication, *Mission Tidings,* was off the press in time for the convention the following year.[33]

In the American Lutheran Church, already prior to 1915, the Literature Committee of the Fremont District, upon request, issued "a small pamphlet containing an outline of material for monthly missionary programs. Beginning in 1916, it published Monthly Missionary Programs.[34]

In February 1921 the *Lutheran Standard* began to carry a "Women's Department" in its publication. At the beginning two pages of the first issue of every month were made available to the organization.[35]

"A literature committee was an important part of the organizational structure of each of the three groups making up the ULCA Society" (United Lutheran Church), says Nona M. Diehl in her book *U. L. C. W. Heritage and History.* "As early as 1911 there had been a joint committee on literature at work. This committee may be said to have been the forerunner of the merger. To continue this important function a literature committee of fifteen members was provided by the Constitution. In 1934 this was designated as the Education Department. Its function was to plan and project monthly programs, direct and promote mission study and the Week of Prayer, and publish *Lutheran Woman's Work.*" [36]

Conclusion

Lutheran women, like those of other denominations, had to be content at first, for the most part, to use their God-given talents and their Christian influence within the sphere of the home. Gradually, however, they began to emerge and expand their activities through the local Ladies Aid. It was not until the organization of women became more widespread on a larger scale that the majority of women began to emerge and find greater avenues of service. Here they have been privileged through women's missionary societies to use the talents with which they have been endowed by a beneficent Creator. In addition, they have found the joy of sharing in the privilege of being "messengers of the King" while at the same time they are developing hidden talents for even greater service.

Notes
III

1. Nona M. Diehl, *U. L. C. W. Heritage and History, 1879—1959* (Philadelphia: United Lutheran Church Women, 1961), pp. 5—6.

2. Ibid., p. 6.

3. Ibid.

4. Martha Reishus, *Hearts and Hands Uplifted: A History of the Women's Missionary Federation of The Evangelical Lutheran Church* (Minneapolis: Augsburg Publishing House, 1958), p. 32.

5. Ibid., p. 31.

6. Ibid., pp. 33—34.

7. Ibid., p. 26.

8. Ibid., pp. 39—40.

9. Ibid., p. 40.

10. Diehl, p. 6.

11. Ibid., p. 6.

12. Ibid., p. 7.

13. Ibid.

14. Ibid.

15. Mrs. Peter Peterson, *These Fifty Years* (Chicago: Women's Missionary Society of Augustana Synod, 1942), p. 23.

16. Ibid.

17. Ibid., p. 24.

18. Ibid., p. 21.

19. Ibid., p. 24.

20. Ibid., p. 25.

21. Ibid., p. 26.

22. Diehl, p. 7.

23. Ibid., pp. 8—9.

24. Ibid., p. 8.

25. Ibid., pp. 8—9.

26. Ibid., p. 9.

27. Katharine Lehmann, *And the Women Also* (Columbus: Women's Missionary Federation of The American Lutheran Church, 1952), p. 3.

28. Reishus, p. 41.

29. Ibid., pp. 46—47.

30. Ibid., p. 50.

31. Peterson, p. 116.

32. Diehl, pp. 16—17.

33. Peterson, p. 28.

34. Lehmann, p. 9.

35. Ibid., p. 7.

36. Diehl, p. 18.

IV
Planting the Seed in "Missouri"

THE SAXONS WHO LEFT GERMANY and came to America in 1839 did so in protest to the wave of rationalism which was sweeping Germany at that time. When they joined with others to form what is now known as The Lutheran Church — Missouri Synod, their church polity was characterized by a determination to cling to the traditional. Even now, after almost a century and a quarter of its existence, this is still evident to some extent today. It has permeated every facet of the work of the church and is responsible, to a great degree, for the role which women have played in the church, and the fact that the establishment of a national organization of women was so long delayed. While it is true that there have always been some individuals who have been more far-sighted than the majority (and because of this have often been censored either by passive resistance or by militant opposition), the greatest percentage have, until very recently, leaned heavily to the side of conservatism. This has been demonstrated both in the doctrinal position of the church and in the practical application of the doctrine. This is also reflected in the attitude of the church toward the role of women. It will be well for the reader to bear this in mind as we trace the development of this role in The Lutheran Church — Missouri Synod.

In 1847, almost 10 years after the arrival of the Saxons on the shores of the Mississippi in St. Louis, the church body which we now know as The Lutheran Church — Missouri Synod was organized as *Die Deutsche Evangelisch-Lutherische Synode von Missouri, Ohio und anderen Staaten* [1] (German Evangelical Lutheran Synod of

Missouri, Ohio, and Other States). It has been commonly known throughout its history as the "Missouri" Synod. The organizers included, in addition to the Saxons, representatives from Ohio, Illinois, Indiana, Michigan, and New York. The Saxons had made contact with these Lutherans in other parts of the country through various means, especially through *Der Lutheraner,* a German publication, established in 1844 by Dr. C. F. W. Walther, who later became the first president of the new organization.[2]

Opposition to the formation of a synod was voiced by Rev. Carl Ludwig Geyer of Watertown, Wis., and his delegate, who opposed such an organization on the grounds that it was unwarranted on the basis of Scripture.[3] Trinity Church, St. Louis, expressed concern over the proposed constitution because it feared the possibility of clergy domination and the authority which the Synod would exert over the local congregation. It therefore submitted an amendment declaring that the Synod in its relation to the self-government of the individual congregation "is to be merely an advisory body, and that its resolutions have no binding effect until adopted by the congregation as not contrary to the Word of God and suited to its condition."[4] The autonomy of the local congregation, as expressed in the resolution of Trinity Church, has remained as a basic tenet of the Missouri Synod to the present time.

Though the amendment proposed by Trinity Church was adopted at the organization of the Synod, the constitution required a unanimous vote of all member congregations to amend it, and since there was no time limit set, it was not until 1853 that it actually became a part of the revised synodical constitution.[5]

Christians all over the world and throughout the history of the Christian church, regardless of sex, have been motivated to put their God-given talents to work, at least in part, by Paul's reminder that God has bestowed certain gifts "to equip God's people for work in His service, to the building up of the body of Christ" (Eph. 4:12 NEB). It is not surprising, then, that the women, too, who came to America from Germany, soon sought and found an opportunity to use their special gifts in His service.

First Women's Organizations

Two societies, begun almost simultaneously, though in widely separated places, marked the beginning of women's organizations in the Missouri Synod. Both were organized for essentially the same purpose: to sew, mend, wash, and iron for students, in the one case at the seminary which the church had in Fort Wayne, Ind., and the other at Concordia Seminary, St. Louis. The exact date of the organization of the Fort Wayne group is not known, but it is presumed to have been in January 1852. By the following year it had a membership of 74.[6] Of this group it is said that by the time the women finished patching and mending a garment "it often reminded one of Joseph's coat of many colors."[7] (Two additional organizations were formed later for the benefit of the college: the Letitia Society in 1888, whose function it was to provide linen for the college sickrooms, and the Martha Society in 1919, which sewed and otherwise provided necessities for the college hospital and kitchen.)[8]

The St. Louis group, popularly known as *Frau Doktor Walthers Naehverein* (Mrs. Walther's Sewing Circle), was organized in the same year as the Fort Wayne group, but several months later.

Rev. August R. Suelflow, director of Concordia Historical Institute, the depository for the archives and history of The Lutheran Church — Missouri Synod, writes about this group of women in St. Louis. He says in part:

"June 2, 1952, marks the centennial of the St. Louis group, when Trinity and Immanuel were the only two Lutheran congregations in that city. The stimulus to organize originated at Immanuel. Though each had its own pastor, the two churches comprised one parish, called the *Gesamtgemeinde* [General Congregation], with Dr. C. F. W. Walther as *Oberpfarrer,* or chief pastor. The voters' meeting of the *Gesamtgemeinde,* May 24, 1852, announced that a ladies' aid would be organized for the purpose of supporting indigent students at the Seminary. 'Each sister, accordingly, is invited to join this praiseworthy society. Even though some may not be able to help with sewing, they may nevertheless support the undertaking financially or help with the washing. All those interested are to meet at J. F. Schuricht's drug store (on Franklin Avenue between First and Third Streets) a week from Wednesday' — June 2."[9]

Further insight into the function of this organization is given in an account in *Die Abendschule*. It enumerates the various items which were made for the students: towels, bedding, handkerchiefs, shirts, etc. These women gladdened the heart of many a student away from home through the motherly concern shown him. This, however, was not the extent of their concern. Mrs. August Craemer, the wife of a member of the seminary faculty during the 1860s, is mentioned for the special work which she did for the students. Single-handed she would go into the surrounding territory with the seminary wagon (sometimes assisted by a young son of a member of the faculty) to the gardeners and farmers in the surrounding area to gather foodstuffs for the seminary.[10]

Leisurely Get-Togethers

The meetings of the St. Louis group, as undoubtedly also of the society in Fort Wayne, were leisurely get-togethers which provided social activity while the women sewed for the students. There was, in the St. Louis group, the customary coffee and coffeecake combined with the usual chatter about subjects of common interest.[11] But it also had its serious moments. "On one occasion the society met during an unusually dry period of the year. Much lamentation regarding the drought was heard at this meeting. After having listened for some time to the complaints, Mrs. Walther arose and said: 'My dear friends, we don't pray enough; this drought is due partly to the lack of prayer. Let us all kneel and fervently petition the Lord to send us rain.' All knelt while Mrs. Walther led in prayer. Thereupon the women busied themselves again with their task of sewing for the needy students, when, lo and behold, from the distance there came sounds of rolling thunder, the sun became obscured, clouds gathered, lightning flashed and even before the meeting adjourned their prayer was answered as a welcome rain refreshed the parched earth."[12]

Circumstances related to the life of women during the third quarter or more of the last century are described by Dr. Ludwig Fuerbringer (1864—1947), who was a professor at Concordia Seminary, St. Louis, for 50 years, the last 12 of which he served as its

*The Old Sewing Circle of Holy Cross Lutheran Church, St. Louis, Mo.
(1870s): Left to right: Mrs. Stoeckhardt, Mrs. Schaller, Mrs. Gast, Mrs.
Volk, Mrs. Heins, Mrs. Walther, Mrs. Meyer (kneeling), Mrs. Steinmeyer,
Mrs. Schumann, Mrs. Tschirpe, Mrs. Schuricht, Mrs. Lange (standing),
Mrs. Barthel, Mrs. Kalbfleisch*

president. While he is writing primarily about the lives of pastors'
wives, the situation as he describes it is representative of life in
general during that time.

The women lived a quiet life, their interests centered in their
responsibilities as wives and mothers. They did not have much
money, nor did they have the conveniences which women have
today. Consequently, their housework demanded more time and
labor than at present, particularly if they had a large family. Recall-
ing his own boyhood, Dr. Fuerbringer recounts that, as long as she
lived, his mother did all of the baking for the family, including, of
course, all the bread. She also did all of the sewing, including in
addition to shirts, blouses, and underwear, also suits. Dr. Fuerbringer
acquired his first ready-made suit when he was 10 or 11 years old.
There was very little activity outside the home for the woman. No
meetings were held, and there were virtually no organizations except
in the city congregations, where there was a *Frauenverein* (Ladies'
Aid) or a *Naehverein* (Sewing Circle).[13]

As Dr. Fuerbringer indicates, the Ladies' Aids which did exist were largely in the cities. There is evidence that such a *Frauenverein* existed in St. Matthew's Lutheran Church (America's oldest Lutheran church), New York City, in 1861. Under that date a pamphlet was published which was dedicated to the *Frauenverein* of that congregation. It was written by the pastor on the occasion of the 85th anniversary of the nation.[14]

Another Ladies' Society, older than its parent congregation, was organized in 1866. "The women's group of Martini Lutheran Church in Baltimore was organized two years before the congregation when members of St. Paul's Lutheran Church split into three groups to serve different areas of the growing city. The group assisted in raising funds for the building of the facilities of Martini congregation in South Baltimore."[15] The ladies of this same congregation were later instrumental in founding "The Ladies' Society of the Augsburg Home for Orphans and the Aged" in 1892.[16]

Attitude Toward Women

The general attitude which prevailed in the church toward the role of women was expressed by Dr. Wilhelm Sihler, long the pastor of St. Paul's Church and president of the college in Fort Wayne, Ind. His article on "Woman's Vocation and Its Deterioration," which appeared in the *Lutheraner* (Feb. 1, 1872), contained the following views on the subject:

God's original purpose for woman was that she be a helpmeet to her husband, especially to bear children, and, in that role, to preserve the human race and bring up her children according to the will of God.

Though the original purpose of woman was not essentially changed by her fall into sin, the righteous God nevertheless imposed on her the wholesome punishment: "Thy desire shall be to thy husband, and he shall rule over thee." She is to submit herself to the man as her superior in marriage, in everything that is not contrary to God's will and command. This, Dr. Sihler says, is not in conflict with Gal. 3:28, which says: "There is neither Jew nor Greek, there is neither bond nor free, there is neither male nor female; for ye are all one in Christ Jesus." While the woman by common faith in Christ has no less in and of Christ and His spiritual blessings than does her husband, yet God's marriage ordinance requires that the woman in this life be subject to the man and acknowledge him as lord.

Thus, in her domestic and maternal calling, according to God's will and ordinance, the purpose of woman is fulfilled. The man's calling is different. It is he alone who is to make laws, supervise their enforcement, institute justice and righteousness on earth, and render due obedience to existing laws. He alone according to God-given gifts, is appointed, according to his calling, within the community, either to till the soil or to convert raw materials into manufactured products for the common good, for this purpose even to harness the powers of nature, such as steam, water, light, electricity. It is he alone through whom, according to the special gifts of God, by his calling, the world of the sciences and the fine arts is opened up; yes, also in the community of the church it is the man alone — for "the women are to keep silence in the church" — who is officially to administer God's Word and sacraments publicly.

Dr. Sihler particularly deplores the fact that, in addition to the desire of women for suffrage and a share in the government of the land, the deterioration of woman's vocation is evident in other areas. He cites the fact that "ladies" are to be found at the institutions of higher learning — in 1870 there were over 20 of them enrolled at the University at Ann Arbor — in order to engage in formal studies, e. g., medicine, law, the fine arts, etc., with the purpose of later applying such knowledge and skills as they acquired in a professional way as doctors, lawyers, and professors.

Dr. Sihler concludes that most daughters of the immigrant Germans were best suited as maids or to do sewing (the more talented ones being able to do finishing and even cutting out of women's garments), which would not conflict with woman's calling. Within certain limits, he even sanctions teaching by young ladies, especially for small children or for the upper classes in girls' schools. Most women, he says, would probably be less suited as teachers for growing boys because they need a teacher with a better knowledge of foreign and ancient languages and because they demand the discipline which only a man can give them for a wholesome influence on the entire development of their character.[17]

Oddly enough, the year after the appearance of Dr. Sihler's article denouncing the training of women in schools of higher education, Trinity Lutheran Church of Springfield, Ill., conceived the idea of purchasing a building which had been erected in 1854 for the Illinois State University in Springfield. The Lutheran Pennsylvania Synod had acquired it in 1870, when the university failed, and had offered to sell the property to the Missouri Synod in 1873. However, the Missouri Synod failed to accept the offer. It was the intention of Trinity Church to open a girls' school and teachers' seminary for women by Jan. 1, 1874. An association was formed which was called "The Evangelical Lutheran Female College and Normal School Association." Though definite plans were made, few students applied, and the school never became a reality.[18] Instead it became the campus of the practical seminary when this was moved to Springfield in January 1874.[19] Actually the Missouri Synod trained no women teachers until 1919, when a small beginning was made at the hitherto all-male teachers college at Seward, Nebr.,[20] and it was not until 1938 that Concordia Teachers College at River Forest, Ill. opened its doors to women.[21]

In view of pronouncements such as those made by Dr. Sihler in the official publication of the church, it is not difficult to see why women's organizations other than the local *Frauenverein* did not become a reality early in the history of the Missouri Synod.

Organizations Multiply

Despite the attitude which prevailed in the church, little by little women broadened the scope of their activities in response to various challenges which presented themselves. One such challenge, which resulted in the establishment of the first orphanage in the Missouri Synod, came when a member of Pastor Buenger's congregation, who had been called into the service of his country during the Civil War, brought his child to the pastor. The child's mother had died, and the father did not know what to do with it. Pastor and Mrs. Buenger took the child into their own home and cared for it. Subsequently other children, who for one reason or another had lost their home, were taken in by the Buengers. As a result, the first orphans' home began functioning as such in July 1868. Mrs. Buenger, of course, had played a prominent role in the events which led to the establishment of the home, and groups of women in St. Louis, i. e., ladies' aids and sewing circles, began at once to work for this institution. While women were associated with the home in this manner from the very beginning, their society, known as the "Lutheran Orphans' Home Ladies' Aid Society," joined other women at the turn of the century in organizing the "Woman's Auxiliary to the Lutheran Hospital," representing women's groups of the St. Louis congregations who served both institutions.[22]

From the beginning of the 20th century on, new organizations began to spring up whose goal was serving various charitable institutions, and the word "mission" began to appear in the names of these organizations. In St. Louis the "Lutheran Ladies' Mission Aid Society" was organized in 1901 to assist the city missionary, Rev. F. W. Herzberger, although a group of women had been meeting for about a year previously in the home of its founder, Mrs. Alexander Rohlfing, who was also president of the "Woman's Auxiliary to the Lutheran Hospital."[23]

The picture was beginning to change in Fort Wayne too. On Sept. 26, 1904, a group of women organized "The Ladies' Aid of the Lutheran Hospital." Its purpose was to sew, or otherwise prepare for use, linens and other materials for all departments of the hospital.[24]

About the same time an India Mission Society was organized in Fort Wayne, which in turn served as the spark that lit the fire for a similar organization in St. Louis. Mrs. F. Zucker from Fort Wayne, whose husband had been a missionary to India for many years, visited her daughter, Mrs. Ludwig Fuerbringer, in St. Louis in the fall of 1906. During her visit she spoke to Mrs. George Stoeckhardt, wife of a seminary faculty member, about the Fort Wayne society. Mrs. Stoeckhardt was genuinely interested, but she was somewhat hesitant about organizing a new society, though she had discussed the matter on several occasions with other women. Encouraged by her husband, Mrs. Stoeckhardt invited a group of women to her home on Feb. 27, 1907, at which time the "India Mission Ladies' Society" became a reality. At this meeting the women began to sew for India missions. Later, when the China mission field was opened, the society added this field to its objectives, and the name was changed to "The Foreign Mission Ladies' Aid Society."[25]

Auxiliary Groups

During the next 20 years organizations sprung up all over the country to aid various charitable institutions or endeavors in one way or another. These include the following:

The Ladies' Auxiliary of the Lutheran Hospital, Brooklyn, N. Y., was organized in September 1912 for the purpose of supplying linens, blankets, etc., for the hospital.[26]

Concordia Ladies' Aid Society of Pittsburgh, Pa., was organized in the fall of 1915, its purpose, according to its constitution, that of "giving aid to the Concordia Orphans' Home and the Old Folks' Home at Marwood, Pa., to give aid to any other institution of our Synod when deemed necessary, and to promote interchurch sociability among Lutherans who are one with us in faith."[27]

Bethlehem Ladies' Aid Society for the Bethlehem Orphans' Home, Staten Island, N. Y., began in 1916 with a membership of 288 and had as its sole purpose "the maintenance of the household of the Bethlehem Orphans' and Half-Orphans' Home."[28]

The Women's Auxiliary of the Lutheran Hospice of Buffalo, N. Y., was organized in 1915 and, oddly enough, began with the same number of members as the organization for the orphanage at Staten Island, 288. In addition to the Lutheran Hospice, it supported Lutheran institutional missions in Buffalo.[29]

An organization whose function was somewhat different was formed in the Twin Cities — St. Paul and Minneapolis, Minn. — in 1922. While this organization did some sewing for children in hospitals, it also paid "such incidental expenses of the mission-workers as prayer-books, catechism, Sunday-school literature, tracts, a subscription of 500 copies a month of the *Good News,* as well as emergency orders for groceries, milk, medicine, carfare, etc."[30]

Meanwhile other organizations had come into existence in St. Louis, too, i. e., organizations of women for the Lutheran Altenheim (Old People's Home) and the Lutheran Ladies' Aid for Colored Missions.[31] A unique organization came into being there as a result of a plea to the Lutheran Ladies' Mission Aid Society by Pastor Herzberger and Mrs. Anna Vellner, a Lutheran social worker in the City Hospital. Their plea was for a home for convalescents under Lutheran supervision and was directed to the Lutheran Ladies' Mission Aid Society in 1915, at a time when women were engaged in volunteer services in connection with World War I. As a result the matter was deferred until after the war, when the women who had served on the Council of Defense, finding that they had a small balance in their treasury, looked around for a place to use it.

"In May, 1919, the Lutheran Ladies' Mission Aid Society voted to use $500 out of its treasury to establish the Lutheran Convalescent Home Fund," which by the following year had reached a total of $3,236. With this they purchased a home, and the indebtedness of $15,000 was liquidated in the short period of 3 years and 8 months. This society is unique in that, from the beginning, the administration of the home was entirely in the hands of women, and still is today (1967).[32]

New Role for Women

The first opportunity for women to band together and serve the church on a larger scale came with the organization of the Walther League. Dr. C. F. W. Walther (1811—87) had made an effort as early as 1851 to gather all organized youth groups into a synodwide federation. In fact, such a federation was formed in 1854, but soon dissolved.[33]

Several similar attempts were made later (one in 1882 by the Young Men's Club of Trinity Church in Buffalo and another a few years later by a group in Detroit), but both of these efforts failed. Then, in June 1892, the Young Men's Clubs of Trinity and St. Andrew's Churches in Buffalo began to publish a paper to serve as a means of contact between the societies of the various churches and to stimulate interest in a larger organization. It was called *Der Vereinsbote* (The Society Messenger). The original plan of the two men's societies in Buffalo when they began to publish the paper in 1892 was to organize a young men's society. However, when the convention of interested people gathered in Buffalo in May 1893, the group was organized as "The General Society of Young People's and Young Men's Societies."[34]

Preliminary meetings had been held in Buffalo, and even before the 1893 convention, applications were received for membership from a number of societies. These included The Lutheran Young People's Society of Zion Church, Dallas, Tex.[35] Of special significance is that the officers of this society, listed in the May 1893 issue of *Der Vereinsbote,* included two women: Miss Josie Ax as president and Miss Hulda Thomas as vice-president.[36]

By January 1894 the *Vereinsbote* reported a membership of 15 societies, with a total membership of 708. Of these, in addition to the Young People's Society of Zion Church, Dallas, there were young people's societies from Holyoke, Mass.; St. Matthew's, New York; and Emmaus, New York, included in the list.[37] In the convention later that year (1894) the name of the organization was changed to the Walther League.[38]

"It was a small beginning," says W. G. Polack in a booklet commemorating the 50th anniversary of the league, "and there were many who viewed with alarm this projected union of young people's societies in our Missouri Synod. Their fear was that such an organization might encroach upon the rightful domain of the local congregation and interfere with the organized work of Synod. . . . Such ideas, however, did not enter the minds of the founders of the Walther League. Their aims were to place the organization into the service of the church."[39] However, the Walther League was not officially recognized by Synod until 1920.[40]

The organization of the Walther League, with the inclusion of women in its membership, marked a turning point in the role of women in the Missouri Synod. Heretofore the activities of women in the church were carried on largely by the older women. Now the younger women, who were to be the leaders of the future, were being drawn into action and training for the role they were to play in the years to come. It also marked another "first" in that, while the organized work of women, as well as of the church as such, was conducted almost exclusively in the German language, the Walther League helped to pave the way for the introduction of English.

The transition was not made so quickly, however. At first the meetings, the minutes and the publication of the Walther League were in both German and English, but slowly the change became more apparent. Dr. Walter A. Maier wrote about this situation in an article, "Shall We Remain Lutheran Though We Stay German?" in the *American Lutheran* (April 1922). He says, in part:

"The real impetus to the English work in our Church, after the weak beginnings which date back to the early '80's, was furnished only within the last ten or fifteen years, and especially as a result of the lamented world war, when by urgent necessity or by prudent choice, many congregations introduced English worship.

. . . .

"Yet: with almost one hundred million people in this country who cannot understand the German language . . . the last available statistical records show that German services still exceed the English by about fifty per cent.

. . . .

"If the past belongs to the German, the future belongs to the English."[41]

Deaconess Work Begins

The path was opened for women to serve the church in another area at the convention of the Associated Lutheran Charities in Fort Wayne, Ind., in 1911, when it was known as the *Evangelisch-lutherische Wohltaetigkeitskonferenz* (Evangelical Lutheran Conference on Welfare). At this convention the question of training deaconesses within the Synodical Conference was officially discussed for the first time. Pastor Herzberger of St. Louis, pioneer worker in the city mission field, had been asked to present a paper on the "Female Diaconate" at this convention. Being an enthusiastic champion of this cause, he welcomed this opportunity.

Already prior to this convention in 1911, Pastor Herzberger had stressed the need of trained women workers in the field of missions and charities. "He realized from his experience in this field the great opportunity for effective service that presented itself to trained women assistants in this work. He had seen the work done by deaconesses of other churches and saw that we were handicapped to a certain extent in our work in these fields because we lacked such trained helpers."[42]

"No immediate results of Pastor Herzberger's plea for Lutheran deaconesses were apparent. The members of our Church have always been very conservative and therefore slow to support any new and unknown movement. But people were beginning to think about the question."[43]

Prior to the convention of the Associated Lutheran Charities in 1919 Pastor Herzberger wrote a tract entitled, "Woman's Work in the Church," in which he stressed the need for women workers. He illustrated his point with a story about two farmers, A and B, who, seeing storm clouds coming, reacted in two different ways. The first called on his womenfolk to assist him before the storm, the second did not, with the result that the first man got his crops harvested before the storm, the second did not. Pastor Herzberger compared Farmer A to other Protestant churches who were utilizing the talents of women. Farmer B he compared to the Synodical Conference. "Why have we Lutherans of the Synodical Conference failed so far," said Pastor Herzberger, "to make use of the many gifted and pious women the Lord has given also to us for work in the fields entrusted to our stewardship? Are we living in a different world from that in which Christians of other denominations are living — a world less affected by sin and want and woe than theirs? Certainly not. We meet the same wants and afflictions they have to contend with in their church work. As they, so do we need the assistance of trained women workers in our various harvest fields."[44]

When the Associated Lutheran Charities met in Fort Wayne in July 1919, it decided to organize a Lutheran Deaconess Association with headquarters in Fort Wayne. In addition, it voted to request the Fort Wayne Lutheran Hospital Association to admit students to its training school who wished to become deaconess nurses.[45]

Woman Suffrage Stirs Clergy

The woman suffrage movement had demanded more and more attention through the years until, in 1919, Congress approved the Nineteenth Amendment, which gave women the right to vote. It was ratified by 36 states and became law on Aug. 26, 1920. The church could not but be affected by this new role of women in the country. Rev. Louis J. Sieck (1884—1952), pastor of Zion Lutheran Church in St. Louis for many years and during the last years of his life the president of Concordia Seminary (1943—52), read a paper to the Pastors' and Teachers' Conference of St. Louis and vicinity on "Attitude Lutherans Should Take Toward Woman's Suffrage." It was printed by resolution of the conference in the *Lutheran Witness* in three installments. Pastor Sieck said in part:

"Many of us have been accustomed to regard Woman Suffrage as too insignificant and too absurd to deserve serious attention. Most of us felt like the writer of this essay that we could never be induced to discuss this question earnestly. We actually avoided it, hoping secretly that it would die a natural death. Instead of favoring us with an early and natural death, the Woman Suffrage movement has grown to such proportions that the time has come when it cannot be disregarded by the Church, which is to show us from the Scriptures our attitude also toward such questions. Nor can it be disregarded by any citizen, as equal rights of women, or suffrage, constitutes one of the profoundest questions which can arise in human government."[46]

Pastor Sieck outlined the role of woman in the home, the church, and the state. Regarding woman's place in the home, Pastor Sieck said: "This is woman's place and sphere in the world, and God surely knows what is best for women. . . . To change this sphere of woman and create for her a sphere outside of the home is to overthrow God's ordinance and unsex woman."[47]

Concerning woman's place in the church Pastor Sieck said: "We find, then, that the woman occupies an equal position with man in the Church in the offers of God's grace in the Gospel, equal privilege of service, the right to meet with the Church, the right quietly and unostentatiously to express her opinion, but that she is not granted suffrage nor leadership in the congregation and is barred from the public ministry."[48]

Finally, treating the role of woman in the state, Pastor Sieck said: "But what about the Christian women in the States in which suffrage has been granted? Should Christian women not use the ballot? Since it is something which God neither forbids, nor commands, it is a Christian woman's liberty to vote or not to vote."[49]

During the observance of the 75th anniversary of the organization of Synod (1922), the *American Lutheran* published an editorial which not only deplored the mistakes of the past but looked to a better future. The editorial says in part:

"Whereas the Church's doctrinal program is divinely fixed and therefore unchangeable, its practical program, its policy of methods, must be kept flexible enough to adapt them readily to the rapidly changing demands of the conditions about us. . . . We have sometimes permitted our grateful appreciation of the accomplishments of the past to blind us to a degree to the opportunities of the present and the vast responsibilities of the future." [50]

The editorial calls for a reshaping of the church's program, with special attention to its missionary policy. It then concludes as follows:

"The adaptation to changing conditions is, within our circles, a slow process. . . . There may be some impatience because of the slowness of the process and the resultant detriment to the Church, but it must never displace the cheerful confidence that God's grace, which has been so evidently with us in the past, will also be with us in the future."[51]

That the women of the church had the patience to bear with the conservatism which shunned change and that at the same time they had the confidence that the time would come when they could serve more effectively in the Kingdom is evidenced by the events in the years that followed.

Notes

IV

1. *Lutheran Cyclopedia,* ed. Erwin L. Lueker (St. Louis: Concordia Publishing House, 1954), p. 609.

2. Ibid., p. 608.

3. A. C. Stellhorn, "Carl Ludwig Geyer," *Concordia Historical Institute Quarterly,* XII (April 1939), 10.

4. *Lutheran Cyclopedia,* p. 608. For full text of the amendment in English see August R. Suelflow, "Walther and Church Polity," *Concordia Theological Monthly,* XXXII (Oct. 1961), 636.

5. Suelflow, pp. 636—637.

6. August R. Suelflow, "Ladies' Aid Centennials," *Lutheran Witness,* LXXI, No. 11 (May 27, 1952), p. 5.

7. *The Concordian, Centennial Edition, 1839–1939* (Fort Wayne: n. p., n. d.), p. 63.

8. *Lutheran Laymen's League Bulletin,* II (March 1, 1931), 107.

9. Suelflow, "Ladies' Aid Centennials," p. 5.

10. [Louis] W[agner], *Die Abendschule,* LVII, No. 22B (May 18, 1911), p. 33.

11. Ibid.

12. "The Centennial Church: 'Old Trinity,' St. Louis" (St. Louis: Literature Committee of the Lutheran Woman's League), Topic 61, mimeographed, p. 3.

13. Ludwig Fuerbringer, *Persons and Events* (St. Louis: Concordia, 1947), pp. 64—65.

14. Carl Fr. E. Stohlmann, "Zum fuenfundachtzigsten Geburtstage unserer Union" (New York: Ludwig, 1861), front cover.

15. *Lutheran Witness Reporter,* II, No. 11 (June 5, 1966), p. 9.

16. *Lutheran Laymen's League Bulletin,* II (Nov. 17, 1930), 62.

17. Wilhelm Sihler, "Ueber den Beruf des Weibes und seine Entartung," *Der Lutheraner,* XXVIII (Feb. 1, 1872), 65—67.

18. August C. Stellhorn, *Schools of The Lutheran Church — Missouri Synod* (St. Louis: Concordia, 1963), pp. 250—251.

19. Carl S. Meyer, *Log Cabin to Luther Tower* (St. Louis: Concordia, 1965), p. 49.

20. Stellhorn, *Schools of The Lutheran Church — Missouri Synod,* p. 232.

21. Ibid., p. 430.

22. "Lutheran Women's Work in Greater St. Louis" (n. d.), pp. 16—19.

23. Ibid., pp. 20—24.

24. *Lutheran Laymen's League Bulletin,* II (Aug. 1, 1930), 15.

25. "Lutheran Women's Work in Greater St. Louis," pp. 25—30.

26. *Lutheran Laymen's League Bulletin,* I (June 16, 1930), 127.

27. Ibid.

28. Ibid., II (Aug. 1, 1930), 15.

29. Ibid., p. 16.

30. Ibid., II (Oct. 22, 1930), 45. See also *History, Minneapolis Lutheran Mission Auxiliary, 1923—43,* p. 4.

31. "Lutheran Women's Work in Greater St. Louis," pp. 31—39.

32. Ibid., pp.40—45.

33. *The Encyclopedia of the Lutheran Church,* ed. Julius Bodensieck (Minneapolis: Augsburg, 1965), Vol. III, p. 2552.

34. *Walther League Messenger — Vereinsbote* (25th-anniversary number), XXV (June and July 1917), 357.

35. *Der Vereinsbote,* I, April 1893, p. 1.

36. Ibid., I, May 1893, p. 1.

37. Ibid., II, Jan. 1894, p. 1.

38. *Walther League Messenger — Vereinsbote,* op. cit., p. 357.

39. William F. Weiherman, ed., *Fifty Years of Service to Lutheran Youth (1893—1943)* (Chicago: Walther League, 1943), p. 16.

40. *Walther League Manual* (Chicago: The Walther League, 1935), p. 21.

41. Walter A. Maier, "Shall We Remain Lutheran Though We Stay German?" *American Lutheran,* V (April 1922), 47—48.

42. H. B. Kohlmeier, "The Twenty-fifth Anniversary of the Lutheran Deaconess Association Within the Synodical Conference" (manuscript, Fort Wayne, 1944), p. 1.

43. Ibid., p. 2.

44. Ibid., pp. 3—4.

45. Ibid., p. 4.

46. Louis J. Sieck, "Attitude Lutherans Should Take Towards Woman's Suffrage," *Lutheran Witness,* XXXVIII (May 13, 1919), 149.

47. Ibid., p. 150.

48. Ibid., May 27, 1919, p. 162.

49. Ibid., June 10, 1919, p. 179.

50. *American Lutheran,* V (April 1922), 35.

51. Ibid., p. 36.

V
The Seed Sprouts

Transition

THE PACE OF THE CHURCH quickened at the beginning of the second decade of the 20th century, largely because of factors outside the church which nevertheless had a profound effect on the work of the church in many areas. In fact, 1920 marked the beginning of a new era in the Missouri Synod. Just what were these conditions which brought about the change, and how did they affect the history of the church, particularly so far as the role of women is concerned?

The mission outreach of the Missouri Synod had been directed largely to the many German immigrants coming to America. The efforts to gain these people for the church were commendable, particularly because the proportion of pastors to immigrants was relatively small. Nevertheless, the Missouri Synod had not made much of an effort, generally speaking, to reach the English-speaking people in America. Circumstances beyond the control of the church served to bring about a gradual change in this pattern.

World War I had necessitated a deemphasis of the German language. Even before the close of the war, the synodical convention had voted in 1917 to eliminate the word "German" from its official name. But as already indicated, change comes slowly. A summary of the status of the church at that time is given in *Moving Frontiers* (Carl S. Meyer, editor), from which we quote in part:

"The Missouri Synod in 1920 seemed to be very much like the Synod at the end of the Civil War. . . . The consequences of the language transition were far-reaching and of basic significance but were not evident till the second and third quarters of the 20th century. After World War I the supply of German immigrants was shut off. By 1920 the Synod as a whole seemed ready to accept the challenge of English mission work at home and the pressing challenge of mission work in one shrinking world."[1]

Along with other changes, a change was beginning to take place in the thinking regarding the professional services that women might render in the church. The synodical convention in 1917 had authorized an Educational Survey Committee. This Committee recommended to the 1920 convention "the erection of a ladies' seminary in order to give young ladies opportunity to secure a higher education at a synodical institution as well as to train them up for teachers in our schools and assistants in our heathen missions." The matter was placed in the hands of a committee with instructions to report to the next convention.[2]

When the above committee reported its findings to the 1923 convention, the result was that "Synod declined to erect a Ladies' Seminary. [This was to be a college rather than a seminary in the sense of a theological institution to prepare women for the ministry.] Instead, the Districts were urged to provide Lutheran Centers and chapels in the immediate vicinity of a number of colleges and universities."[3]

The matter did not end here, however. The next convention, in 1926, passed a resolution approving the work that was then being carried on, i. e., that of educating women teachers at Seward, Nebr., "which is carried on without particular expense to Synod," with the stipulation that, as in the past, the enrollment of "female pupils" should not exceed 20 percent of the total enrollment. In addition, it voted to permit the college in Edmonton, Alta., Canada, to enroll girls in the same way, with the same restrictions.[4]

The attitudes which had been prevalent during the last century had not died, however. Dr. Franz Pieper, for many years professor at Concordia Seminary, St. Louis, and also its president, voiced this sentiment in an article translated from the German and quoted in *Moving Frontiers*. Dr. Pieper first quotes the following from an Associated Press release: "On this day [Jan. 20, 1925] a woman assumes the gubernatorial seat of Texas, which heretofore has been occupied only by men." He then comments: "There are other things which offer even more definite proof that even before its end the world has completely lost all common sense."[5]

Women Organize in Districts

The '20s also brought far-reaching changes in the role of women in church organizations. The time had come when women were to experience the joy of joining hands with their sisters in the faith in larger organizations to serve the church more effectively.

History was made when ladies from six congregations met at Zion Lutheran Church in Oklahoma City on March 11, 1928. They had assembled for the purpose of organizing Mission Circles in the Lutheran churches of Oklahoma and chose as the name for their new organization, "The Lutheran Women's League of Oklahoma."

The following year at its convention this group decided to adopt mite boxes for the collection of moneys to be used for furnishing St. John's College, Winfield, Kans., with bed linens. In addition, it decided to promote a statewide canning project for the college and for the Lutheran Home Finding Society of Winfield, for which it had agreed to solicit memberships as one of its projects. Two factors were responsible for the selection of institutions outside the state of Oklahoma: the church had no benevolent institutions in that state; and until 1924 the Oklahoma congregations had been members of the Kansas District of Synod.[6]

Dr. Alfred M. Rehwinkel, at that time president of St. John's College, Winfield, attended the 1929 convention of the Lutheran Women's League of Oklahoma. He reported his reactions in an article in the Lutheran Laymen's League *Bulletin,* in part as follows:

"One of the most interesting meetings that I have ever attended was the recent Convention of the Lutheran Women of Oklahoma. . . . It occurred to me that here was the beginning of a movement that is bound to spread to wider circles and that will bring into more active service a force which has been more or less dormant in our Church.

.   .   .   .

"Very interesting to me was the fact that all the lady delegates took an active part in the discussions. I have attended many synodical conventions and meetings of young people, and I found that usually the lay delegates have had little to say, the pastors being obliged to do the greater part of the speaking. It was different here. These women delegates were here to discuss their business and not to have it discussed for them. If they wanted advice or direction, they called on one of the pastors whom they had elected as official adviser of their organization."[7]

Central District

Close on the heels of the Oklahoma organization came another effort in the Central District (comprising Indiana, Ohio, part of Kentucky, and West Virginia). The Pastoral Conference of Fort Wayne, Ind., and vicinity had submitted an overture to the District convention requesting that the convention "instruct its Home Mission Board, together with District representatives for Foreign and Negro Missions, to get in touch with the women's auxiliaries of our District, for the purpose of enlisting their interest and cooperation in an expanded mission program."[8]

The above overture was actually the culmination of earlier efforts to effect an organization of women in the Central District. In the fall of 1927, Rev. Frederick Wambsganss, then Director of the Home Mission Board of the District, had approached the Northern Indiana Pastoral Conference with a plan to form a missionary association of women in the District. The object of this organization would be to augment the mission treasury of the District. The plan met with opposition on the part of the pastors and did not materialize.

At the same time a group of women in Fort Wayne, who had had the formation of a Synodwide organization of women in mind for some time, got together to make plans. Their object was not to form a new organization but to federate the existing organizations and coordinate their work for the benefit of missions and charity, particularly for women and children. Both of these plans included an educational program as one of the main features.

A committee of women, with the approval of Pastor Wambsganss, contacted a large number of pastors and women's societies, either personally or by correspondence. The encouragement received through these contacts prompted a petition to the Pastoral Conference of Fort Wayne in the spring of 1928 to permit the women to organize. Both the proposal of Pastor Wambsganss and that of the women were given to a committee for consideration, resulting in a compromise which was then presented to the District convention in the form of the above overture.[9]

As a result of this overture, the District adopted a resolution on June 27, 1928, which recommended that (1) the women of the District, particularly in the Fort Wayne area, and the Mission Board, be commended for their missionary zeal; and (2) the District accept the suggestion of the Mission Board to utilize the existing Ladies' Aids to create a greater interest in mission projects not included in the District budget and to enlist their financial assistance for such projects.[10]

The Executive Home Mission Board of the District, together with the Director of Missions, was to constitute a ways and means committee which was to direct and promote the above endeavors. This committee was also empowered to augment its membership by adding the District representatives of the Foreign and Negro Mission Boards to determine the projects of the women's organization and to supervise the proper distribution of moneys collected.[11]

Actually the Central District Missionary Endeavor was no organization at all in the usual sense but was a project which was administered by the clergy to carry out a program which they planned, through the Home Mission Board of the District. Consequently there were no meetings, no committees, no conventions, and no minutes except the record kept by the Mission Board.[12]

Despite the fact that this effort was sponsored by the clergy and endorsed by the District convention, there was much misunderstanding about it, in fact, it was even viewed with alarm by some. To clarify its function the Endeavor *Quarterly* published a detailed outline of the Plan (December 1929), which embodied, in addition to the provision of the resolution of the District convention that the existing Ladies' Aids be the functioning unit, the following points:

The existing Ladies' Aids should, if possible, enlist *all* the women of the congregation; the Lutheran Women's Missionary Endeavor *Quarterly* would serve as the means of communication and would be made available to *all women* of the congregation; this publication would be distributed by a Missionary Committee of the Ladies' Aid, who would also furnish mite boxes to all women in the congregation who were ready and willing to participate. In addition, these mite boxes would be collected at the time the *Quarterly* was distributed or be brought to the quarterly meeting. At these meetings a missionary topic would be discussed, "usually under the leadership of the pastor." Finally, the plan provided that "the guidance of the Endeavor was the responsibility of the District Mission Board which also edited the Endeavor *Quarterly* and determined how the mite box offerings were to be used."[13]

Not Yet Generally Accepted

It is interesting to note that, while women's work was expanding, their role was not yet generally accepted. Prof. Martin Sommer of the St. Louis seminary, also an editor of the *Lutheran Witness,* had repeatedly written editorials on the status of women in the church, always reiterating the theme of woman's silence in the church (this despite the fact that his wife, the former Mrs. Stoeckhardt, played such an active role in women's work).

Such an editorial appeared after the synodical convention in June 1929 at River Forest, Ill. Prof. Sommer says in part:

"The status of women in the Church was not even discussed at the meeting of Synod. . . .

"And yet the ladies were there; they visited the sessions and conducted themselves in an exemplary manner. They sang in the services and at the concert of the Bach Chorus. They prepared and served the meals. Some took dictation and prepared manuscripts. In their homes many entertained their friends and their husbands' friends.

.   .   .   .

"Again and again we have noticed that in these external matters God's Word and natural good sense agree. The Bible does not condemn nature, but sanctifies it. St. Paul, when speaking of the question of women's conduct in the Church, appealed to his readers' natural sense of propriety, 1 Cor. 11, 14. And thus it happens that those women show the best judgment who follow the directions of the Bible."[14]

Despite the opposition to any widespread organization of women in the church which was still prevalent in the second decade of the 20th century, the movement continued like the incoming tide, slowly but surely gaining momentum.

LLL Calls for Action

When the Executive Committee of the Lutheran Laymen's League, which had been organized in 1917 to help wipe out Synod's debt, met in St. Louis on Sept. 3, 1929, the matter of women's role in the church was discussed and resulted in a resolution which called for action. It read: "Resolved to put the question of a 'National Ladies' Aid Federation' as an auxiliary body to the Lutheran Laymen's League before the Board of Governors at its next meeting."[15]

At its meeting on Sept. 11 (just a little over a week after the meeting of the Executive Committee), the Board of Governors considered the recommendation of the Executive Committee and decided to "recommend for favorable consideration at the next Convention of the LLL the establishment of a national organization of women to be affiliated with the LLL." It further resolved that in the interim a survey of the situation should be made by the Executive Committee and that they offer the women their assistance and facilities in the effort to organize.[16]

The Board of Governors later that month reiterated its intention to continue its efforts through the Executive Committee to be of assistance to the existing women's organizations in bringing about a national organization.[17] Letters were sent to various parts of the country securing the names of prospective representatives of Ladies' Aids and other interested women to attend the preliminary meeting of the "National Lutheran Ladies Aid," which was to be held in St. Louis on November 5.[18]

Such a letter was received by Mrs. J. H. Deckman of Minneapolis from Mr. A. G. Brauer, secretary of the Board of Governors of the LLL, and reads in part:

"For many years there has been sporadic and isolated 'talk' on the feasibility of bringing about a National Lutheran Women's Organization with specific objectives and coordinated efforts. In some localities state or district organizations have been formed. The success of these smaller organizations tends to show that a national organization of our more than two thousand Ladies' Aid Societies would prove a tremendous success and would work untold good for the work of our Church at home and abroad. The Lutheran Laymen's League believes that the time has come to informally discuss the proposition, and it has consented to become instrumental in calling a meeting for this purpose." The letter was dated Oct. 22, 1929.[19]

1929 Meeting

A month later, in response to the invitation of the Lutheran Laymen's League, 16 Lutheran women from various parts of the country were present at meetings held on Nov. 5 and 6 in St. Louis. Those present were:

Mrs. H. F. Beckmann, Indianapolis, Ind.
Mrs. Ernest Brand, Pittsburgh, Pa.
Mrs. Frederick Brand, St. Louis, Mo.
Mrs. A. G. Brauer, St. Louis, Mo.
Mrs. J. H. Deckman, Minneapolis, Minn.
Mrs. Charles Franz, Indianapolis, Ind.
Mrs. A. A. Grossmann, St. Louis, Mo.
Mrs. H. J. Heitner, St. Louis, Mo.
Mrs. H. Kionka, South Orange, N. J.
Mrs. W. A. Maier, St. Louis, Mo.
Mrs. L. Meyer, St. Louis, Mo.
Mrs. Anna Roehrkasse, Pittsburgh, Pa.
Mrs. Otto F. Schmitt, St. Louis, Mo.
Mrs. E. W. Schultz, Sheboygan, Wis.
Mrs. M. Sommer, St. Louis, Mo.
Miss Marie Zucker, Fort Wayne, Ind.

In addition to the above women, the following men were present:
Mr. A. G. Brauer, member, Executive Committee of the LLL
Mr. A. A. Grossmann, member, Executive Committee of the LLL
Mr. Louis H. Waltke, member, Executive Committee of the LLL
Rev. L. T. Buchheimer, Field Secretary of the LLL
Rev. Henry Kowert, Advisory Member of the LLL
Rev. L. Meyer, Executive Secretary pro tem of the LLL

Mr. Grossmann informed the group that "the Lutheran Laymen's League had been approached regarding the feasibility and advisability of organizing a National Lutheran Ladies' Aid, and that it had consented to become instrumental in calling a meeting for the purpose of discussing the matter."[20]

Mrs. Otto F. Schmitt of St. Louis was chosen to serve as temporary chairman, whereupon she invited the men present "to remain in the meeting and lend their counsel and advice."[21]

Areas Report

Then followed reports of various women on the work that was being done in their respective areas. Mrs. Kionka from New Jersey reported that "nothing definite had been taken up by the Ladies' Aids either individually or collectively" in her area. Mrs. Franz of Indianapolis and Miss Zucker of Fort Wayne both spoke on the work of the Lutheran Women's Missionary Endeavor in the Central District. Miss Zucker stressed the fact that this organization fostered the work of both home and foreign missions and that it had a quarterly publication. Mrs. Deckman of Minneapolis reported that a large number of the societies in the Twin Cities region had formed an association and that, while attempts were being made to organize the societies of the entire state, this had not yet materialized. Mrs. Schultz of Sheboygan indicated that the ladies of her District, according to the sentiments expressed by a representative group which had met at her home, were eagerly awaiting the formation of a national organization.[22]

A report of the work being done by the Oklahoma District was made by Rev. L. Meyer, who described the group as "well organized." It was his opinion that the "objectives of the national body in question would be so stated that the objectives of all existing organizations be embodied therein."[23]

"Wide and Deep"

After a number of those present expressed their opinion concerning the objectives of the proposed organization, Mr. Waltke explained the objectives of the Lutheran Laymen's League as outlined in its constitution. He then "suggested that the foundation for this new organization be laid wide and deep" and "encouraged the ladies to choose objectives that would cover a large field of work."[24]

Mr. Grossmann's view was somewhat different. Regarding the

objectives he said: "The first and foremost objective must ever be to keep the work of the local congregation in mind as has been done in the past." As further objectives he cited a continuance and enlargement of aid extended to communities, particularly of a charitable nature; assistance to Districts; and cooperation in any other projects which might present themselves in relation to the work of Synod.[25]

Of special significance was the suggestion that educational programs be a part of the objectives of the organization, particularly in the areas of charitable and social work, which would improve and enlarge such work then being done.[26]

The opinion was also expressed that "one special goal should be chosen, preferably missions, and others taken up as opportunity presents itself."[27]

Pastor Kowert, the synodically appointed advisor to the LLL, cited the work of various women in the Bible and in church history, including also the work that women had been doing through the local Ladies' Aids throughout Synod. He pointed out that every man and woman is a priest of God and that the societies which now exist in the local congregation are evidence that such societies had the approval of the congregation. The aim of the national society would be to get these societies together and coordinate their activities for greater results.[28]

The advantages of a national organization were defined as being of benefit not only to societies but also to individual members, who would receive "more definite information on the work in question through prepared programs for meetings, mission programs and educational programs which would tend to make their work more practical. An open forum conducted at the society meeting would give an opportunity for an exchange of ideas. A national organization would assist materially in accomplishing these things on a larger scale."[29]

Mrs. W. A. Maier, who prior to her marriage had served as the first Junior Secretary of the Walther League at its headquarters in Chicago, emphasized that a national organization would benefit not only the societies in the cities but those in the smaller communities as well. She cited the work which the Walther League had done in arousing interest among the young people of the church beyond the interests of the local society.[30]

In answer to the concern expressed over the fate of existing organizations for various charitable endeavors, it was suggested that these might be united to form the nucleus for a national organization.[31]

District or National?

The question was also raised whether the district or the national would be organized first. The sentiment expressed was that the best procedure would be to have the national organize independently of either state or district organizations with the intention of working them into the national organization later.[32] In this connection, Mrs. Sommer, who had long been active in women's organizations in St. Louis, expressed the opinion that it was very necessary at this time to have a head or central body to give direction to the existing Ladies' Aid societies.[33]

As a result of these discussions the following resolution was unanimously adopted by a standing vote:

"Resolved, that we record it as the consensus of opinion of this meeting that we consider an attempt to organize the women of our church into a national federation as advisable."[34]

In the afternoon the discussions took the form of more detailed plans for organization. The Lutheran Laymen's League offered its assistance, as well as its office facilities, to the women.

The following procedure for organizing was suggested:

"That a temporary committee of five or seven members be elected to submit organizational plans, ways and means of raising funds, and a tentative or proposed constitution.

"That these plans and constitution be then submitted at the next meeting of the National Organization of Lutheran Women for approval. It was suggested that this general meeting be held in connection with the next meeting of the Board of Governors and district representatives of the Lutheran Laymen's League which was tentatively planned for Chicago during the first week in December."[35]

A motion followed calling for the election of a committee of seven "to draw up a constitution and lay the foundation and plans for a National Organization." The following were elected:

Mrs. L. Meyer, St. Louis, Mo.

Mrs. W. A. Maier, St. Louis, Mo.

Mrs. E. W. Schultz, Sheboygan, Wis.

Mrs. H. Kionka, South Orange, N. J.

Miss Marie Zucker, Fort Wayne, Ind.

Mrs. J. H. Deckman, Minneapolis, Minn.

Mrs. Charles Nehring, New York City

The committee was authorized to enlarge itself as it saw fit.[36]

The method of raising funds to effect the organization came under consideration next. Suggestions included (1) a general call to all Ladies' Aids to contribute toward such a fund, (2) contacting individuals for donations, and (3) having those present approach their own societies.[37]

Mr. Waltke offered a loan of $1,000 in the name of the Lutheran Laymen's League to start the fund. It was then resolved to establish an organization fund by soliciting private donations, the method of gathering these private funds to be at the discretion of the Organization Committee. Mrs. Schmitt was authorized to serve as temporary treasurer. A number of the women present pledged a total of $700 for this fund.[38]

The Organization Committee was also authorized to use its discretion as to who of those invited to attend the next meeting ought to be informed that, if necessary, the expenses may be equalized. The women who were present at this meeting had paid all of their own expenses.

In another resolution the Executive Committee of the Lutheran Laymen's League, together with Rev. L. Meyer, Executive Secretary pro tem of the LLL, were asked to act as an advisory body to the Organization Committee.

Other resolutions stipulated that "the National Organization of Lutheran Women be an organization of societies belonging to congregations of the Missouri Synod only" and "that temporary headquarters be maintained in the office of the Lutheran Laymen's League, 3558 So. Jefferson Avenue, St. Louis, Missouri." [39]

In the discussion which followed, regarding whether the organization should be an independent organization or an auxiliary to the Lutheran Laymen's League, there was a divergence of opinion. When no agreement could be reached, it was decided to postpone action until the Organization Committee had made a study of the matter and reported its findings.[40]

In response to the question of an official organ, Mr. Waltke suggested that the committee keep in mind the possibility of a joint Lutheran publication. The offer of Mr. Grossmann to use the LLL *Bulletin* for publicity purposes was accepted, and Rev. L. Meyer was asked to write news items on this meeting for the various church publications.[41]

A discussion of a name for the organization drew the following suggestions: Lutheran Women's League; Lutheran Daughters of the Reformation; and International Lutheran Women's League.[42]

Decide to Meet Again

The group thanked the Lutheran Laymen's League for the assistance they were giving the women in their effort and asked them, if possible, to arrange the next meeting of their Board of Governors for January instead of the first week in December, as indicated previously.[43] (This request was granted at a meeting of the LLL Executive Committee on Nov. 14, 1929.)[44]

The arrangements for this meeting of the National Organization of Lutheran Women, to be held in conjunction with the next meeting of the Board of Governors of the LLL and its district representatives, were to be made by the Organization Committee.[45]

By resolution of the group, Pastor Kowert was requested to be the synodical representative at the meetings of the organization.[46]

An announcement of the proposed meeting was carried in the *Lutheran Laymen's League Bulletin* (Jan. 1, 1930) as follows:

"On January 17 and 18 in Chicago, at the Palmer House, there will be held a meeting of representative women from all parts of our Church.

"At this meeting definite steps for the organization of a national league of Lutheran women will be taken. A committee elected at the St. Louis meeting has prepared an extensive program and will also present a proposed constitution for a national organization." [47]

Meantime the Organization Committee had been busy since the November meeting in St. Louis drawing up a constitution and discussing ways and means of collecting organization funds. In a letter dated Nov. 25, 1929, the committee informed those who had attended the November meeting that the committee had met immediately following the meeting on Nov. 5, and again on Nov. 14. At the latter meeting, they said, a constitution was presented and discussed point for point. Since it was "so closely in accord with the opinions expressed at the meetings of November 5 and 6, your committee thought it advisable that instead of going to the expense of having the constitution mimeographed first, we would have it set up in type as it will appear in the printed constitution eventually, this type to be held until our January meeting when this tentative constitution will be presented, discussed, and adopted or changed as the assembly will see fit." [48] (Actually, the constitution was printed prior to the January meeting.)

In connection with the method of collecting organization funds, the committee indicated that a brief pamphlet was being prepared which would enlarge on the objective of the proposed organization with the view to create an interest in such a venture. This, it was hoped, would make it easier to get donations toward the Organization Fund.[49]

Another letter, dated Jan. 13, 1930, signed by the secretary, Mrs. W. A. Maier, called attention to the space which the *Lutheran Laymen's League Bulletin* had given the proposed organization and stated that the *Bulletin,* together with a letter, had been sent to "all of our 3500 pastors in Synod as well as to the president of every Ladies' Aid Society through the respective pastors." [50]

1930 Meeting

In addition, letters of invitation were sent to a number of women throughout the country who, it was thought, might be interested in the proposed organization. The *Lutheran Laymen's League Bulletin* reported that the response to these letters was overwhelming. "At one time," it said, "no less than 200 letters were stacked up on the desk of the L. W. L., and all but three voiced the hearty approval of those who had been invited to the meeting." While distance, expense, and household duties prevented many from coming, the attendance at the meeting ranged from 100 to 125.[51]

Mrs. Otto F. Schmitt of St. Louis was elected temporary president and Mrs. E. Riep of Albany, N. Y., secretary. Mr. A. A. Grossmann, Rev. Henry Kowert, and Prof. Theodore Graebner were asked to serve as advisors for the meeting. [52]

Mrs. E. W. Schultz, of Sheboygan, Wis., had been requested by the committee to speak on "The Present Status of Ladies' Organizations Within Our Church." She cited the various district federations which had been formed, such as the Lutheran Women's Missionary Endeavor of the Central District, the Lutheran Women's League of Oklahoma, and also the efforts which were being made along that line in the St. Paul-Minneapolis area. "In many circles," Mrs. Schultz said, "the thought has been expressed that it would be to the advantage of all concerned if these independent local and state organizations could be brought together on common ground with common objectives in a national organization."[53]

The objectives of the projected federation were presented by Mrs. W. A. Maier of St. Louis, who spoke on the question "Shall We Form a National Women's Organization?" She said in part:

"Women are able to serve our Church in a far greater capacity than has hitherto been the case. What forces have not been released through the work of the Walther League in bringing our young people to a realization of their opportunities? When, before a national association was formed, did our young people have systematic Bible study, missionary endeavors, hospice work, and educational features?" Mrs. Maier also cited the influence the LLL had had to make the laymen active in a wider sphere. "If the ladies' aid has been a helpful organization in thousands of our congregations," continued Mrs. Maier, "why should these ladies' aids not act jointly for the support of missions and charities? They are not indeed to become collection agencies for the Synod, but they may foster many causes of a charitable nature. . . . Through national cooperation an educational program may be fostered which will bring into every ladies' aid suggestions and material for inspirational addresses and for a study of topics in which women are particularly interested." [54]

Favor National Organization

While the discussion which followed elicited numerous responses, the women expressed hearty approval of a national organization.

Attention was called to the fact that other denominations had such women's organizations and that the women of our church ought to have the same.

Mrs. Deckman of Minneapolis read a letter dated Dec. 16, 1929, from Pastors Paul Lindemann and E. G. Nachtsheim, both of the Twin Cities, which she had received in answer to her inquiry about their reactions to a national women's organization. The views expressed contain the following:

"First of all, we wish to state that a movement of this kind should be completely independent of any other organization now in existence and should not have the position of being a mere auxiliary of some other body. There ought to be in such an organization freedom of action undirected by any other body of a similar character, subject only to the necessary synodical limitations in order that there might be no conflict between the interests of the Women's Society and those of Synod.

"Another point which we think ought to be stressed is this, that the women have complete jurisdiction over their own funds and that these funds be not used for the fostering of the aims and purposes of an organization of which it is merely the auxiliary.

"We also believe that the funds of such an organization should not flow into the regular channels of the Church but should be used for missionary purposes in conjunction with the work of the Church but for the carrying out of which the Church has not the necessary means. The utilization of the funds for the regular missionary treasuries of Synod would tend to hamper the devolpment of regular, systematic giving for outside purposes through the regular channels of the Church on the part of the individual members. There are many projects of the Church of a missionary character which the Church cannot properly develop, and which could be undertaken by an organization of this kind."

The letter further warned that a committee of individual women has no power to call a permanent organization into existence. It granted that such a group could meet in a preliminary way to launch such an organization but that only after a sufficient number of societies had ratified such a venture could it become a reality. "The meeting in Chicago should not elect permanent officers," they said, "nor has it the power to adopt a permanent constitution. Its resolutions must be only suggestive and in every way preliminary. The organization itself must be effected by the women's societies of which the organization is to consist."

The letter concluded by expressing a genuine interest and approval of a national women's organization, with the hope that such an organization would be called into being "along lines which are entirely unobjectionable and which will be of great value to the Church." [55]

Mrs. Paul Heckel of New York reported that many organizations in the East were heartily in favor of a national organization and pointed out that "some women and groups of women have joined with societies of other denominations and taken up some special work in their organization just because there is nothing to do, owing to lack of information and knowledge of what should be done at the meetings of our Ladies' Aid Societies." [56]

Cautions

Mr. Eugene Wengert, a lawyer and member of the Board of Directors of Synod, had been requested by the board to attend the women's meeting. He addressed the group and commended them for the spirit that had brought about such a meeting. At the same time he pointed out a number of dangers which he cautioned the women not to overlook:

1. That all action taken by the group must be referred to the proper channels for ratification. These, he said, would include not only the Board of Directors of Synod but beyond that.

2. That it may not succeed because of lack of support in Synod. "The Board of Directors feels that this organization may be for good, but can easily be for things that are beside the point."

3. That the things at home may be neglected as the result of a national organization.

4. That a national body may not be able to function as efficiently as a local body.

Mr. Wengert did, however, conclude with a word of encouragement. He felt, he said, that a women's organization "can be used for much more extensive work today; it can influence the men of our church to much more decided activity and decided liberal support of the undertakings of Synod, which should not be overlooked in this attempt." [57]

In concluding the morning session, Mr. Grossmann cautioned the women "to faithfully follow the advice and warning that we should comply with every detail necessary in order to do the things required, and also realize that our success hinges on that very thing." He also pointed out that there were both advantages and disadvantages in such a proposed organization but that, in his opinion, the advantages outweighed any "doubt that may exist in the minds of some." He was convinced, he said, that an association of women's societies could be made to function "for good and good only." In concluding his remarks, Mr. Grossmann said that it ought to be determined whether there was a need or demand for the kind of organization that was proposed.[58]

In the afternoon session, Prof. Theodore Graebner addressed the group. He pointed out that, in connection with synodical regulations, two things needed to be kept in mind: (1) the objective of the constitution and (2) whether the constitution contains anything that would conflict with the rights of the individual congregation. He referred to the provision of the synodical Constitution which made the congregation supreme. Therefore, he said, "the congregation must be asked for permission to organize." [59]

Mr. Grossmann pointed out that since the tentative constitution had been drawn up a number of factors had developed which necessitated a revision of the constitution and suggested that a committee of seven or more be appointed to consider various forms and plans of organization, to be presented at the meeting the next morning.

Such a committee, consisting of nine to 12 or more ladies, was authorized and a resolution passed providing for representation on this committee from all sections of the country. The following were appointed to this committee:

Mrs. J. H. Deckman, Minneapolis, Minn.
Mrs. F. R. Zucker, Fort Wayne, Ind.
Mrs. M. L. Wyneken, Los Angeles, Calif.
Mrs. E. Riep, Albany, N. Y.
Mrs. Paul Heckel, New York City

Mrs. E. W. Schultz, Sheboygan, Wis.
Mrs. L. J. Reindel, Detroit, Mich.
Mrs. W. G. Bohnsack, Chicago, Ill.
Mrs. E. Wengert, Milwaukee, Wis.
Mrs. E. W. Tatge, Evanston, Ill.
Mrs. F. Krueger, Chicago, Ill.
Mrs. C. Schicht, Chicago, Ill.
Mrs. H. F. Rohrmann, Wilmette, Ill.
Miss M. Zucker, Fort Wayne, Ind.
Mrs. W. A. Maier, St. Louis, Mo.
Mrs. L. Meyer, St. Louis, Mo.

In addition to these women, the following men were asked to attend the meeting of the committee: a committee of the LLL appointed by them; the representatives of the Board of Directors of Synod — Pastor Henry Kowert and Mr. E. Wengert; and the counselors and advisors of the women's group — Prof. Theo. Graebner, Mr. A. A. Grossmann, and Rev. L. Meyer.[60]

When the sessions convened on Saturday morning, Mr. Grossmann gave a brief outline of the proposed constitution, and Mrs. L. Meyer was asked to present the constitution article by article. The constitution, with the changes which were adopted, reads as follows:

Proposed Constitution

Article I. — Name

The name of the association shall be: The Lutheran Women's League of the Evangelical Lutheran Synod of Missouri, Ohio, and Other States.

Article II. — Objectives

A. The objectives of the Lutheran Women's League shall be: —

1) To encourage one another to give assistance to our home congregations according to local needs.

2) To create a greater interest in the mission-work of our Church by providing opportunity and material for the study of missions.

3) To cooperate in charitable endeavors.

4) To furnish practical material and helps for the meeting of local women's societies.

B. The better to execute these objectives, the Lutheran Women's League shall have the power to hold, purchase, lease, sell, exchange, and receive, by gift, devise, or bequest, all kinds of property, real and personal, and to do all things necessary to carry out the objects of the organization.

Article III. — Memberships

The Lutheran Women's League is an association composed of women who are communicant members within congregations of the Evangelical Lutheran Synod of Missouri, Ohio, and Other States.

All women's organizations of any congregation affiliated with the aforesaid Synod are eligible to membership.

Article IV. — Officers

1) The officers of the Lutheran Women's League shall be: a president, four regional vice-presidents, a recording secretary, a treasurer, and a financial secretary.

2) The affairs of the Lutheran Women's League shall be governed by a Board of Governors, consisting of the president, the treasurer, five members elected by the Lutheran Women's League, one clergy-man, as an advisory member, appointed by the Board of Directors of the Missouri Synod, and one advisory member appointed by the Board of Governors of the Lutheran Laymen's League.

Article V. — Meetings

The Lutheran Women's League shall meet annually for the purpose of directing the affairs of the association.

Article VI. — Amendments

This Constitution of the Lutheran Women's League may be amended by a two-thirds majority vote at any regular meeting of the Lutheran Women's League, provided that notice of proposed changes has previously been published.

Article VII. — By-Laws

The affairs of the Lutheran Women's League shall be governed by such by-laws as the Lutheran Women's League may from time to time adopt, not inconsistent with these articles, or the Constitution of the United States, or the laws of the State of Missouri, or the tenets of the Evangelical Lutheran Synod of Missouri, Ohio, and Other States.[61]

After the adoption of the constitution with the necessary changes, it was resolved (1) to form a preliminary association under the constitution as proposed, (2) to elect officers to serve until the next convention, and (3) to have the chairman appoint a nominating committee.[62] In another resolution it was decided to have the convention of the Lutheran Women's League at the same time and place as the Lutheran Laymen's League.[63]

From the slate of candidates presented by the nominating committee the following were elected:

President:	Mrs. Otto Schmitt
Secretary:	Mrs. Ida Kellerman
Treasurer:	Mrs. H. J. Heitner
Vice-Presidents:	Mrs. W. Bohnsack
	Mrs. J. H. Deckman
	Mrs. Henry Dahlen
	Mrs. M. L. Wyneken

The following were elected to the Board of Governors: Mrs. E. W. Schultz, Sheboygan, Wis.; Mrs. W. F. Drexmit, Chicago, Ill.; Mrs. L. Meyer, St. Louis, Mo.; Mrs. L. J. Reindel, Detroit, Mich.; and Mrs. Ben Pritzlaff, Milwaukee, Wis.[64]

One of the final resolutions called for the soliciting of "voluntary contributions from individuals and interested societies to carry on the work of the association until the next convention." [65]

Hopes Soon Shattered

The women left Chicago with high hopes that a national women's organization would soon be a reality, despite the misgivings of the Board of Directors of Synod as expressed by Mr. Wengert. The events which followed proved that their hopes were soon to be shattered.

Several months after this historic convention in Chicago, women from churches throughout Kansas met in Wichita on March 30, 1930, to organize "The Lutheran Women's League of Kansas." As the result of the talk made by Mrs. L. Meyer of St. Louis about the proposed national organization of women, the women, 170 in number, representing the majority of the congregations in the state, voted to urge individual ladies' organizations in Kansas to join the tentative national organization. They also passed a resolution declaring that "it shall be the object of this organization to be of service to the Church and that whatever projects this organization may favor, support, and carry on shall be in keeping with true Missouri Synod Lutheran church practise, and that we stand ready to aid our home congregations and the Church at large." [66]

A meeting of the temporary Board of Governors of the proposed Lutheran Women's League was held in St. Louis on Feb. 27, 1930, which was also attended by two members of the advisory board: Mr. A. A. Grossmann and Rev. A. Ullrich, the latter representing the College of Presidents.

Reporting on this meeting, the *Lutheran Laymen's League Bulletin* said:

"The present movement in our circles for more effective work and wider fields of organized Lutheran womanhood was again discussed, including a study and survey of the reaction of this movement up to the present time and a careful and conscientious consideration of the wisest and most proper steps next to be taken." [67]

The article pointed out also that, while "all the ladies present manifested a profound spirit of loyalty to our Lutheran Church and its Scriptural principles" there existed differences of opinion as to the feasibility of such an organization. As a result, it was resolved "to submit this important matter also to the College of Presidents for counsel and advice, which body will meet in St. Louis during the last week in May." [68]

Prior to the meeting of the College of Presidents an article entitled, "Aims and Ideals of a Federation of Ladies' Aid Societies" appeared in the women's section of the LLL *Bulletin*. This article undoubtedly was intended to clarify the purposes for which such an organization of women was desired on a national scale. "The demand for a Lutheran Women's League," said the article, "has risen spontaneously. In half a dozen areas of our Synod they are already uniting into federations, some District-wide. The ideals which called forth this activity are such as naturally grow out of the soil of Christian character." [69]

Synodical Committee

When the College of Presidents met on May 27 and 28, 1930, the matter was presented by Mr. Louis H. Waltke and Mr. A. A. Grossmann. The various aspects of such a venture were discussed, and President Pfotenhauer was authorized to appoint a committee to advise the sponsors of the proposed Lutheran Women's League.[70] Rev. J. Schinnerer, President of the Michigan District; Rev. Paul Schulz, President of the Central Illinois District; and Rev. Alex Ullrich, President of the Northern Illinois District, were appointed to this committee.[71]

Meanwhile the temporary officers of the League, which constituted its Board of Governors, was to meet on Sept. 5 to formulate plans for an organization meeting to be held in October 1930. This meeting was to be open to delegates from all societies which had registered, to representatives of other ladies' societies, and to all women of the church interested in the movement.[72]

The Board of Governors met again on Sept. 25, together with the Advisory Committee and the synodically appointed Committee. At this meeting Rev. Ullrich reported the results of the discussion concerning an organization of Lutheran women on a synodical scale which had taken place at the meeting of the synodical District Presidents the preceding day. He stated that the Presidents advised against the organization of this federation along the lines submitted for the following reasons: "1) The need for such an organization was not admitted, as it would seem that even with their present organizations our women have ample opportunity for service; 2) a survey taken among quite a number of pastoral conferences revealed a great deal of adverse opinion; 3) ministers and teachers are becoming overburdened by societies and an additional organization will mean more work." [73]

The men pointed out that, while the College of Presidents is not a body "that can forbid or grant anything," its voice ought to be heeded because it reflected the sentiments prevalent in the Districts.[74]

In view of the "mandate" from the College of Presidents, Mr.

Grossmann "definitely recommended the abandonment of the idea of a national organization at this time." Instead he suggested "that Synod itself might institute some department in order to give the assistance that is necessary if the services of ladies' aids are to become more proficient and the value of their work is to be enhanced." [75]

Since the women present at this meeting had been elected to represent a larger body and had been given definite directives, they felt that the temporary organization had no right to disband "without having given an account of its activities and of the expenditures which have been made during its lifetime." A resolution was therefore passed calling for a meeting of women on Nov. 19 in Chicago, at which time the following proposals would be presented:

"Resolved, That because of the situation as it has developed and presents itself to us, we recommend to the next assembly of women that no permanent organization be formed, but that other ways and means be found to meet existing needs.

"Resolved, That we invite all those who are interested in solving our problem to be in attendance at the meeting." [76]

The members of the Advisory Committee and also the synodical committee were asked to serve the women and to attend all meetings, including the meeting in Chicago.[77]

When the meeting in Chicago on Nov. 19, 1930, was convened, Pastor Fred Wambsganss of Fort Wayne gave a thorough presentation of the work which the women in the Central District were doing. He was followed by Pastor W. Birkner, also of Fort Wayne, who said that "the fear expressed that the regular budget would suffer had been unfounded." They (the Central District) found that the "miting" congregations came closer to meeting all the requirements of the budget than those that did not "mite." The ladies' aids also had increased in membership, Pastor Birkner said.

Pastor Schulz, one of the synodically appointed representatives, suggested, among other things, that the women "resubmit a new plan to the College of Presidents at their next meeting in June 1931." He indicated that it was necessary to determine what was really needed, also "what problems we wish to take up but not to organize at the present time." To this Mr. Grossmann replied that the women were not ready to organize but that the matter ought not be dropped, and concurred in the suggestion that the matter be presented to the College of Presidents again.[78]

Pastor Ullrich, the other synodical representative, indicated that "the consensus of opinion of the College of Presidents was that the movement is a good one and Synod appreciates the services of the women in our Church, therefore, the project ought to be considered from all angles. The College of Presidents did not mean to condemn the organizing of an L. W. L., however, they studied the matter and feel that all purposes are answered by the present number of organizations and they fear very much the danger of over organization." [79]

Pastor Schulz answered questions which were asked concerning the attitude of the College of Presidents by stating that (1) the "home is being disturbed by too many societies; and (2) the pastors are becoming over-burdened by societies, which causes them to neglect their duties." He assured everyone that the matter was not clear to the College of Presidents. The women should be kindly disposed to the ministers, he said. He also suggested that they appeal again to the College of Presidents, stressing the many and various needs of the Ladies' Aids in their work for the church.[80]

"Find Ways and Means!"

As a result of the foregoing, the following resolution was adopted:

"Resolved that we refer the matter of a national women's association to the College of Presidents with the request that they assist us in finding ways and means of accomplishing the objectives of the proponents of this movement, principally a deeper interest in the work of Synod and greater activities on the part of Lutheran women in their proper sphere." [81]

A thorough discussion on the proper procedure in view of the above produced resolutions authorizing the present Board of Governors, together with the acting officers and advisors, to constitute a committee to work out a plan of its needs to be presented to the College of Presidents; the addition of Mrs. William Bohnsack of Chicago to the committee; and authorization for Mrs. Walter A. Maier to act as vice-president.[82]

At the afternoon session, Mr. Grossmann requested the assembly to select a committee to confer with representatives of the College of Presidents to determine the procedure to be followed in the future. His request was granted, and the following were placed on the committee: Mrs. O. Schmitt, Mrs. H. Heitner, Mrs. I. Kellermann, Mrs. W. A. Maier, Mrs. L. Meyer, Mrs. W. F. Drexmit, Mrs. E. W. Schulz, Mrs. L. J. Feindel, Mrs. Wm. G. Bohnsack, Mrs. E. Wengert; the Advisors: Pastor Kowert and Mr. Grossmann; and the representatives of the College of Presidents: Pastors Ullrich and Schulz. The committee was empowered to call a meeting at a later date.[83]

In conclusion, those present were advised "not to become discouraged, but to continue working for this wonderful cause, slowly and carefully in the right Christian spirit." [84]

Several meetings were held, both by the advisors and the Executive Committee, to try to determine the course to be pursued. Various possibilities were discussed. Finally, at a meeting of the Executive Committee on April 20, 1931, six possible ways of proceeding were presented for consideration. Following are the six ways suggested:

1. Again to present our matter to the College of Presidents.

2. To send an overture to the next plenary session of Synod.

3. To associate ourselves with the Lutheran Laymen's League.

4. To postpone attempted organization.

5. To disband and drop the matter entirely.

6. To proceed with organization irrespective of the advice given.

"After all these points had been thoroughly discussed, it was decided to seek to accomplish our objectives without organization, possibly through an association with the LLL." [85]

At another meeting of the tentative Lutheran Women's League in Chicago, on May 22, 1931, in which the whole matter was reviewed again, the chairman presented two alternatives:

"1. To request the LLL to institute a women's division of the LLL, which is to be headed by a council of women, under the direction and guidance of the Board of Governors of the LLL.

"2. To start locally in districts according to the boundaries of districts of Synod." [86]

Mr. Grossmann explained that the first alternative embodied

three parts which had been agreed upon by the Advisors in a meeting on April 20, 1931. Their recommendations were:

"1. To offer their assistance in enrolling sustaining members for the LLL.

"2. To request the LLL to institute a women's division of the LLL which is to be headed by a Council of Women under the direction and guidance of the Board of Governors of the LLL.

"3. This department is to give the women individually an opportunity to assist the LLL in its endeavor and is also to furnish helpful material to Ladies' Aids in order that they may make their meetings as profitable as possible." [87]

Go Independent

Mrs. W. A. Maier objected to the idea of joining the LLL for the following reasons:

"1. It makes all thoughts of the original plan impossible. It provides only for individual members, whereas our original purpose was to unite ladies' aids.

"2. It has a national scope which has provoked the criticism of the representatives of conferences.

"3. The LLL is misunderstood and misrepresented in many sections of the Church, a fact which will immediately antagonize the women of those sections.

"4. The LLL is burdened with its own problems with hardly enough time for them and can't take care of a women's department.

"5. If the LLL fails to grow, the women's cause in our Church is lost for this generation.

"6. The women can still work with the LLL and have an organic union. It is still possible for the LLL to form a women's division which can enlist the support of the women, but does not constitute a substitution for the original plan." [88]

The six alternatives which had been discussed at the April 20 Executive Committee meeting were read again. Finally the following resolution was adopted:

"Resolved, that in accordance with the advice of the Synodical representatives we postpone the organization of a National Women's League for the present."

Another resolution, however, encouraged the women who were eager to serve the church more effectively to work both individually and collectively in their own areas to create a better understanding of what the group was trying to accomplish through a national organization.[89]

Dean Fritz Encourages

Dr. John H. C. Fritz, the first and long-time dean of Concordia Seminary in St. Louis, was an ardent supporter of the Lutheran Laymen's League, particularly in its formative years and especially in connection with its radio ministry. He was also serving at this time (1930—31) on a committee of the LLL to try to secure closer cooperation between the laymen and synodical officials. The LLL had effected a reorganization several years previously which broadened the scope of its activities and resulted in misunderstanding and apprehension. Dr. Fritz was also interested in the formation of a national women's organization. In fact, he was present at a meeting of the LLL Board of Governors on April 28, 1931, when the women's movement was discussed.[90] He undoubtedly had either or both of these efforts in mind when he wrote the following editorial in the *Lutheran Witness,* Dec. 9, 1930:

" 'Vast enterprises are never born of the masses, but of individuals.' In my reading recently I came across this sentence. It expresses a truth well established by experience: First the apostles, then the churches; first Luther, then the great Reformation; first a few Saxon immigrants, then the large Missouri Synod. The leaders of great enterprises at the beginning usually meet with much opposition and many difficulties; the apostles did, so did Luther, so did the founders of our Synod. And some opposition, strange to say, at times comes from their own friends, who directly discourage the undertaking or at least will not encourage it and will not cooperate with them. These friends do not mean to discourage a good cause, but nevertheless they do. For the leaders of any great movement those are trying times. They need enlightenment, courage, and zeal, which alone God can give them. Let us thank God whenever He gives us such leaders." [91]

Notes

V

1. *Moving Frontiers,* ed. Carl S. Meyer (St. Louis: Concordia, 1964), p. 376.

2. *Proceedings of the Thirty-First National Convention of the Ev. Luth. Synod of Missouri, Ohio, and Other States,* Detroit, June 16—25, 1920 (English ed.), p. 29.

3. *Proceedings of the Thirty-Second Regular Meeting of the Ev. Luth. Synod of Missouri, Ohio, and Other States,* Fort Wayne, June 20—29, 1923 (English ed.), p. 11.

4. *Proceedings of the Thirty-Third Regular Convention of the Ev. Luth. Synod of Missouri, Ohio, and Other States,* St. Louis, June 9—18, 1926 (English ed.), p. 77.

5. *Moving Frontiers,* p. 380.

6. "History of the Oklahoma District Lutheran Women's Missionary League," undated manuscript, Concordia Historical Institute, p. 1; *Proceedings of the Thirty-Second Regular Meeting of the Ev. Luth. Synod of Missouri, Ohio, and Other States,* p. 45.

7. *Lutheran Laymen's League Bulletin,* I (Jan. 1, 1930), 46. (Hereafter cited as *LLL Bulletin*)

8. *History of Central District Lutheran Women's Missionary Endeavor 1928—1942 and Lutheran Women's Missionary League 1943—1964* (1966), p. 6.

9. Minutes, Organization Meeting, Lutheran Women's League, Jan. 17—18, 1930, p. 1.

10. *Proceedings of the Fifty-Fifth Convention of the Central District of the Ev. Luth. Synod of Missouri, Ohio, and Other States,* Fort Wayne, June 24—29, 1928, p. 78.

11. Ibid.

12. *History of Central District Lutheran Women's Missionary Endeavor, etc.,* p. 9.

13. Ibid., pp. 7—8.

14. *Lutheran Witness,* XLVIII (July 9, 1929), 234—235.

15. Minutes, Lutheran Laymen's League Executive Committee, Sept. 3, 1929, p. 46.

16. Ibid., Sept. 11, 1929, p. 52.

17. Ibid., Sept. 27, 1929, p. 56.

18. Ibid., Oct. 10, 1929, p. 58.

19. From the file of Mrs. J. H. Deckman.

20. Minutes of the Meeting of Representative Lutheran Women Held at the Missouri Athletic Association, St. Louis, Nov. 6, 1929, pp. 1—2. From the file of Mrs. J. H. Deckman.

21. Ibid., p. 2.

22. Ibid.

23. Ibid., p. 3.

24. Ibid.

25. Ibid.

26. Ibid.

27. Ibid.

28. Ibid., p. 4.

29. Ibid., p. 3.

30. Ibid., p. 4.

31. Ibid., p. 3.

32. Ibid., p. 4.

33. Ibid.

34. Ibid.

35. Ibid., p. 5.

36. Ibid.

37. Ibid.

38. Ibid., p. 6.

39. Ibid.

40. Ibid., pp. 6—7.

41. Ibid., p. 7.

42. Ibid.

43. Ibid.

44. Minutes, Lutheran Laymen's League Executive Committee, Nov. 14, 1929, p. 67.

45. Minutes . . . Representative Lutheran Women, p. 7.

46. Ibid.

47. *LLL Bulletin,* I (Jan. 1, 1930), 48.

48. From the file of Mrs. J. H. Deckman.

49. Ibid.

50. Ibid.

51. *LLL Bulletin,* I (Feb. 7, 1930), 59.

52. Minutes of Organization Meeting, Lutheran Women's League, Jan. 17—18, 1930, Chicago, p. 1. From the file of Mrs. H. J. Heitner.

53. Ibid.

54. *LLL Bulletin,* I (Feb. 7, 1930), 59.

55. From the file of Mrs. J. H. Deckman.

56. Minutes, Organization Meeting, Lutheran Women's League, p. 5.

57. Ibid., pp. 5—7.

58. Ibid., pp. 7—8.

59. Ibid., p. 8.

60. Ibid., p. 9.

61. Ibid., pp. 11—12; Proposed Constitution and By-Laws of the Lutheran Women's League of the Ev. Luth. Synod of Missouri, Ohio, and Other States (St. Louis: Concordia, 1929); *LLL Bulletin,* I (Feb. 7, 1930), 63.

62. Minutes, Organization Meeting, Lutheran Women's League, p. 12.

63. Ibid.

64. Ibid., p. 13.

65. Ibid., p. 12.

66. *LLL Bulletin,* I (April 15, 1930), 92—93.

67. Ibid., I (March 26, 1930), 75.

68. Ibid., pp. 75—76.

69. Ibid., I (May 15, 1930), 107.

70. Ibid., I (June 16, 1930), 125.

71. Ibid., II (Aug. 1, 1930), 11.

72. Ibid.

73. Ibid., II (Oct. 22, 1930), 44.

74. Ibid.

75. Ibid.

76. Ibid.

77. Ibid.

78. Minutes, Lutheran Women's League, Chicago, Nov. 19, 1930, p. 1. From the file of Mrs. H. J. Heitner.

79. Ibid., p. 2.

80. Ibid.

81. Ibid.

82. Ibid.

83. Ibid., p. 3.

84. Ibid.

85. Minutes, Executive Committee, Temporary Women's League, St. Louis, April 20, 1931, pp. 1—2.

86. Minutes, Tentative Lutheran Women's League, Chicago, May 22, 1931, p. 2.

87. Ibid.; also Minutes, Advisors to the Lutheran Women's League, April 20, 1931 (one page only).

88. Minutes, Tentative Lutheran Women's League, Chicago, May 22, 1931, p. 2.

89. Ibid., p. 3.

90. Minutes, Lutheran Laymen's League Board of Governors, April 28, 1931, pp. 276—277.

91. *Lutheran Witness,* XLIX (Dec. 9, 1930), 420.

VI

The Seedling Is Nourished

THE ESCALATING ECONOMY in the United States in the '20s, particularly in the last few years of that decade, came to an abrupt halt with the stock market crash in October 1929. This produced a chaotic state not only in the country as such but in the lives of millions of individuals as well. Millionaires were reduced to paupers overnight, and the appalling suicide rate that followed gave evidence of the extent to which America had come to rely on material things. Virtually no one remained unaffected in some way by this catastrophe. Millions of people lost their employment and with it, of course, their source of income. The '30s, which came to be known as the years of the Great Depression, are still vivid in the minds of many individuals today.

The church, of course, could not escape the effects of this situation either. Dr. Pfotenhauer, President of the Missouri Synod, presented the grave financial picture of Synod at that time in an article in the *Western District Lutheran*. He pointed out that, while it had been possible previously for Synod to borrow money to meet the regular expenses if there was not sufficient money in the synodical treasury, the banks now refused to make further loans. "The dwindling receipts in the congregations," said Dr. Pfotenhauer, "are a cause for deep concern. The Synodical treasurer has reached the end of resources." Dr. Pfotenhauer urged every member in Synod to purchase notes at the rate of 4% and appealed particularly for more regular contributions. "It is apparent," he said, "that unless our appeal is answered a catastrophe will come over Synod which will leave in its wake devastating effects, noticeable upon every branch of our church work, if not upon the very organization of our Church." [1] During this period, too, many young men preparing for church professions were left standing idle in the marketplace for want of financial resources to place them into the service of the church.

The Lord often uses adversity to achieve His purposes. The history of Israel shows how God time and again used chastening of one kind or another to rekindle an awareness in His people of their sins with a resultant spiritual renewal. The depression of the '30s, too, caused the leaders of the church to reevaluate the program of the church and to launch various programs to improve the spirituality of its members. One such effort was the Mission Forward Movement, which had as its goal "the awakening and deepening of missionary zeal on the part of the clergy and laity, setting forth the grave responsibility of every Christian as missionary and the abundant mission opportunities." [2] In connection with this effort a series of outlines for mission lectures was printed and distributed for use by pastors to stimulate interest in the cause of missions.

There was also a development during this period of educational features for young people's societies and for ladies' aids. The *American Lutheran* published numerous articles during the '30s on women's societies in the church, with special emphasis and suggestions for educational programs. One such article, "Lutheran Women's Societies," was written by Oscar E. Feucht, then pastor of Calvary Lutheran Church, Kansas City, Mo. Pastor Feucht explained in great detail the program of Christian Knowledge and Christian Service which was being successfully carried out by the women in his parish. "We need a constructive program for all our women's societies," said Pastor Feucht, "that can be used in replacing the program which most ladies' aids still have . . . a definite program of Christian Knowledge and Christian Service; a program that continues the work begun in good young people's societies." [3]

It was also early in this decade, as previously stated, that the movement for a national federation of women in the church likewise suffered a "depression." This resulted from the advice of the College of Presidents of Synod not to proceed with plans for such an organization at that time. Tentative objectives adopted by officers of this women's group (March 16, 1931 — prior to the directive from the College of Presidents) include the following: To aid the Evangelical Lutheran Synod of Missouri, Ohio, and Other States in its financial needs, particularly in reference to missions; to create a greater interest in the mission work of our church by providing opportunity and material for the study of missions; to furnish practical material and help for the meeting of local women's societies.[4] These objectives coincided with the emphasis in Synod as a whole at that time.

In addition to the fear of overorganization which existed among the clergy in Synod and was expressed by the College of Presidents, there was opposition to the proposed organization on the basis that the objectives of the proposed organization were those which properly belonged to the local congregation. Furthermore, it was felt that because of the depression and other projects under way in the church, the time was inopportune.[5] That the concerted efforts of the woman-power in the church could be utilized to help the church solve its problems apparently did not receive serious consideration. Though the spirits of the women who had championed the cause of a national organization were crushed by the directive of the College of Presidents, they were by no means broken.

The Temporary Lutheran Women's League, meeting on May 22, 1931, had authorized the formation of a committee to serve as "a clearing house for suggestions, advice or information for ladies' aids," and the committee which had been serving was asked to continue. It was also authorized to enlarge itself as it saw fit.[6]

In view of the financial status of the temporary organization, a resolution was also passed asking the LLL to "bear with us . . . until we can afford to pay them." The resolution also thanked the LLL for the assistance it had given. At the same time the group promised to support the LLL in the future.[7] When the Acting Committee met the following month (June 9, 1931), the debt was discussed further. In addition to the resolutions of the previous meeting, it was agreed that, because of the amount owed to the LLL in July, $1,354.75, the Acting Committee would be unable to pay for additional space in the *LLL Bulletin.* It was agreed that "if, however, the LLL should at any time care to present items of interest to women, we accept such courtesy with gratitude." [8]

The Acting Committee, meeting again on Nov. 3, 1931, after a long summer recess, discussed the matter of an enlarged committee and decided that the committee should not be increased at that time beyond the five individuals who had been agreed upon at the previous meeting. Dr. Theo. Graebner and Rev. Lawrence Meyer were asked to continue as advisors. In addition Dr. W. A. Maier was to be requested to serve. It was suggested that the synodical District and circuit plan be studied with a view to using a similar plan for the LWL. [9]

In January, however, the committee enlarged itself by the addition of two members. (The entire committee, including the officers, were all from St. Louis.) Because of Mr. Louis H. Waltke's keen interest and helpful assistance in an unofficial capacity from the beginning of the effort to form a women's federation, he was asked to serve as one of the official advisors. The matter of the indebtedness to the Lutheran Laymen's League was again discussed at length, but since there was no change in the financial status of the group, no action could be taken. [10] This matter resolved itself a few months later when the LLL indicated that it had never charged this amount against the Lutheran Women's League. [11]

St. Louis Women Organize

About this time Valparaiso University sent representatives to St. Louis, as well as to other cities, to interest Lutheran women in forming chapters for the university, to provide financial assistance to the school and to recruit students. This was the spark that rekindled the flames of enthusiasm among the women, at least in some quarters. The matter was discussed in a meeting of the Enlarged Committee, together with specially invited guests on Feb. 19, 1932, resulting in an agreement to combine the Valparaiso effort under the banner of the Lutheran Women's League rather than have too many organizations. [12] Dr. Graebner expressed the opinion that two organizations would be impossible and that the greatest benefit would accrue to Valparaiso University if it were a part of the program of the Lutheran Women's League. [13]

Of special significance at the above meeting was the encouragement received by the women from Dr. Richard Kretzschmar, President of the Western District, who said that, while he could not at that time encourage the formation of a national organization, he heartily approved of the formation of a Lutheran Women's League of Greater St. Louis. He suggested that the committee petition the Pastoral Conference of St. Louis for its approval. He felt sure, he said, that if such an organization could be made to work satisfactorily in the St. Louis area, it would ultimately spread through the entire District. As a result the Enlarged Committee passed a resolution requesting the approval of the Pastoral Conference in this matter.[14]

The letter of the committee to the Pastoral Conference expressed surprise that the representatives of Valparaiso were permitted to organize chapters in various conferences when the temporary Lutheran Women's League had been requested to refrain from attempting to organize nationally as the Lutheran Women's League. Assurance was given the Pastoral Conference that, if approval were forthcoming, the organization would consist of a federation of the ladies' aid societies and would be only local in scope. The letter stated that this Lutheran Women's League would take over the Valparaiso project as one of its chief efforts and thus immediately preclude the establishment of another organization. In addition, it said it had what it believed to be a wide and helpful program in educational, missionary, and social features which, under divine blessing, would offer a very decided help to the cause of the church, especially in St. Louis.[15] Though the women indicated that the organization would be "only local in scope," it is evident that they never really lost sight of their goal to achieve a more general organization.

The results of the letter were not long in coming. On March 4, 1932 (less than a month after the request was made to the St. Louis Pastoral Conference), it was reported at a meeting of the Enlarged Committee of the Lutheran Women's League that the Pastoral Conference had expressed its approval of a Greater St. Louis Lutheran Women's League and wished it God's blessing.[16]

The wheels were quickly set in motion to implement the action of the St. Louis Pastoral Conference. Letters were sent to each pastor and ladies' society in the St. Louis area informing them of the proposed organization and asking that they send the chairman of their Aid, plus as many additional women as were interested, to a meeting on March 18, which would mark the beginning of the new organization.[17]

At this meeting Dr. Kretzschmar pointed out that the methods employed by the organization should be based on sound Christian principles and that the principle of the supremacy of the local congregation must be kept in mind. He spoke of the opportunities for women, who had helped from the beginning of time, and encouraged those present to "show leadership here in St. Louis to form a federation, which, under God's guidance, may be an influence felt by other organizations." [18]

The motion to organize was carried and the object of the organization stated as follows: "The object of this organization shall be to interest, inspire, and federate our Lutheran women and women's organizations for concerted service which can be rendered to our Church in various Christian endeavors by united efforts of women." [19] The missionary and educational emphasis adopted tentatively by the officers earlier were not spelled out when the new organization was formed.

At a subsequent meeting (April 15, 1932) 42 women joined as charter members, a constitution and bylaws were adopted, and the name "Lutheran Women's League of Greater St. Louis" was selected as the official name of the organization.[20] (The name was changed in September of the same year to "Lutheran Women's League, Missouri Synod" and in February 1938 to "Lutheran Woman's League, Missouri Synod.")[21] Charter membership was held open until the June meeting, when the election of officers took place. At that meeting eight societies were represented, and 50 members were present. The constitution provided for both individual and society memberships. Societies were represented by two delegates from each society. Dues for societies were optional, dues for individuals $1.00 or more per year. Mrs. Otto F. Schmitt, who had so ably led the effort to organize nationally, was elected as the first president of the St. Louis organization, a position she held until 1940.[22]

Unlike the other districts which had organized previously, whose objectives were largely missions or benevolent institutions or both, the St. Louis group, as its objectives indicate, adopted a diversified program. As a result its method of collecting funds was also different. Though mite boxes were introduced to gather funds for its mission projects, the method of collecting funds was left to the discretion of the individual societies. The program of the organization was carried on largely by committees, each of which functioned virtually as an organization within an organization. At the outset these committees were the Mission Committee, Valparaiso Committee, Literature Committee, Educational and Program Committee (planned programs for LWL meetings), and Students' Welfare Committee. Later a Music Committee was added.[23]

The Mission Committee's major project, one that continued until the formation of the national LWML in 1942, was the chapel at Columbia, Mo., the location of the University of Missouri. The women's project began in 1932.[24] Interest payments were made until 1935, when it was decided to liquidate the bonds from time to time and thus reduce the principal.[25] Approximately $6,000 had been gathered by 1940.[26] A campaign was then launched as the result of a resolution of the Western District of the Synod to enlist the assistance of every woman in the District to wipe out the remaining $20,000 debt over a 2-year period.[27] This meant an average of only 50¢ a year for each woman in the District. However, at the termination of that time only $10,406.14 of the $20,000 goal had been raised.[28] The Western District Mission Board then took over the remainder of the debt.[29] In addition to the Lutheran Woman's League, there were numerous other women's organizations serving as auxiliaries to various charitable endeavors of the church in the St. Louis area. This no doubt was responsible, in part, for the difficulty in collecting the desired amount for the Columbia Chapel. However, the fact that the program of the Lutheran Woman's League was so diversified, and that missions were only one phase of its work, no doubt played a big role in its failure to achieve the desired goal. Another factor which must not be overlooked is that there was delegate representation at meetings rather than general representation, making for a less general interest in the work of the organization. This custom still prevails in St. Louis in 1967.

The Valparaiso Committee sponsored an annual Christmas

Candlelight Service by the St. Louis A Cappella Choir and the Students Chorus of Concordia Seminary for the benefit of Valparaiso. It also held an annual rally for the benefit of Valparaiso and encouraged young people and parents to take advantage of the opportunities which a Lutheran university afforded. This committee later became the nucleus for the St. Louis chapter of the Valparaiso Guild.

The Literature Committee supplemented the usual programs of ladies' aids by providing papers on a monthly basis (10 per year) based on Biblical characters and other topics of general interest which would stimulate women to become more active in the Kingdom. These papers were prepared by women under the supervision of the counselors and were sent free of charge to all member societies. Others could purchase them for a nominal sum. Subsequently they found their way into as many as 32 states, four Canadian provinces, and even to Alaska and Australia.[30] The papers were sent also to Wheat Ridge Sanatorium in Colorado and to "all local [Lutheran] institutions." [31] Some of the papers were reprinted in publications of other Districts including the Central and Northern Illinois Districts.[32] In 1940 the Publicity Department of Synod purchased about 150 of these study topics for use in connection with its "Call of the Cross" conferences throughout Synod.[33]

The first task of the Literature Committee had been the preparation of a model constitution for distribution to societies desiring such a guide. This was later included in a 36-page Guide Book published by the committee in 1937, which contained, besides the constitution, hymns and prayers for use in meetings.[34]

The Students' Welfare Committee, as its name implies, served the interests of students at Concordia Seminary, St. Louis. This was accomplished by means of an annual "Jelly Shower" (later called Donation Day) in the fall of the year. Before the first such event in the fall of 1932 the committee met at the home of the chairman, Mrs. J. H. C. Fritz (the mother of this writer), to make plans. The women had no idea how many to expect and were thinking in terms of perhaps 40 or 50. The event was to be held in the Fritz home. Each woman on the committee volunteered to bring a few cups, some silverware, and cookies. Just before the conclusion of their meeting, Dean Fritz came home. When he heard their plans he suggested that, instead of having the "Jelly Shower" in the home, it be held at the seminary, that the seminary serve lunch to the women, and that he assist by providing a program consisting of student talent. Imagine the surprise of the committee when the reservations began to come in, and even more so on the day of the "Jelly Shower," when 1,100 women appeared, bringing a total of 1,700 jars of home-made jellies and preserves. In addition, the voluntary contributions at the luncheon table amounted to $113.89.[35] This became an annual event which drew not only the women of St. Louis and surrounding area but also a group of 250 women from Chicago in 1937 and another group from Milwaukee in 1941.[36]

In addition, the Students' Welfare Committee prepared boxes of sweets for students who were not able to go away for the Christmas vacation, served a luncheon to the graduates and their parents, gave each graduate a small gift, and provided $50 from time to time for the dean to assist students in need. This committee, too, eventually grew into the present Seminary Guild.

The Music Committee sought to create an appreciation for both good sacred music and secular music of a classical nature. Its function was therefore largely cultural. This it accomplished by presenting musical programs of various types. Proceeds were used for music scholarships for seminary students.

The Lutheran Women's League, St. Louis, extended its interest and influence beyond the confines of the church by its concern for certain social problems outside the sphere of the church. In February 1934 the League ratified the signing, by its president, Mrs. Schmitt, of a protest against the Child Labor amendment.[37] The following year it sent two representatives to Jefferson City, the state capital, to a hearing on this matter.[38] The League also sent two representatives regularly to the St. Louis Civic Union, an organization committed to safeguarding the public from obscene literature and objectionable movies. Dr. Theodore Graebner was president of this organization. [39]

Beginning in March 1939 the St. Louis Lutheran Woman's League published *The Lutheran Woman,* an 8-page quarterly publication. This was continued until December 1942, when it was replaced by the *Lutheran Woman's Quarterly.*

Evening Division Organized

Another long-felt need was met when the Evening Division of the Lutheran Women's League was organized Oct. 15, 1934. Miss Anna Beck, who had been an active Walther Leaguer, had attended a mission rally of the LWL and as a result joined the League. She soon found, however, that it would be impossible for her to attend any of the meetings of the group because she was employed during the day. It occurred to her that there were others like herself who had outgrown the Walther League but yet had no other organization in the church in which they could become active. She spoke with a number of her friends who shared her enthusiasm for an organization to fit their situation. She then contacted both Mrs. Walter A. Maier and Mrs. Otto F. Schmitt. A preliminary meeting was held at the home of Mrs. Maier. Twelve young women were present, representing six churches. After discussing their problem, Mrs. Maier was asked to obtain permission from the Lutheran Women's League for them to organize an Evening Division of this group, thus eliminating the necessity of organizing another society. This request was granted, and Mrs. Maier was appointed as the contact member between the two groups. Eighty-nine women were present for the first meeting.[40]

Rev. L. Meyer, one of the pastors who spoke to the group at the organization meeting, pointed out the deficit in the church, the number of idle candidates, the new interest evident in church work, and the various efforts of the Missouri Synod at that time. The new awakening in the church, he said, was due to a great extent, as it had been in New Testament times, to the women of the church.[41]

At this meeting Miss Anna Beck was chosen to serve as temporary chairman and, fittingly, at a meeting a few months later was elected as the first regular president, an office she held until 1938.[42]

The educational program for the first year was geared to acquaint the members with various aspects of the church's work so that a definite type of project or projects could be adopted. The theme for the year was "My Church" and included its early history, missions, education, social service, and finances. The presentations were made by both members and guest speakers in the course of the year.

Dr. P. E. Kretzmann presented opportunities in the field of social service; as a result, the organization launched a series of social-service projects which culminated in the establishment of a community center, begun as a project with members serving on a volunteer basis. In 1947 Miss Anna Beck, who had been the driving force in this effort from the beginning, became full-time director, a position she still holds, directing a large group of volunteers in the operation of three centers in the inner city. For her outstanding service to the under-privileged through the years, Miss Beck was awarded the Mind of Christ award at the 17th annual convention of the Lutheran Human Relations Association of America in 1966.[43]

Prior to the operation of the community centers, the Evening Division, in cooperation with the St. Louis Provident Association, shared the salary cost of a Lutheran social worker in St. Louis who served Lutherans in the community. In addition, through the society's connection with the St. Louis Provident Association, Sherwood Forest Camp near St. Louis was made available to underprivileged boys and girls (ages 12—16), beginning in 1938.[44] This project, too, has grown through the years and is still being carried on. Dr. Kretzmann continued to give lectures each year for a number of years on various aspects of social work involvement, as a series separate from the educational program presented at the meetings of the organization.

In 1941, when it became evident that the organization of a na-tional women's group was about to become a reality, the Evening Division, whose scope of activities and method of operation were so different from that of the Day Division, and because it did not wish to become national, requested its release from the Lutheran Woman's League. It then became the "Lutheran Business Women." [45] The membership had reached 237 by 1940, over 100 of whom were serving on committees.[46]

The desire for organized women's work on a larger scale con-tinued to grow. An informal meeting of representative women of Cleveland, Ohio, and others, numbering 75, met during the general convention of the Ev. Lutheran Synod of Missouri, Ohio, and Other States (June 24, 1935) for the purpose of sharing information about the work women were doing in various parts of the country. After hearing reports from women representing various types of societies from different locations, the following resolution was unanimously adopted:

"Resolved that we, the Lutheran women assembled in meeting at the Cleveland Hotel on June 24, 1935 heartily commend the efforts of the women of the Lutheran Church in various localities for the advancement of the church and that we whole heartedly pledge our continued support to the extension of our Savior's cause and furthermore that we encourage all women upon returning to their respective localities to seek and to create an interest for organized women's work." [47]

The work of the Lutheran Woman's League in St. Louis became known all over the country largely through the papers of the Literature Committee, and little by little societies far removed from the St. Louis area applied for membership. In addition to societies and individuals from the Western District, the Lutheran Woman's League by 1941 numbered among its members societies and individuals from Indiana, Texas, Louisiana, Illinois, Oregon, Ohio, Florida, and Montana. It was, in effect, national in scope even though it was not recognized as such officially.

Organizations in Other Districts

Of the three districts which had organized prior to the failure of the initial effort of the women to organize nationally in 1930, and the formation of the St. Louis Lutheran Women's League which followed, only Kansas ceased functioning when the President of the synodical District, together with the Board of Directors, terminated the organization after the failure of the national effort.[48] The other two, Oklahoma and Central, continued to function and to flourish.

The Oklahoma District published a quarterly bulletin almost from the beginning and used mite boxes to gather its funds. In 1932 it inaugurated a unique project when it voted to sponsor loans to parochial schools and Sunday schools for necessary equipment, etc. It undertook to pay off the debt on the first Negro mission established in Oklahoma in 1935. The same year it sought and received official recognition by the synodical District. It was among the 15 Districts who sent delegates to the organization meeting of the national Lutheran Women's Missionary League in Chicago in 1942.[49]

The Central District, though different in structure, constituted a mighty force of women committed solely to the cause of missions. It, too, had a quarterly publication, the Endeavor *Quarterly,* which also found its way into other parts of the country through requests from individuals and groups. Of special note is that in 1930 (a year after it began publication) 500 copies of the *Quarterly* were sent to Oklahoma.[50] From the middle of 1929 to the organization of the national Lutheran Women's Missionary League in 1942, its membership increased from 71 to 125 Ladies' Aid societies. During this period it collected $78,401.26, of which $63,049.60 (80%) was used to participate in 26 major and 7 minor projects.[51] The Central District, too, had other women's missionary societies in Fort Wayne, as well as auxiliaries for various charitable endeavors and for the college in Fort Wayne.[52]

The organization of Lutheran women into units of district proportions continued to grow. The North Dakota and Montana District authorized the formation of a Districtwide women's organization at its convention in June 1937, which was called the Lutheran Women's Missionary Endeavor. As in the Central District, it had no officers but functioned under the direction of the synodical District Mission Board through the District's Mission Secretary. Its membership numbered 32 society units which gathered $2,251.84 by means of mite boxes up to October 1942. It, too, had a quarterly publication in the form of a mimeographed bulletin, which contained a topic study and District news.[53]

Following close behind North Dakota and Montana was the formation of the Lutheran Women's League in the Southeastern Conference of the English District. In answer to an invitation extended by the Mission Committee of the Southeastern Conference of the English District to all ladies' organizations in the Southeast, 49 women, representing eight congregations, met at Hickory, N. C., on April 24, 1938, to hear a plan for a Lutheran Women's League in the Southeastern Conference. Rev. James L. Summers, pastor at that time of St. Stephen Church, Hickory, and representative of the General Home Mission Board, made the presentation. He pointed out that "the purpose of such an organization would be the study of the work of missions in our Church and the promotion of this work wherever and in whatever manner possible." [54] The organization was effected at this meeting, but the first regular meeting was held in November of the same year at Charlotte, N. C. Already at the meeting in April the use of mite boxes was explained as having proved successful in the Central District and was recommended. In an Executive Board meeting prior to the November meeting it was decided to issue a quarterly bulletin, which would contain topics written by pastors in the Southeast. The first four topics chosen were in the nature of an introduction to missions in its various categories. [55] Projects gave assistance to new missions in the area, where Synod at the time was starting missions at an accelerated rate as a result of the Missionary Forward Endeavor.

The first women's mission rally of the Northern Illinois District was held at River Forest in 1938 and was attended by 500 Lutheran women from 33 congregations. It was the result of a resolution adopted at the convention of the District to call into being such an organization. It chose as its name "The Lutheran Women's Mission Endeavor of Northern Illinois." "Since the District has endorsed this missionary endeavor," wrote District President Rev. Ernest T. Lams in the first issue of the quarterly publication *The Harvest Call,* "all our congregations will naturally open wide their doors to this missionary society and accord it the support which it merits." [56] Its purpose was stated as follows: "(1) to develop and maintain a greater mission consciousness in the Lutheran womanhood within the District, and (2) to gather funds for the support of such District and Synodical mission projects for which no adequate provision has been made in the budgets." [57] Mite boxes served as the medium for the collection of moneys to implement projects which were suggested from time to time by the District Mission Board, as well as the Board of Foreign Missions. The projects were endorsed by the District Board of Directors and were then selected in each case by the Endeavor itself. [58]

Synod Reconsiders Women's Federation

The biggest event in the '30s so far as the women of the church were concerned was the action taken by the synodical convention in St. Louis in June 1938. This convention had before it memorials from both the Central District Home Mission Board and the Lutheran Woman's League, St. Louis, concerning the formation of a churchwide federation of women. The overture submitted by the Central District board read as follows:

WHEREAS, The women of the Church, through the existing ladies' societies, offer a potential and frequently almost neglected source of positive power in the Lord's kingdom; and

WHEREAS, Experience has demonstrated that ladies' societies often appreciate the opportunity for systematic education in missionary tasks confronting the Church and thereby stimulating sympathy and zeal in an increasing measure for the cause of Christian Missions; and

WHEREAS, Ladies' societies have been found willing to place a portion of their collective financial resources at the disposal of the Church in her endeavors to extend the boundaries of God's kingdom; and

WHEREAS, An encouraging example of such united action on the part of the women of our Church is seen in the Central District, where 112 ladies' societies, numbering 11,200 members, have assembled for quarterly missionary meetings during the past decade and have collected $48,235.49 through mite-boxes within that time; and

WHEREAS, A careful survey, also by officials of Synod who are not members of the Central District, has resulted in the conviction that no Scriptural principles governing woman's position in the Church have been sacrificed and that the funds collected through mite-boxes have in no way detracted from the regular contributions through the established congregational channels, which are conceded priority rights; and

WHEREAS, This plan of developing powers for good, dormant in a great section of our communicant membership, has the triple advantage of being developed under the immediate auspices of the Church, of not contemplating regional, State and national conventions, and of making the work of Christian missions, which has a *universal* appeal for every group of church-members, the one aim of its endeavor; therefore be it

Resolved, That we petition the Delegate Synod to sanction a Synod-wide Women's Missionary Endeavor; and to that end be it further

Resolved, That the proposed Synodical Women's Missionary Endeavor have as its local unit existing ladies' societies, thereby avoiding the creation of additional societies within our Church; and be it further

Resolved, That through these existing ladies' societies, as agents, efforts be made to enlist the active support of all ladies in our congregations in the objectives of the endeavor, both educational and financial; and be it further

Resolved, That the proposed Synodical Women's Missionary Endeavor be administered by the Board for Home Missions in North America and its Executive Secretary, who would operate through the Home Mission boards of the respective Districts; and be it further

Resolved, That a women's missionary journal, containing informational and inspirational articles as well as a mission-study outline, be published quarterly under the auspices of the Board for Home Missions in North America for free distribution to all ladies in congregations where ladies' societies are participating in the proposed Synodical Women's Missionary Endeavor and that this Board also furnish gratis necessary mite-boxes; and be it further

Resolved, That the collection of funds in the proposed Synodical Women's Missionary Endeavor be limited to these mite-box contributions in such a manner that no interference will occur with any financial duty to be performed through customary congregational channels; and be it further

Resolved, that 75 per cent of the funds thus collected through the mite-boxes be retained by the respective District Home Mission Board and that the remaining 25 per cent be placed at the disposal of the Board for Home Missions in North America with the understanding that this Board defray all the expenses of the proposed Women's Missionary Endeavor out of its 25 per cent and use the balance to advance missionary projects having a general appeal; and be it further

Resolved, That for the purpose of determining from time to time the particular missionary project or projects to be advanced, a meeting of representatives of all mission boards of our Synod and of the Synodical Conference be called by the Secretary of Missions; and be it further

Resolved, That no expenditure of funds be made by any board of the Districts or of Synod which will necessitate a continuous subsidy in order to save the original investment, all donations toward any project being one-time grants; and be it finally

Resolved, That authority shall be, and herewith is, given to the Board for Home Missions in North America to proceed at once in establishing this proposed Synodical Women's Missionary Endeavor.

Respectfully submitted,

CENTRAL DISTRICT HOME MISSION BOARD

F. WAMBSGANSS, *Chairman*

THEO. WYNEKEN, *Secretary*

E. WEBER

A. H. SCHROEDER

F. BREDEMEIER

W. C. BIRKNER, *District Secretary*
of Missions

Fort Wayne, Ind., March 29, 1938 [59]

The overture submitted by the Lutheran Woman's League of St. Louis was not so specific in its recommendations but rather requested assistance of Synod in working out the details in connection with the formation of the desired federation. Its recommendation read as follows:

It is well known that our Lutheran women are giving valuable organized help in their recognized sphere and under proper guidance to their congregations, to charitable and educational organizations, to Districts, and to Synod at large.

We have women's societies in almost all our congregations. Other organizations of women for special efforts are increasing, we might say, in some sections alarmingly. Some of our Districts have found it very advisable to favor a District organization among their women.

Is it not therefore quite natural that our Lutheran women would also desire to effect a closer relation and a helpful cooperation among the various organizations, somewhat as it is found among our young people in the Walther League?

We therefore respectfully petition Synod in behalf of the Lutheran Woman's League, which has received the recognition of the Western District and of that section of the English District, to permit some kind of federation among the various District women's organizations which would be in keeping with sound Lutheran principles, with the understanding that the District organizations would remain under control of the respective District, while a general organization would come under the control of Synod.

We also petition that Synod will lend its help, possibly through its Praesidium or an appointed committee, to study the various problems connected with this proposition and to solve them with those that are interested under the guidance of the Holy Spirit to the best interests of the Church.

> CLARA S. SCHMITT, *President of the L.W.L.*
> BERTHA G. MEYER, *Secretary of the L.W.L.*
> PASTORAL ADVISERS OF THE LUTHERAN WOMAN'S LEAGUE
> HERBERT C. CLAUS, Western District
> HOBART MEYER, English District [60]

The day prior to the opening of the synodical convention in St. Louis which was to consider these proposals the Lutheran Laymen's League met in convention. In this connection a meeting for women was arranged by the Lutheran Woman's League of St. Louis and was attended by 225 persons. After hearing about the work of the Lutheran Woman's League of St. Louis and other women's groups in various parts of the country, the group adopted a resolution for submission to the committee which had the memorials concerning a women's federation under consideration. The resolution expressed the wholehearted approval of those present for a Synodwide federation of women. Another resolution called for the appointment of a committee to draw up resolutions for presentation to another meeting of women to be held several days later on June 17.[61]

The latter meeting drew an attendance of 350 persons. It was likewise arranged by the Lutheran Woman's League of St. Louis. In welcoming those present, Mrs. L. C. Tirmenstein of St. Louis called attention to the fact that it was just a hundred years since the Saxon "foremothers" had left their homes in Germany for the uncertainties of their new homeland. "As we enter upon the second century of our church in this country," she said in part, "let us reconsecrate ourselves and dedicate ourselves to service for our church." [62] This group, like the one which had met several days previously, passed a resolution to go on record as favoring a Synodwide federation "for greater activities in church and home" and to bring the resolution to the attention of Committee No. 18, which had the memorials concerning such a federation under advisement.[63]

Floor Committee 18 at the synodical convention reported that it was convinced that the request for permission to effect a Synodwide organization of women was prompted by a desire to utilize to the fullest extent the talents with which the Lord had endowed the women of the church and to use them in the most effective way possible. The committee also felt that the church had an obligation to help its members perform the work of the church so that the greatest possible good would result.[64] Its recommendations reflected these conclusions.

The first resolution which the committee submitted called for the appointment by Synod of a Survey Committee to consist of two pastors, one teacher, and two laymen, who would consider the entire question of women's work and organizations in the Synod. The committee would also "gather information concerning the problem . . . formulate a practicable program of missionary and educational features which would be helpful to all, and submit definite proposals to Synod at its next meeting." In this connection it was recommended that the Survey Committee "consider the advisability of establishing a Committee on Women's Work similar to the now existing Committee on Young People's Work." The second resolution recommended "that Synod gratefully recognize the zealous endeavor of our women for the cause of Christ and His Church." Both resolutions were adopted.[65]

The synodical resolutions gave the women new hope that their long-cherished dream of a national federation of women in the church might soon become a reality. They looked with eager anticipation to the recommendations of the Survey Committee which would be presented to the next synodical convention 3 years hence. After almost a century of existence as a church body in America, the Ev. Lutheran Synod of Missouri, Ohio, and Other States was recognizing more fully that women, too, had a definite and rightful role in the Kingdom.

Notes

VI

1. *Western District Lutheran,* IX (June 1933), p. 821.

2. Ibid., Sept. 1933, p. 845.

3. *American Lutheran,* XX (April 1937), 10.

4. Minutes, Active Officers, Temporary Lutheran Women's League, March 16, 1931. File of Mrs. H. J. Heitner.

5. Minutes, Executive Committee, Temporary Lutheran Women's League, April 20, 1931, p. 1. File of Mrs. Heitner.

6. Minutes, Tentative Lutheran Women's League, May 22, 1931, p. 3. File of Mrs. Heitner.

7. Ibid.

8. Minutes, Acting Committee, Temporary Lutheran Women's League, June 9, 1931, p. 1. File of Mrs. Heitner.

9. Ibid., Nov. 3, 1931 (one page). File of Mrs. Heitner.

10. Ibid., Jan. 25, 1931 (one page). File of Mrs. Heitner.

11. Minutes, Executive Committee, Lutheran Laymen's League, April 21, 1932, p. 408.

12. Minutes, Enlarged Committee, Lutheran Women's League, Feb. 19, 1932 (one page). File of Mrs. Heitner.

13. Ibid.

14. Ibid.

15. From the file of Mrs. L. C. Tirmenstein.

16. Minutes, Enlarged Committee, Lutheran Women's League, March 4, 1932 (one page). File of Mrs. Heitner.

17. Ibid.

18. "History of the Lutheran Woman's League, Missouri Synod," unprinted manuscript, p. 7. On file at Concordia Historical Institute. (Hereafter cited as "History of LWL.")

19. Ibid., p. 8.

20. Ibid.

21. Ibid., p. 9, minutes of Sept. 16, 1932; p. 15, minutes of Feb. 21, 1938.

22. Ibid., p. 27, minutes of June 17, 1932; p. 27, minutes of May 17, 1940.

23. Ibid., p. 8, minutes of April 15, 1932; p. 9, minutes of June 17, 1932.

24. Ibid., p. 9, minutes of Sept. 16, 1932.

25. Ibid., p. 13, minutes of Feb. 15, 1935.

26. *Lutheran Witness,* LX (Nov. 11, 1941), 386.

27. "History of LWL," p. 26, minutes of Feb. 16, 1940.

28. Minutes, Lutheran Woman's League, Sept. 18, 1942, p. 32 (bound minutes book in LWL file. Hereafter cited as Minutes of LWL).

29. Ibid., p. 34.

30. "History of LWL," p. 18, minutes of Sept. 17, 1937; Minutes of LWL, May 16, 1941, p. 12.

31. "History of LWL," p. 18, minutes of Feb. 18, 1938.

32. Ibid., p. 22, minutes of Feb. 17, 1939; p. 27, minutes of May 17, 1940.

33. Ibid., p. 26, minutes of Feb. 16, 1940.

34. Ibid., p. 9, minutes of Sept. 16, 1932; p. 18, minutes of Nov. 19, 1937.

35. Ibid., p. 10, minutes of Nov. 18, 1932.

36. St. Louis *Globe-Democrat,* Nov. 2, 1937, p. 1. Minutes of LWL, Nov. 21, 1941, p. 20.

37. "History of LWL," p. 12, minutes of Feb. 16, 1934.

38. Ibid., p. 14, minutes of May 17, 1935.

39. Ibid., p. 15, minutes of Sept. 20, 1935.

40. Report on the Evening Division of the Lutheran Woman's League, Nov. 16, 1934, n. p. File of Mrs. W. A. Maier.

41. Minutes, Evening Division, Lutheran Woman's League, Oct. 15, 1934. File of Mrs. W. A. Maier.

42. Ibid., Oct. 15, 1934; Dec. 10, 1934; Nov. 14, 1938.

43. *St. Louis Lutheran,* XXI, No. 22 (July 30, 1966), p. 1.

44. Minutes, Evening Division, May 9, 1938, p. 2.

45. Minutes of LWL, Sept. 19, 1941, p. 18.

46. Minutes, Evening Division, Jan. 8, 1940, pp. 1—3.

47. Minutes, Lutheran Women's Meeting, Cleveland, Ohio, June 24, 1935, in "History of LWL."

48. Letter from Mrs. C. A. Hass, Oct. 10, 1966. In LWML file.

49. "History of Oklahoma District of the Lutheran Women's Missionary League," unprinted manuscript on file at CHI and LWML office.

50. Minutes, Organization Meeting, LWL, Jan. 17—18, 1930, p. 4. File of Mrs. Heitner.

51. *History of Central District Lutheran Women's Missionary Endeavor,* etc., pp. 17, 21—22.

52. Convention booklet, LWML, Aug. 31, Sept. 1, 1943, p. 9.

53. "The North Dakota District of the Lutheran Women's Missionary League," unprinted manuscript on file at CHI and LWML office, n. p.

54. "History of Southeastern District of the Lutheran Women's Missionary League (Carolinas and Georgia)," unprinted manuscript on file at CHI and LWML office, n. p.

55. Ibid.

56. *The Harvest Call,* I (Sept. 1938), 1—2.

57. Ibid., p. 17.

58. Ibid., pp. 4—5.

59. *Reports and Memorials for the Twenty-Second Delegate Synod,* St. Louis, Mo., June 15—25, 1938, pp. 130—132. Also in *Proceedings of the Thirty-Seventh Regular Convention of the Ev. Lutheran Synod of Missouri, Ohio, and Other States,* St. Louis, Mo., June 15—24, 1938, pp. 342—344.

60. *Reports and Memorials,* etc., 1938, pp. 276—277. Also in *Proceedings,* etc., 1938, p. 344.

61. Women's Meeting, June 14, 1938, St. Louis, pp. 1—2. File of Mrs. L. C. Tirmenstein.

62. Women's Meeting, St. Louis, June 17, 1938, p. 1. "History of LWL."

63. Ibid., p. 2.

64. *Proceedings,* etc., 1938, p. 345.

65. Ibid.

VII
A Tree Grows

ONCE AGAIN, IN THE '40s, the chastening hand of God reached down to touch the world, which for the most part had forgotten Him. The events of that infamous day in December of 1941 ignited the spark that produced the worst holocaust the world has ever seen. While it brought bitter heartache to thousands whose loved ones sacrificed their lives, it gave impetus to an economic prosperity which was also without precedent in our country. The demand for arms and other commodities of war, plus the shortage of manpower because of that war, drew women into the ranks of the employed in such proportions that it gave new dimensions to the role of women all over the world and, as a result, also in the church. It was in this setting that the Lutheran Women's Missionary League came into existence.

A major factor in making the organization of the Lutheran Women's Missionary League possible was the report which the synodical Survey Committee, appointed in 1938, presented to the 1941 synodical convention. The committee, consisting of Pastors Rudolph H. C. Meyer and Fred Wambsganss, Prof. F. H. Schmitt, and Messrs. J. Ohlis and Lawrence Rupprecht, found that "the women of the Church offer a potential but heretofore oft-neglected power in the Church." This dormant power, the committee felt, could be enlisted for the benefit of Synod without sacrificing any of the Scriptural principles governing women's position in the church. It called attention to the fact that other Protestant church bodies had long realized the potentialities of women and had sponsored nation-wide women's organizations for many years under the direct supervision of the respective church bodies.[1] The committee also pointed out that, while Synod had not officially organized women's work, several Districts in Synod had Districtwide women's organizations. "These women," they said, "are motivated by the love of Christ and the spirit of helpfulness to expend their talents in the interest of their respective Districts, and they are anxious to extend their efforts beyond the boundaries of their Districts and to assist Synod at large in some of its undertakings." [2]

The Survey Committee suggested that this laudable intention ought to be encouraged. It therefore submitted a plan to enlist the interest and cooperation of the women of our Synod in concerted and united work for Synod. A combined activity, "which would have a general appeal, be wide in its scope, attainable, and worthy of every thought and participation that may be accorded it" was suggested. The church's teaching regarding women's work in the church was taken into consideration, and a proposal was therefore made that an activity be carried on by the women of our Synod under the sympathetic direction and guidance and also the helpful cooperation of Synod itself.[3]

A very lengthy and detailed plan for such a women's organization was submitted which, under God, it was hoped would be helpful in carrying on an expanded missionary and educational program.[4] The Committee then presented the following resolutions:

"1. That Synod recognize the plan as outlined above as an activity for the benefit of Synod and its respective Districts so general in scope and attainable of purpose as to enlist the interest and cooperation of our women throughout Synod;

"2. That Synod in no wise, by the introduction of a District- and Synod-wide FLW [Federation of Lutheran Women], hinder or retard the work of already existing women's groups or organizations which are organized to promote and to assist local or regional charitable, educational, local missionary, or cultural endeavors." [5]

To help bring about a national women's federation, suggestions were made for local, District, and national levels. Synod was asked to urge congregational ladies' aids to adopt a resolution making the plan a part of their regular activities. Where no such congregational unit existed, the committee recommended that a congregational committee be appointed to carry out the work of the congregational group.[6]

Synod was also requested to petition the Districts to see that District officers be elected who would direct and lend helpful cooperation to the work within the District according to stipulations included in the report of the committee. After the formation of such District organizations, it was recommended that circuit or regional groups be formed.[7]

In order to effect a Synodwide federation of women, the committee recommended that Synod encourage the calling of a meeting of interested women representing the Districts to organize a Synodwide federation at the time of the Delegate Synod. The function of the synodical committee would be to direct and assist in the work of the women's federation in its relation to Synod.[8]

The committee also reported that it had considered the advisability of establishing a committee on woman's work similar to the present Committee on Young People's Work. "Your Committee," it said, "is of the opinion that, if the women of our Synod will be organized along the plan mapped out above, there will be no need of a synodical committee on women's work, as under the proposed plan such an organization will operate under the supervision and guidance of constituted authorities." [9] The committee had also considered an unprinted memorial calling for recognition by Synod of three major organizations: the Walther League, the Lutheran Laymen's League, and the Lutheran Woman's League, and a coordination and gradation according to age of these three. It recommended that no action be taken on this matter until after the organization of the women's federation.[10] The floor committee concurred with the Survey Committee in this matter.[11]

Floor Committee 14 of the synodical convention, which was charged with studying the report of the Survey Committee and of making recommendations to the convention, submitted a number of other resolutions which were subsequently adopted. Among these was one giving approval and encouragement for the creation of a national women's organization in the church, in keeping with the Scriptural principles involved in women's position in the church. Another resolution suggested that the details of such organization, "such as the choice of name, scope, purpose, membership, and the constitution in general be left to a committee of women, properly elected and constituted by the women themselves, assisted by a committee of pastors to be appointed by the President." [12]

Other resolutions called for (1) each District President to appoint a committee of three pastors in his District, to bring into existence an organization within the District from which two delegates would be sent to represent the District at a national convention; (2) the appointment of a committee of counselors by the President of Synod, who would be empowered to call a national meeting of District representatives, not later than July 1942; (3) and the stipulation that the constitution adopted by the national organization be submitted to the College of Presidents for approval.[13]

Just 10 years had elapsed since the effort to organize a national women's group in the church had been curtailed by the directive of the College of Presidents to desist. Now, however, the women were poised and ready to go into action to accomplish such an organization with the blessing of the church. Besides the Districts which already had organizations, i. e., Oklahoma, Central, and Western (Lutheran Woman's League in St. Louis), several additional Districts had formed organizations during the '30s. The North Dakota Missionary Endeavor was organized in June 1937, and both the Northern Illinois Missionary Endeavor and the Southeastern Lutheran Women's Missionary League (Carolinas and Georgia) in May of 1938.[14] An organization representing congregations in East Tennessee, though actually members of the Western District, organized in 1938 and called itself the East Tennessee District.[15] Another such organization, representing a section of a synodical District, was organized as the East Bay Lutheran Women's Council in Northern California in 1937.[16]

After the passage of the synodical resolution in 1941 authorizing the formation of a national women's organization, machinery was set in motion in other Districts, as well as the above. Interested women in each District gathered to elect delegates to represent them at the meeting to form a national organization.

The Committee for a Synodwide Women's Organization appointed by Dr. J. W. Behnken, President of Synod, consisted of the following: Pastors Rudolph H. C. Meyer; W. C. Birkner, secretary;

J. H. Deckman, Oscar Fedder, and A. H. Semmann. Under date of Jan. 15, 1942, this committee issued a digest of information and suggestions for synodical Presidents in connection with preliminary District activity relative to a Synodwide women's organization. Several items of special interest are contained in this digest. They read in part as follows:

"District Conventions should be scheduled as soon as possible during the Spring of this year with a representative Ladies Aid Society acting as hostess. . . . (Representatives of Ladies Aid Societies should pay their own traveling expenses or have their local Society assume this obligation)." It was suggested that Districts pay the expenses of their delegates to the national meeting.

"Ladies Aid Societies of English District Congregations should be invited to participate by the District in whose territory they are located. . . .

"In deliberating on the 'character, scope, and purpose' of the proposed Synod-wide Women's Organization, the three Pastors who act as District Counselors might emphasize that this hoped-for Organization should focus its attention on the Church's main objectives — Missions. Every reasonable purpose of a *Synod-wide* Women's Organization could be included under the general subdivisions in the wider sense of the terms: Missionary Inspiration; Missionary Education; Missionary Service."

The committee called attention to the fact that existing District organizations ought not be disrupted but could rather be made the basis for District units. It stated furthermore: "In reviewing these matters the Committee became convinced, as discussion proceeded, that it would be wise policy to give the greatest possible latitude of action to the various Districts, thereby enabling the Districts which were organized — such as the North Illinois District, the Central District, the Oklahoma District, and others, — to continue their programs which have found District favor. At the same time it was also realized that the objectives and the method of organization should be sufficiently definite to prevent exploitation of the entire organization, or one of its District affiliates, by any of the many private groups that were existing within the frame-work of the Church for only one specific purpose, often local in character and in interest."

Ladies Wurttemberg Maennerchor Outing, Summer 1971

The committee agreed tentatively on July 7—8, 1942, as the date for the meeting and to accept the offer of a member of the committee, Pastor Oscar Fedder, to hold the meeting at his church, St. Stephen's, in Chicago.[17] Midway between the synodical convention and the time set for the organization meeting in Chicago, there came that fateful day in December known as "Pearl Harbor Day," which marked the entrance of the United States into World War II. Begun in Europe in 1939, the war was now extended to the islands of the Pacific. What effect these events would have on the decision of the synodical convention to ratify a national federation of women had they come before the convention is, of course, difficult to say. The timeliness of the 1941 synodical decision, however, was demonstrated through the ensuing years, as we shall see later.

The meeting at St. Stephen's Church, in Chicago's south side, July 7 and 8, 1942, marked the culmination of many years of waiting, working, and praying on the part of Lutheran women all over the country. Twenty-eight women, representing 15 Districts, were present as delegates. In addition there were about 100 visitors during the 2-day period. One District, Oregon-Washington-Idaho, was not represented because it was erroneously informed that the meeting had been canceled.[18] The following delegates were present:

1. Atlantic	Mrs. Dorothea Priebe	Woodhaven, L. I., N. Y.
	Mrs. Flora B. Hecker	Belmont, Mass.
2. California-Nevada	Mrs. H. W. Lembke	San Leandro, Calif.
	Mrs. Arthur Klugow	Tracy, Calif.
3. Central	Mrs. Fred Wambsganss	Fort Wayne, Ind.
	Mrs. Lydia Lichtsinn	Indianapolis, Ind.
4. Iowa East	Mrs. Eliz. Petershagen	Williamsburg, Iowa
	Mrs. Walter Widmann	Waterloo, Iowa
5. Michigan	Miss Lena Welsch	Port Hope, Mich.
	Mrs. H. F. Hensieck	Dearborn, Mich.
6. Minnesota	Mrs. A. Rubbert	Minneapolis, Minn.
	Mrs. Al. Bakke	Crookston, Minn.
7. North Dakota	Mrs. George Skinner	Grandin, N. Dak.
	Mrs. A. G. Kellam	Grand Forks, N. Dak.
8. Northern Illinois	Mrs. E. W. Heidorn	Hillside, Ill.
	Mrs. John W. Busse	Arlington Heights, Ill.
9. Northern Nebraska	Mrs. L. C. Heine	Omaha, Nebr.

10. Oklahoma	Mrs. L. Baccarini	Oklahoma City, Okla.
	Mrs. B. J. Theimer	Oklahoma City, Okla.
11. South Dakota	Mrs. Earl Heldt	Waubay, S. Dak.
	Mrs. A. H. Meitler	Aberdeen, S. Dak.
12. Southeastern	Mrs. F. A. Freed	Hickory, N. C.
	Miss G. Ressmeyer	Baltimore, Md.
13. Southern Nebraska	Mrs. C. H. Riggert	Seward, Nebr.
	Mrs. Raymond Roehrkasse	Grand Island, Nebr.
14. Texas	Mrs. D. E. Ressel	Tyler, Tex.
15. Western	Mrs. R. C. Jahn	Chattanooga, Tenn.
	Mrs. Otto F. Schmitt	St. Louis, Mo.

There were mixed feelings on the part of the women present at that historic event. On the one hand, they were eager to do the Lord's work to the fullest extent possible, but on the other hand, some were apprehensive, because they had had no experience in leadership on such a large scale. This was apparent when names were proposed for various offices. There was hesitance on the part of some to accept the nomination, unqualified rejection on the part of others. However, they received encouragement from one of the pastors present who told them, "When the Lord taps you on the shoulder and says, 'I need you for this job,' you must not turn Him down." With this awareness of its challenge, the convention moved on to make decisions which the women were well aware would have to be adjusted and improved upon from time to time, but which nevertheless proved to have far-reaching effects down to the present.

Officers were chosen, a constitution was adopted, and a name selected. The nominating committee attempted to prepare a slate which would supply representation from various parts of the country. Mrs. Otto F. Schmitt was elected president on the second ballot; the first ballot had resulted in a tie. Mrs. Schmitt's experience as president of the Temporary Lutheran Women's League from 1928 to 1931, and the same position in the Lutheran Woman's League, Missouri Synod (St. Louis) from 1932 to 1940, made her eminently well qualified to fill this position. In addition, she was a woman of rare ability, serving as an active partner in business with her husband during the entire 50 years of their marriage (42 at this time) while at the same time serving her church actively as Sunday school teacher and presi-

Mrs. Otto F. Schmitt
First President, 1942—1947

dent of the Ladies' Aid for many years. Both her mother and mother-in-law lived in the Schmitt home for many years, and when the son-in-law died, the Schmitt home was opened to their daughter and her five small children. Above all, she was a humble, dedicated servant of the Lord, who gave freely of herself to advance His kingdom.[19]

Other officers elected were: First Vice-President, Mrs. H. W. Lembke, San Leandro, Calif.; Second Vice-President, Miss Gertrude H. Ressmeyer, Baltimore, Md.; Secretary, Mrs. Walter Widmann, Waterloo, Iowa; Corresponding Secretary, Mrs. Raymond Roehr-kasse, Grand Island, Nebr.; Financial Secretary, Mrs. B. J. Theimer, Oklahoma City, Okla.; and Treasurer, Mrs. A. H. Meitler, Aberdeen, S. Dak.[20]

The selection of a name for the new organization was perhaps the most controversial matter to come before the convention. Even though this matter was presented on the afternoon of the opening day, it was not until late the next afternoon that an agreement was finally reached. Ten names were suggested in all. There were some who insisted on the inclusion of the word "Missionary" to identify the objective of the organization, while others favored a shorter name. A motion was finally made to add the word "Missionary" to a proposal to adopt the name "Lutheran Women's League." Balloting showed 15 in favor and 10 opposed. The original motion, with the amendment, was then unanimously adopted, making the official name "Lutheran Women's Missionary League." [21]

The other item which drew the greatest discussion was the inclusion of a treasurer in the list of officers. The Central District (also North Dakota District), which had existed previous to the new organization, had operated without such an officer (any officers in fact) and instead channeled all its moneys through the Treasurer of the synodical District. After much debate the proposed article of the constitution dealing with officers was amended to include a treasurer.[22]

The Constitution as finally adopted read as follows:

CONSTITUTION — Lutheran Women's Missionary League

I. Name.

The name of this organization shall be: *Lutheran Women's Missionary League.*

II. Objectives.

The objectives of this organization shall be

a. to develop and to maintain a greater mission consciousness among the women of Synod: *Missionary Education — Missionary Inspiration — Missionary Service;*

b. to gather funds for mission projects, sponsored by Synod, especially such for which no adequate provision has been made in the budget.

III. Membership.

a. All women's organizations within the congregations of the Evangelical Lutheran Synod of Missouri, Ohio, and Other States, which have expressed their desire to join, have followed the mode of procedure laid down in the constitution, and have made the object of the League their own, may join.

b. Wherever there is no women's organization, the pastor with the consent of the congregation may organize a congregational group of women, which body may join by the regular procedure.

IV. Meetings.

The National Convention of the League shall be held biennially.

V. Representation.

The National Convention of the League shall be a delegate body organized in the following manner: All Districts arrange their organizations into groups of seven to ten societies. These groups will be known as Circuits, Zones, Regions, etc. These Circuits, Zones, Regions, etc., elect one representative and an alternate for the National Convention at the District Convention. The credentials shall be in the hands of the National Recording Secretary at least four weeks before the Convention.

VI. Officers.

1. The officers of the League shall be a President, a Vice-President, a Second Vice-President, a Secretary, a Corresponding Secretary, a Treasurer, and a Financial Secretary, who shall be elected at the general convention and whose term of office shall be two years. All of these officers shall be eligible to not more than two re-elections.

2. The officers shall be elected by ballot at the National Convention of the League. A nominating committee appointed by the Executive Board shall propose a slate of candidates to the National Convention.

VII. Executive Board.

a. The Executive Board shall consist of the District Presidents and of the officers of the League.

b. An Administrative Committee consisting of the president, the recording secretary, the treasurer, and the financial secretary shall act in matters requiring immediate attention and shall report to the Executive Board.

VIII. Counselors.

a. The Convention shall elect three pastoral counselors from a list of names submitted by the President of Synod.

b. The counselors shall be held to attend the meetings of the Executive Committee, the Administrative Committee, and the National Convention.

IX. Projects.

The National Body shall not undertake, at any one time, more than two projects, to be submitted to the Convention by the Executive Board after ratification by the President of Synod, the

Executive Secretary of Synod's Board for Home Missions, and the Counselors.

X. District Organization.

The Districts are requested to adopt as far as practical the model constitution for Districts presented by the National Body. Essential requirements in the adoption of the District Constitution are the following points:

1. Maintaining the basic principle of group representation.

2. Arranging for supervision by synodical District.

3. Fostering Missionary Education.

4. Contributing approximately 25 percent of all missionary contributions toward approved national projects in fairness to all other member Districts.

XI. Amendments.

The Constitution may be amended by a two-thirds vote of the members present at any regular convention of the League, provided notice of the proposed amendments has been presented at a previous meeting of the League or has been published in the League's national magazine at least six months before the time of the general convention.

BY-LAWS

I. Duties of Officers.

a. The President shall preside at the general convention of the League, at the meeting of the Executive Board, shall be a member ex officio of all committees, and otherwise perform the duties pertaining to her office.

b. The Secretary shall keep a record of the proceedings of the general convention and the minutes of the Executive Board meetings and report to the general convention.

c. The President and the Secretary shall announce the convention in due time.

d. The Corresponding Secretary shall conduct the official correspondence of the League and report to the Executive Board and to the general convention of the League.

e. The Treasurer shall receive all moneys from the Financial Secretary, keep an accurate record of all receipts and disbursements, and make all payments authorized by the Administrative Board. All vouchers shall be signed by the President and the Recording Secretary. — The Treasurer shall furnish a fiduciary bond at the expense of the League. The Treasurer shall deposit money in the bank or banks designated by the Administrative Board.

f. The Financial Secretary shall receive all moneys and keep accurate record of all receipts and disbursements made to the Treasurer of the League.

g. In case of emergency the authority of the Executive Board shall not exceed the expenditure of four hundred dollars ($400.00) for the biennium in the furthering of any new project. It is understood that an emergency grant made by the Executive Board will not commit the League to the new project.

II. Standing Committees.

a. A Committee on Literature consisting of five members shall be elected by the Executive Board for a term of two years, eligible to two re-elections, and shall report to the Executive Board. This committee shall have charge of the publication of books, a quarterly national magazine, and tracts and programs under the direction of the Executive Board. One of the counselors shall be chosen by the Executive Board to be ex officio an additional member of the Committee on Literature.

b. A Committee on Constitution shall consist of the two Vice-Presidents and one District President appointed by the Executive Board. The duties of this Committee shall be to propose and announce necessary changes in the Constitution and to examine all District constitutions as to the essential requirements. (Confer Article X.)

c. The reporters for the official church papers shall be appointed by the Executive Board.

d. The books of the Treasurer shall be professionally audited once a year.

III. Contributions.

The Contributions for the National Body are ordinarily received from the Districts, which are requested to forward approximately 25 per cent of their missionary contributions to the National Body. See District Organization.

IV. Change in By-laws.

The by-laws of this Constitution may be changed or amended by a two-thirds vote of a National Convention after such proposed changes have been presented for consideration to the Executive Board.[23]

Jan. 1, 1943, was designated as the day when the Lutheran Women's Missionary League would begin to function officially, and the various Districts which intended to participate in the organization were to use the intervening months to adjust their local affairs accordingly.[24]

Upon recommendation of Dr. Behnken, President of Synod, the Counselors who had been appointed by him were to be retained until the next convention, when they would be chosen as prescribed by the Constitution.[25]

The Executive Board was authorized to hold a preliminary meeting prior to Jan. 1, 1943. It was also resolved to approach the Board of Directors of Synod through the Counselors requesting a loan not to exceed $1,000 to help the organization get started.[26]

Two projects were suggested by the convention and referred to the board: postwar missions, and chapels for deaf-mute congregations. The convention offering of $44.75, received at the opening service, was designated for synodical postwar relief missions.[27]

A resolution was passed to hold the first regular convention the following year, time and place to be decided by the Executive Board. In view of existing conditions, as a result of the war, the possibility of not being able to hold a convention was realized. If such should prove to be the case, the Executive Board was empowered to transact the necessary business.[28]

Though the convention had engaged in serious deliberations of far-reaching proportions, it was not without its lighter moments. Despite differences of opinion, a genuine Christian spirit prevailed, and friendships were formed which lasted through the years.

The first Executive Board meeting was called for Oct. 6, 1942. At that time Pastor Birkner informed the board that the College of Presidents suggested that the word "national" be omitted in the constitution of the Lutheran Women's Missionary League because it was restrictive.[29] Though there had been much discussion by the College of Presidents about the constitution, it had finally been approved unanimously.[30] Pastor Birkner likewise reported that an advance of $1,000 had been made from the treasury of the Missouri Synod to the Lutheran Women's Missionary League.[31] (This was repaid in full Dec. 17, 1943.) He also offered a loan from the Central District. The Mission Board of the Central District subsequently voted the sum of $2,500 as a loan to the Lutheran Women's Missionary League, which represented a balance in the treasury of the Central District

First Executive Board, 1942

Women's Missionary Endeavor. (This note, dated Jan. 15, 1943, and payable on Jan. 15, 1946, was paid in full on Oct. 26, 1944.)[32]

The finances of the new organization were further enhanced by the presentation of $61.09 by Mrs. H. J. Heitner, who had served as treasurer of the Temporary Lutheran Women's League (1929 to 1931). This represented the balance in the treasury of that organization.[33] The treasurer of the Lutheran Women's Missionary League was authorized to open an account in the name of the organization. Both treasurer and financial secretary were instructed to open their books and to keep them to conform to the system in use in the Fiscal Office of Synod.[34]

The importance of publicity for the fledgling organization was not overlooked. The board appointed a Publicity Committee which was to publish a manual and such other materials as it deemed necessary for publicity purposes.[35] Other items of business approved by the Executive Board at its first meeting included the appointment of a Constitution Committee,[36] a resolution to make available uniform collection devices to all who wished them,[37] and the publication of the quarterly periodical of 16 pages (6×9 in.), to be known as the *Lutheran Woman's Quarterly*.[38]

The presence of delegates from organized Districts at the meeting in Chicago several months earlier was interpreted as being a declaration of intent on the part of those Districts to affiliate. However, charter membership was held open throughout 1943 to permit still others to join.[39]

Rev. Elmer A. Kettner of Wollaston, Mass., had long promoted the formation of a Lutheran Women's League in Synod. After the 1941 convention of Synod he was one of the pastors appointed by the Atlantic District President to help organize the women in that District and became one of its first counselors. Shortly after the organization of the Lutheran Women's Missionary League in Chicago, Pastor Kettner was approached by Mrs. Flora B. Hecker, first president of the Atlantic District women's organization, to write a song for the Lutheran Women's Missionary League. (Pastor Kettner had written a school song for his Alma Mater, Concordia College, Fort Wayne, Ind., during his student days.) A feeling of inadequacy prompted him to procrastinate. Before long, however, he was hospitalized.

There, with plenty of time to meditate, Pastor Kettner wrote words to the tune "St. George," which he dedicated to the Lutheran Women's Missionary League. The song was sung at the first meeting of the board in October 1942 and was published in the first issue of the *Lutheran Woman's Quarterly.* It ultimately became the official League song. It reads as follows:

> Lutheran Women, one and all
> We have heard the Gospel call,
> We by faith have seen our Lord
> Crucified and then restored.
> We have seen Him pay the price,
> For our sins a sacrifice.
> Him we Lord and Christ acclaim,
> And unite to praise His name.
>
> Lutheran Women, young and old,
> Well we know His challenge bold:
> "Help to take the Gospel light
> To a world in darkest night,
> By example in the home,
> By inviting those who roam,
> By your prayers for sinners lost,
> By your gifts for missions' cost."
>
> Lutheran Women, coast to coast,
> In the Lord a mighty host,
> Let us all united be
> In the Holy Trinity.
> One in faith, in hope, and love
> Working for the Lord above,
> Till, our earthly labors done,
> We, in heaven, shall all be one.[40]

The foundations for the Lutheran Women's Missionary League had been laid. Mr. Louis H. Waltke had suggested in 1929 that the foundations for a national women's organization be laid "wide and deep." The Synodical Survey Committee likewise had recommended an organization which would "be wide in its scope." The committee appointed by the President of Synod to implement the synodical resolution authorizing a national women's organization suggested that "this hoped-for organization should focus its attention on the Church's main objective — Missions." It added, however, that every reasonable purpose of such an organization could be included under the *wider* sense of the terms: Missionary Inspiration, Missionary Education, and Missionary Service. The program of the Lutheran Women's Missionary League, as it has developed through the years, serves as the barometer which indicates the extent to which this initial goal has been realized.

Notes

VII

1. *Proceedings of the Thirty-Eighth Regular Convention of the Ev. Lutheran Synod of Missouri, Ohio, and Other States,* Fort Wayne, Ind., June 18—27, 1941, p. 393.

2. Ibid., p. 394.

3. Ibid.

4. Ibid.

5. Ibid., p. 397.

6. Ibid.

7. Ibid.

8. Ibid.

9. Ibid., p. 404.

10. Ibid.

11. Ibid., p. 410.

12. Ibid., p. 405.

13. Ibid.

14. "The North Dakota District of the Lutheran Women's Missionary League," (in file of District LWML histories at Concordia Historical Institute, St. Louis, and in LWML office), n. p.; *The Harvest Call,* I (Sept. 1938), 20; *Southeastern Lutheran Women's Missionary Society Quarterly,* I (Jan. 1939), 1.

15. "History of the Lutheran Woman's League, Missouri Synod," p. 22, minutes of May 19, 1939; *Lutheran Witness,* LXI, Western District edition, Nov. 10, 1942, p. 1.

16. *Lutheran Witness,* LVIII (Jan. 10, 1939), 2.

17. "Digest of Information and Suggestions for District Presidents Concerning Preliminary District Activity in Connection with a Synod-wide Women's Organization" (mimeographed copy on file at LWML office), pp. 1—2.

18. Report of District Executive Board, Oregon-Washington-Idaho LWML District Convention program, April 19, 1944.

19. Copy of dialog between Mrs. J. H. Deckman and Rev. H. Claus, presented over Radio Station KFUO in June 1951, pp. 2—3. From file of Mrs. Deckman.

20. "Minutes of the Convention of the National Body of the Lutheran Women's Missionary League," July 7—8, 1942, p. 8. Mimeographed copy on file in LWML office.

21. Ibid., p. 6.

22. Ibid., p. 2.

23. *Lutheran Woman's Quarterly,* Jan. 1943, pp. 19—20.

24. Minutes, 1942 Convention, p. 7.

25. Ibid., pp. 5—6.

26. Ibid., p. 7.

27. Ibid., p. 6.

28. Ibid., pp. 6—7.

29. Minutes, Executive Board, Lutheran Women's Missionary League, Oct. 6, 1942, p. 1.

30. Minutes, College of Presidents, Aug. 5, 1942, p. 1.

31. Minutes, LWML Executive Board, Oct. 6, 1942, p. 1.

32. Memo to Lutheran Women's Missionary League Executive Board from W. C. Birkner, Dec. 21, 1942, p. 1.

33. Minutes, LWML Executive Board, Oct. 6, 1942, p. 4.

34. Ibid., p. 3.

35. Ibid., p. 4.

36. Ibid., p. 1.

37. Ibid.

38. Ibid., p. 3.

39. Ibid., p. 1.

40. *Lutheran Woman's Quarterly,* Jan. 1943, p. 6.

VIII
Strengthening the Roots

LAUNCHING AN ORGANIZATION of nationwide proportions is not easy at any time. The first few years of the Lutheran Women's Missionary League's existence were complicated by the fact that the country was engaged in a global war. While this imposed certain restrictions, including the cancelation of the convention in 1945, it also presented a challenge which the women readily accepted and which served to strengthen the bonds that had brought them together.

Those who attended the League's conventions in 1942 and 1943, and those who attended the Administrative Committee and Executive Board meetings during the remaining war years, did so under very trying, though sometimes amusing, circumstances. Travel by car was virtually impossible because of gasoline rationing, and transportation by train was almost as prohibitive. Servicemen had priority, with the result that civilians never knew when they started out whether or not they would be displaced by a serviceman. Even if they were able to board a train, the accommodations were anything but ideal. It was not uncommon for members of the Executive Board and Administrative Committee to have to stand in the aisle of a train for long distances. Every available piece of equipment was put into service, and some of it had not been in use for many, many years. Dining-car service for civilians was almost nonexistent, and most civilians who had to travel any great distance tried to provide themselves with sufficient food to last the duration of their trip. If this was not possible,

Officers and Counselors, 1943: (Seated left to right) Mrs. Raymond Roehrkasse, Mrs. H. W. Lembke, Rev. W. C. Birkner, Mrs. Otto Schmitt, Mrs. Walter Widmann, Rev. R. H. C. Meyer, Miss Gertrude Ressmeyer. (Standing) Mrs. C. A. Hass, Mrs. A. H. Meitler, Rev. Oscar Fedder

they would have to hurry out and buy what they could while the train stopped to discharge and receive passengers.

The Lutheran Women's Missionary League also had other problems during those first years which were not related to the war situation. They were charting a new course — there were no precedents to follow — so guidelines had to be drawn up and policies determined. Until this was accomplished, some things were done without the more rigid regulations which followed later. This was true not only on the national level but even more so in the Districts. For example, in one District a woman who had joined the local Ladies' Aid after her husband returned from the war was elected president of her local group at the meeting after she joined and at which she was not present. What's more, the following year she was introduced to the Lutheran Women's Missionary League when her husband read her a headline from the daily paper stating that she had been elected President of the District, which was holding its convention in another town.

These formative years also imposed obligations on individuals which were beyond the usual sphere of duty for their respective roles. The President, Mrs. Schmitt, for instance, conducted heavy correspondence of all kinds, including correspondence with societies and individuals who inquired about the procedure necessary for them to affiliate with the League. She also mailed out mission boxes and *Quarterlies* to such societies when they requested them. Many of these societies, though unaffiliated with the Lutheran Women's Missionary League, adopted its program. Prior to the 1943 convention Mrs. Schmitt had mailed 2,000 copies of the *Handbook* and almost 50,000 mission boxes to all member societies, in addition to application cards for membership and certificates of membership.[1] She explained in a letter to one of the District Presidents that, while it was unusual for the President to take care of all these details, it was the most satisfactory arrangement under the circumstances. In addition, Mrs. Schmitt stored all extra copies of back issues of the *Quarterly* so that they would be preserved. (There was no storage space available at Concordia Publishing House.)[2] It is not surprising that by 1946 Mrs. Schmitt suffered a breakdown which necessitated hospitalization followed by a long period of rest. In 1945 the Executive Board had finally granted the President an allowance of $50 a month for secretarial help.[3]

Another example of such service in the formative years of the Lutheran Women's Missionary League was that given by Mrs. R. H. C. Meyer, Circulation Manager of the *Quarterly*. As such she handled all the details pertaining to the printing and to subscriptions to the *Quarterly* from her home, from the time of her appointment as Circulation Manager in November 1943 to 1947, at which time the *Quarterly* had 109,000 subscribers.[4] Although many of the details connected with the printing and circulation of the *Quarterly* were handled in the League office after a part-time secretary was engaged in the fall of 1947, Mrs. Meyer continued as Circulation Manager until the summer of 1948.

The first officers of the Lutheran Women's Missionary League and the District Presidents, who constituted the Executive Board, realized that there was much to be done to lay the groundwork for a solid organization. They therefore considered the matter of a convention in 1943 at their October 1942 board meeting. They realized that it was problematical whether this would be possible because of world conditions. However, the District Presidents were instructed to determine whether such a convention might be held in their area and, if so, to extend an invitation.

First Regular Convention

The Administrative Board (now known as the Executive Committee) discussed the matter of a convention in April 1943. It decided that, since there were so many things needing clarification and since the government had encouraged the holding of church-related conventions, they would proceed with plans for a convention. Two invitations had been received: one from St. Louis, the other from Fort Wayne. Since the facilities of Concordia College would be available if the convention were held prior to the opening of the school year, the invitation of the Fort Wayne group was accepted. The convention dates were set for August 31 and September 1. The Executive Board was to meet the day prior to the opening of the convention. Both delegates and guests were to be assessed a registration fee of $1.00.[5]

Plans for the first regular convention of the League were announced in the *Lutheran Woman's Quarterly* (July issue). A limited number of visitors, it said, could be accommodated in the dormitory where delegates were to be housed. Requests for such accommodations would be honored in the order in which they were received. The charge for such housing would be $.75 per night, and "if the food supply is sufficient to serve meals to visitors also, in the College Dining Hall [a reflection of the limitations imposed by the war], a charge of $.25 for breakfast, $.50 for dinner, and $.35 for supper will be made." [6]

The convention motto chosen by the Central District, "Serve the Lord with Gladness" (Ps. 100:2), was adopted at the convention as the permanent motto of the League. It was also decided to place this motto in the masthead of the official periodical of the League *(Lutheran Woman's Quarterly)* and on its stationery.[7]

A poem with the convention motto as its theme was written by Prof. Ernest Lewerenz of the Fort Wayne College and dedicated to the League. It was read at the convention and appeared in the *Quarterly* the following October. This poem, which may be sung to the tune "St. Gertrude" ("Onward, Christian Soldiers"), still appears in the *Handbook* of the League and reads as follows:

> "Serve the LORD with gladness!"
> It is He alone
> Who redeemed us sinners,
> Guides us as His own
> To enjoy the blessings
> Of His love and grace,
> Will, at last, in glory
> Meet us face to face.
>
> > Onward, then, for Jesus!
> > Let this be our aim:
> > "Serve the Lord with gladness,"
> > Glorify His name!
>
> "SERVE the Lord with gladness!"
> Us He gave command
> To proclaim His Gospel
> Now in every land,
> So that fellow sinners
> May, like us, be blest;
> Leading them to Jesus
> We can serve Him best.

Onward, then, for Jesus!
Let this be our aim:
"Serve the Lord with gladness,"
Glorify His name!

"Serve the Lord with GLADNESS!"
Is there greater joy
Than to serve the Master
Deigning to employ
Us to build His kingdom?
Angels too rejoice
Over every sinner
Brought to heed His voice.

Onward, then, for Jesus!
Let this be our aim:
"Serve the Lord with gladness,"
Glorify His name! [8]

Since the convention was held on the college campus, there was an informal atmosphere that could not have been duplicated elsewhere. Many of the women appeared at the first session in hats and gloves but by afternoon had discarded them in favor of fans. There was no air conditioning! It was an interesting and unusual experience, too, for the women to be housed in a boys' dormitory. Mrs. Sadie Fulk Roehrs, President of the Central District, who welcomed the women, brought smiles to their faces at the first business session when she promised them "solid" comfort on the college mattresses! The delegates, unconvinced, called them their fox holes because of the deep depression in the center. The sight of women's hosiery drying and cosmetics and feminine apparel hanging all over the dormitory were most unusual sights for this campus which normally housed only young men. [9]

The caliber of the delegates and visitors is attested to by the fact that 85 percent of those in attendance who filled out a questionnaire on their war activities were actively engaged in one way or another in such work. Most of them were in Red Cross work, but a few were serving in a special way. Mrs. Geo. H. Nickles of Oregon City, Oreg., was an observer in the U. S. Air Forces IV Fighter Command Aircraft Warning Service; Mrs. L. Baccarini of Oklahoma City, Okla., was an assistant in the OPA and an aid in WAC recruiting; Miss Marie Ehle of Fort Wayne was on the Allen County Youth Commission on juvenile delinquency; Mrs. J. H. Joesting of Minnesota was chairman of the Salvage Committee of the County Federation of Women's Clubs; and Mrs. Melvin C. Kenn of Berwyn, Ill., was a Braille transcriber.[10]

It is not surprising, then, that during the sessions the dormitory was completely deserted and the women were to be found engaged in the serious business of solving the many problems of this young organization which begged for a solution.

Mrs. Schmitt commended the officers in her president's report for the efficient manner in which they had discharged their duties during the past year. She called particular attention to the Constitution Committee, who, though widely separated geographically (they lived in California, Indiana, and Maryland respectively), had functioned so well.

"Let us not lose sight of our objectives — Missionary Education, Missionary Inspiration and Missionary Service," said Mrs. Schmitt. "This does not mean only financial endeavors, but personal mission service. And let us consider that we are building for the future, paving the way for our younger women, who, with their advantage of higher education, will be kept in the Lutheran fold if we offer them an opportunity to use their talents in the service of the Missouri Synod." [11]

In October 1942 the Executive Board had designated Mrs. Schmitt and Rev. R. H. C. Meyer, one of the counselors, to select a design for a collecting device. It had authorized the Administrative Board to place an order for such a device, stipulating that the Districts were to pay for the collection devices which they ordered.[12] Mrs. Schmitt reported to the convention that such a device had been agreed on in the form of a mission offering box and that an order had been placed for 50,000. By the time of the convention 43,950 of these had been mailed out to the Districts.[13]

The Election Committee presented two resolutions providing for (1) an absolute majority for election to office and (2) the adoption of *Robert's Rules of Order* as the parliamentary authority unless they conflicted with the Constitution. Both were adopted.

Election results were then announced:

President   Mrs. Otto F. Schmitt
                                            Western District

Vice-President	Mrs. H. W. Lembke California and Nevada District
Second Vice-President	Miss Gertrude H. Ressmeyer Southeastern District (North)
Recording Secretary	Mrs. Walter Widmann Iowa District East
Corresponding Secretary	Mrs. Raymond Roehrkasse Southern Nebraska District
Financial Secretary	Mrs. C. A. Hass Kansas District
Treasurer	Mrs. A. Meitler Oklahoma District
Counselors:	Rev. R. H. C. Meyer Western District Rev. W. C. Birkner Central District Rev. O. Fedder Northern Illinois District [14]

Various items came before the convention which reflected the need for establishing certain definite policies to get the new organization to function more effectively. Both the North Dakota-Montana District LWML and the Southeastern District LWML had divided because they found it impractical to retain the boundaries of the synodical Districts. The convention ratified this action but at the same time passed a resolution that in future any such contemplated division be approved by the convention before a division would be effected.[15]

Equalization of Travel Costs

The North Dakota branch of the North Dakota-Montana District submitted an overture calling for equalization of travel costs for delegates to conventions of the League. This matter was considered by the convention in connection with another resolution, submitted by the Resolutions Committee, regarding voting by proxy. A committee of three was appointed to study these matters and report to the next convention. This marked the beginning of recurring requests for equalization of travel costs. A committee appointed in 1947 to study this matter reported at the following convention (1949) that a survey had indicated that 34 percent of the Districts favored some form of equalization and 19 percent were opposed to it. The committee pointed out, however, that 46 percent of the Districts had failed to respond. It presented several resolutions on this matter which were adopted. They suggested that (1) since there did not seem to be a general desire for such an arrangement, no plan of equalization be adopted at that time; that (2) the League declare itself receptive to invitations to hold the general conventions also in the "fringe areas"; and that (3) to compensate Districts which were widely separated from the Midwest, where the concentration of membership was, the Lutheran Women's Missionary League defray the cost of transportation of all District Presidents to general conventions.[16] It was not until 1961 that a plan of equalization was adopted.[17] The matter of voting by proxy was rejected at the 1947 convention.[18]

The League Emblem

Another item to come before the 1943 convention was the request for a League emblem. A committee appointed to investigate the matter [19] presented four designs to the 1947 convention, which chose the design submitted by Mrs. Quin Dennis of Huron, S. Dak. It contained the open Bible, the cross, and the letters L W M L, inclosed in three circles, graduated in size. This has remained the official emblem of the League. The colors of the emblem were left to the discretion of the committee.[20] It was not until 1951 that the Executive Board adopted purple and gold, the colors suggested in the *Handbook* printed in that year, as the official colors of the League.[21]

Missionary Education

While the women were eager to carry out the objective of the League to foster missionary education, correspondence received by Mrs. Schmitt indicated that many, including pastors, were at a loss to know how to go about implementing this objective. They did not know what kind of topics to present or where to get the necessary helps for such topics. The League therefore resolved in 1943 to supply the Districts with information about where additional material for topic study might be had within the Districts.[22]

Historian

The value of recording the history of the League from its beginning was recognized by a resolution authorizing the appointment of a historian. The chair appointed Mrs. Sadie Fulk Roehrs immediately.[23] Her first task was the preparation of a history of the League for distribution at the 1944 convention of Synod. In 1946 a history in dialog form, the first "Facts and Figures" booklet, was written by Mrs. Roehrs. Additional copies were printed later that year. This booklet was reprinted with a 4-page insert in 1947 and was revised further in 1949 during Mrs. Preisinger's term as historian.

War Prevents 1945 Convention

By 1945, when the regular convention of the League should have been held, the war effort had reached its peak. Troops were being moved in ever-increasing numbers across the country and into the Pacific battle areas. In addition, food rationing had become more stringent, as also, of course, travel by any means. In view of all this it would have been impractical if not impossible to hold a convention. Early that year the Oregon-Washington-Idaho District formally requested the LWML to voluntarily postpone its convention.[24] In addition, the government requested the cancellation of conventions. As a result, after consulting the Counselors, Mrs. Schmitt canceled the convention and arranged for a 2-day session of the Executive Board on June 19 and 20 instead.[25]

The matter of holding a convention in 1946 was discussed, but it was agreed not to schedule a convention until 1947 and to have the incumbents remain in office until that time.[26]

First Society Outside Continental U. S.

One of the "firsts" in the history of the LWML came with the affiliation of Our Redeemer Women's Guild of Honolulu immediately after its organization in the summer of 1946 as a member of the California and Nevada District of the LWML. This marked the entrance into membership of the first society outside the continental limits of the United States.[27] It was the author's privilege, as a member of the group, to help organize that society.

Fifth Anniversary

The second regular convention of the League was announced in April 1947, to be held in Chicago in July. Members all over the

Mrs. Sadie Fulk Roehrs
President, 1947—1953

country were eagerly awaiting this event, which marked the fifth anniversary of the League's existence. The League motto, "Serve the Lord with Gladness," was painted on a large scroll which hung in the front of the convention hall.[28]

While the LWML was observing its fifth anniversary, the Missouri Synod was preparing to meet the following week in the same city to observe its centennial.[29]

The 1947 convention brought to a close the long and dedicated service, in an official capacity, of the League President, Mrs. Schmitt. In her place Mrs. Sadie Fulk Roehrs was elected. Though her background was quite different from that of Mrs. Schmitt, she was also eminently well qualified for the position. She had grown up in a Christian family (though not Lutheran), had been trained as a teacher, and then, after teaching several years, had attended International Business College, Fort Wayne, and worked as a bookkeeper prior to her marriage to Mr. Roehrs in 1933. Soon after her marriage she joined the Lutheran Church. She became active in the Ladies' Aid in her congregation in Fort Wayne and served as its president in 1941 and 1942. She also served on the Organization Committee of the Central District LWML and was elected as its first president.[30] She had also been active in the general League from the beginning.

Headquarters Office Established

The extent to which the League had grown during its first 5 years was evidenced not only by the increased interest shown through the attendance at the general convention but in other areas. The fifth-anniversary convention passed a resolution requesting the Executive Board to implement its resolution of November 1946 to establish an office for the League in Concordia Publishing House, St. Louis, as soon as possible. It also authorized the hiring of a part-time secretary (to be under the supervision of the Administrative Committee) to handle official correspondence in connection with the *Quarterly* and send out mite boxes, stationery, and other supplies, etc.[31] A few months later, when the Administrative Committee met, Mrs. Oscar E. Feucht was employed part time, beginning Nov. 20, 1947,[32] at a salary of $20 a month.[33] She had been working part time for the Lutheran Woman's League, Western District,[34] and continued to do so for some time. The Lutheran Woman's League occupied space in the office of the Synod's Western District at Concordia Publishing House. Not until December 1948 was Concordia Publishing House able to make separate office space available for the LWML. At that time arrangements were made for temporary quarters, "with desk, chair, and file included for $7.50 a month." An adding machine, a Royal typewriter, and a steel supply cabinet were purchased by the League. Mrs. Feucht moved into her new quarters on Feb. 1, 1949. During the time that the LWML had occupied desk space in the Western District office the Lutheran Woman's League of the Western District permitted the use of its equipment. To compensate in a measure for the space it occupied, the LWML paid the Western District $5.00 a month.[35] The LWML office has been housed in Concordia Publishing House ever since.

Women of Other Synods

From time to time requests were received from Ladies' Aids who were affiliated with congregations of either the Norwegian or the Slovak Synod. The matter was given careful consideration, and a genuine interest in having these societies affiliate was evident. However, since the constitution provided that only women's groups affiliated with the Missouri Synod were eligible for membership, the societies had to be so informed. (See Chapter IX)

Housing of Missionaries

1947 marked the beginning of a service project which has been carried on through the years, though the nature of the program has changed from its original purpose. The appointment of a committee to cooperate with the Board of Foreign Missions was authorized to provide adequate housing for missionaries and their families in various places throughout the country while on furlough. It was understood that this would involve no financial obligation on the part of the LWML.[36]

Membership

Once the national organization was launched, the response was immediate from many areas. In contrast to the 28 delegates who represented 15 Districts at the Chicago meeting in 1942, 73 delegates, representing 19 Districts, were present the following year.[37] By the time the League observed its fifth anniversary in 1947, the convention was attended by 195 delegates, 44 officials, committee chairmen, and counselors, plus more than 500 visitors who registered.[38] By the end of the decade a total of almost 800 registered for the convention, of which about 500 were visitors.[39]

The increase in attendance at conventions reflected the number of Districts which had been added since the League's beginning and also the increasing number of societies and individuals who affiliated.

When the first regular convention was held in 1943, the number of Districts who were officially received at that time numbered 19: Atlantic, California and Nevada, Central, Iowa East, Kansas, Minnesota, North Dakota-Montana (Montana Branch), North Dakota-Montana (North Dakota Branch), Northern Illinois, Northern Nebraska, Oklahoma, Oregon-Washington-Idaho, South Dakota, Southeastern (Northern Branch), Southeastern (Southern Branch), Southern Illinois, Southern Nebraska, Texas, and Western. Two of the synodical Districts (North Dakota-Montana and Southeastern) had divided prior to the 1943 convention because of the large geographical areas involved.[40]

By 1945 six additional Districts were added to the membership: Colorado, English, Eastern, Michigan, Southern, and North Wisconsin. At that time Montana, which had separated from the North Dakota-Montana District and formed a separate District, was also formally received.[41]

When the League observed its fifth anniversary 2 years later, the membership had increased to 29 Districts, almost double the number who were represented at the organization meeting 5 years earlier. Southern California had become a member in January 1946, Central Illinois in May 1946, and Iowa West in September 1946. South Wisconsin was organized in November 1946.[42]

Another division of two Districts because of large geographical areas involved brought the membership to 31 Districts by the 1949 convention. The two which had divided were the Southern and the Oregon-Washington-Idaho, thus adding the Florida-Georgia District and the Idaho District.[43] A further division of the Southern District was authorized by the 1949 convention, which permitted the Louisiana and Gulf States branches to form the Louisiana District and the Gulf States District.[44]

Both the number of societies and the total membership of the League increased as a result of the affiliation of additional Districts and as evidence of a growing interest in the LWML within those Districts. By the close of the decade 2,525 societies in the United States (including Our Redeemer Women's Guild in Honolulu) and one society in Canada (Bethlehem Missionary Society, Bruderheim, Alta.), with an individual membership of 104,550, made up the membership of the LWML.[45]

Financial Progress

From an organization which began in 1942 without any funds, the LWML had grown by 1949 to the point that it showed total receipts in excess of $275,500 recorded by the Financial Secretary.[46] Though mission offering boxes had been provided from the start, they were not being used by all groups at the time of the '49 convention. However, those districts and local groups who used them reported a sizable increase in their contributions.[47] Of particular interest is that the first check, amounting to $100.00, was received from a layman, Mr. E. Spilman of Baltimore, and was designated for postwar mission expansion.[48]

English District Societies

The committee of pastors who had been appointed by the President of Synod in 1941 (to implement the synodical resolution authorizing the formation of a national women's federation) realized that the women's societies of congregations of the English District would be faced with the problem of affiliation since the English District is made up of congregations located in various parts of the country, within the area of other synodical Districts. Where a number of such congregations were concentrated in a relatively small area, this would pose no problem. On the other hand, in areas where such congregations were not very numerous, such a problem might arise. The pastors therefore suggested in the digest of information and suggestions which they sent to synodical District Presidents on Jan. 15, 1942, that such Ladies' Aid societies "should be invited to participate by the District in whose territory they are located."

When the English District of Synod met in June 1943, the District committee which had been appointed to study the matter made two recommendations, both of which were adopted: (1) that in all congregations some existing society join the new organization and attempt to adapt its program to local conditions; and, odd as it may seem, (2) that in sections where there is a district of the LWML connected with the local (synodical) district, a local English District of the LWML be organized if it is deemed advisable. The committee also recommended that the funds of such a District be divided as follows: "Ten per cent, or at least ten cents a year per member to the 'local,' *e. g.,* Northern Illinois district, as a subscription to their local paper, 25 per cent to the Synod-wide organization, and the remainder be given to any missionary endeavor of which the [English] District may approve, always endeavoring to support some missionary activity which is not supported by Synod." [49]

In connection with the above, the Administrative Board of the LWML agreed (Nov. 10, 1943) to recommend to the English District societies that they join the District in which they reside.[50] At the beginning some such societies affiliated with the LWML of the synodical District in which they were located. However, as the League grew, most societies in this category formed their own groups, which they call chapters, instead of affiliating with the District in which they are located geographically.

Cooperation in Synodical Endeavors

From time to time during the first years of its existence the League sent representatives to meet with the various synodical committees in an effort to assist Synod in carrying out its programs. Such cooperation was designed also to coordinate the program of the League with that of the Synod. The President of the League attended such a meeting of the Adult Education Committee of Synod in 1946, at the invitation of the chairman, Rev. Oscar E. Feucht. Pastor Feucht later addressed the members of the Executive Board (November 1946) and outlined a plan by which a uniform topic study might be conducted for effective group discussion, for Bible study, and for parent education. As a result, representation of the League at future meetings of the Adult Education Committee was authorized.[51]

After Synod passed a resolution at its centennial convention in 1947 urging more general participation of the members of Synod in Bible study and calling upon the auxiliary organizations (Walther League, Lutheran Laymen's League, and Lutheran Women's Missionary League) to assist in the Bible study program, LWML President Mrs. Roehrs attended a meeting of the Adult Education Committee, together with representatives of the other organizations. Purpose of the meeting was to determine what could be done to increase Bible study in each organization. As a result, League members were urged to use helps prepared by Pastor Feucht, Synod's Secretary of Adult Education, to make Bible study a part of the home, the congregation, and the women's organization.[52]

Most significant, perhaps, during the '40s were the developments in the areas of the League's constitution, its *Quarterly* publication, and the projects which it adopted.

Constitution

The constitution adopted by the League at its organization meeting in Chicago in 1942 was amended several times during the '40s. Changes were recommended already at the 1943 convention. These, for the most part a matter of clarification rather than actual change, were accepted, together with suggestions made from the floor, with the understanding that they be ratified by the next convention. The two essential changes were the inclusion of the Corresponding Secretary in the Administrative Committee, and the change in wording in the article on "Representation." The latter provided that Districts "arrange their organizations into groups of 7 to 10 congregations" (each congregation to constitute one unit regardless of the number of societies in the congregation). The fiscal year was also designated to run from May 15 to May 14. The "Temporary, Revised Constitution," with these changes, was printed in the *Quarterly*.[53]

Additional amendments were made at the 1947 convention. These included the addition of the word "approximately" to the above article to read "approximately 7 to 10 congregations." A change in the article on "Amendments" provided that a notice of proposed amendments appear in the *Quarterly* at least 3 months before the convention instead of 6 months as stated previously.[54] The bylaws were amended to provide for publication of a list of the candidates for office in the issue of the *Quarterly* prior to the convention.[55]

As the League continued to grow, the necessity for additional changes in the Constitution became evident. The two vice-presidents were added to the Administrative Committee in 1949. The term of office of the Counselors, who were to be pastors, was set at 6 years without eligibility for reelection (Article IX). Their terms of office were to be staggered so that one new counselor would be elected at each convention from a list of names submitted by the President of Synod. The change became effective in 1949.[56]

Literature Committee

The decision to publish a periodical was made at the first meeting of the Executive Board in October 1942. The necessity for such a published aid to create and sustain interest in the organization was discussed thoroughly. The periodical, it was decided, should be issued quarterly, should be called the *Lutheran Woman's Quarterly,* and should contain one topic study, to be used at the quarterly meeting of the societies. Cost of the publication was to be prorated to the individual Districts, but the first two issues were to be sent to the

Districts gratis for promotional purposes. The Literature Committee of each District was encouraged to supply additional materials for monthly topic study in addition to the topic appearing in the *Quarterly*.[57]

Rev. Walter C. Birkner, one of the Counselors, was appointed by the Executive Board to serve as editor of the *Quarterly* until the first regular convention (1943). He was authorized to choose a committee to serve with him until that time. The committee was also to serve as a clearinghouse for District topic studies and to make them available to societies. In order to make the appointment legal, it was resolved to suspend the paragraph in the Constitution relating to the Literature Committee until the first convention.[58]

Pastor Birkner selected Mrs. Herbert Bredemeier, Fort Wayne, Ind.; Mrs. Ed Klinkerman, Cincinnati, Ohio; and Miss Emelia Wefel, Cleveland, Ohio, as the temporary Literature Committee. Theirs was no easy task. It had been decided to publish the first issue of the *Quarterly* in January 1943. Besides getting the copy together from various people, there was the matter of getting a mailing list of the societies from all the Districts, who were themselves not yet well organized. Despite all these difficulties, the January 1943 issue of the *Quarterly* appeared as scheduled. It contained a message from the President, Mrs. Schmitt; greetings from the President of the Missouri Synod, Dr. John W. Behnken, and from Drs. O. H. Schmidt and F. C. Streufert, synodical mission officials; an article on the responsibility of Christian women in connection with the war effort; and an article by the wife of a foreign missionary.

The first topic study was written by Rev. Martin Ilse, Jr., of Cincinnati, Ohio, on "Women Missionaries in the Foreign Field." It marked the beginning of such topic studies which are still an integral part of the *Quarterly*. Pastor Ilse continued to serve as Topic Editor until April 1956.[59] Through his topics he undoubtedly exerted a great influence on the spiritual development of the League. The first issue of the *Quarterly* also contained a suggested program for a quarterly mission meeting. This feature was discontinued with the January 1945 issue.

The Constitution adopted by the convention in Chicago also appeared in the first issue of the *Quarterly*. In addition, news of each of the 15 Districts represented at the organization meeting was included. As a result of the decision to include all this material, it was necessary to increase the size of the first issue to 20 pages instead of the 16 which had been planned.

The first two issues of the *Quarterly* were sent to the Districts gratis, as intended. 60,000 copies of the January issue were printed and 70,000 of the April issue.[60] Many individuals whose Districts were not yet affiliated with the League were nevertheless desirous of obtaining the *Quarterly*. A resolution was therefore passed at the 1943 convention providing that the *Quarterly* be made available to such individuals for the time being on a subscription basis of 25 cents a year.[61]

The Literature Committee, including Pastor Birkner as editor, had been appointed to serve only until the 1943 convention. Though they expressed a desire on several occasions to be relieved of their duties, the Administrative Board requested them to continue to serve beyond the time specified because of the excellent work they were doing. Pastor Birkner, however, informed the Administrative Board in 1943 that it would be impossible for them to serve beyond the preparation of the January 1944 issue of the *Quarterly*. Their resignation was then accepted, and Rev. Oscar Fedder, another of the Counselors, was appointed to serve as Counselor to the new committee.[62] Named by the Executive Board to the first permanent Literature Committee were: Mrs. M. C. Kenn (Editor), Mrs. A. F. Eilers, Mrs. Robert Magee, Miss Emma Kiefer, and Miss Marie Ehle.[63] Mrs. R. H. C. Meyer had in 1943 been appointed Circulation Manager by the Administrative Committee.[64]

The first meeting of the new committee was held Feb. 19, 1944. Its most urgent business was compiling and editing material for the April issue of the *Quarterly*. The general format of the magazine, they decided, would be essentially the same as it had been. One new feature, however, was the addition of the League motto on the front cover. Another was the introduction of a feature article in each issue about the programs of several of the Districts.

The need for a revision of the *Handbook* was called to the attention of the committee. The first *Handbook* had been published in January 1943 by a Publicity Committee.[65] The revised edition appeared in the fall of 1944 and still another in 1946.[66] In addition, the committee agreed to publish timely tracts and other publicity material.[67]

Before long another problem faced the committee in the form of a paper shortage due to the war. Mrs. Schmitt wrote government officials in Washington twice during 1944 in an effort to get sufficient paper to print the *Quarterly,* and her efforts met with success.[68]

Beginning with 1945 the colors of the cover page of the *Quarterly* were changed to make them more easily identifiable. Tomato, the color which had heretofore been used for all issues, was chosen for the January issue of each year; violet for April; French green for July; and golden orange for October. Otherwise the cover remained unchanged.[69] Another change during this year was the addition of the addresses of the Literature Committee to their names on page 2, beginning with the October issue.

In order to provide continuity, the Executive Board voted in 1947 to stagger the terms of the committee. Two members of the existing committee would serve for two years (1948—50), two for one year (1948—49), and one new member was appointed for 2 years.[70] Though reelected to the editorship, Mrs. Kenn found it necessary to relinquish this position early in 1948. Miss Kiefer succeeded her.[71]

Along with an increase in the number of pages in the *Quarterly* from 16 to 20, the request of Concordia Publishing House to use the back page for advertising purposes was granted.[72] The larger *Quarterly* appeared for the first time in January 1946. The size was increased again in October 1947 to 24 pages.

As the '40s drew to a close, the *Lutheran Woman's Quarterly* had made a good start in bringing the work of the Lutheran Women's Missionary League to the attention of the members of the Missouri Synod. Mrs. Roehrs called attention to the fact that the *Quarterly* "is the only periodical in The Lutheran Church-Missouri Synod circles published solely in the interest of missions for the lay reader." [73] It was also helping the women of the church to carry out the program of the League through the various types of information and helps it offered.

Christ Lutheran Church for the Deaf, Cleveland, Ohio

Projects

Despite the fact that the League was just getting organized and was without funds, it voted at the organization meeting in 1942 to adopt two projects: Postwar Missions and Chapels for Deaf-mute Congregations, and referred the matter to the Executive Board.[74]

Chapel for the Deaf. The following year the President reported that the loans from the Missouri Synod ($1,000) and from the Central District ($2,500) were to be repaid before any national projects would be undertaken. However, the first project adopted in 1943 was designated as a chapel for the deaf at Cleveland, Ohio, but no amount was specified.[75] By 1945 both of the loans had been repaid, and $15,000 was allocated for the project by the Executive Board.[76] Ground was broken Oct. 10, 1948, and the chapel was dedicated June 26, 1949.

Though work had been carried on among the deaf in Cleveland prior to the LWML grant, it had been hampered by the lack of a chapel of its own. The grant therefore marked the beginning of a new era for this work, and under the blessing of Almighty God it has prospered to the extent that the congregation in 1965 numbered over 400 baptized souls and more than 200 communicants.[77]

European Relief. The second project of the League, Postwar European Relief, is unparalleled in the League's history because of the personal involvement of thousands of its members in carrying it out. When the Administrative Board met in November 1943, it took steps to implement the resolution of the convention several months earlier to adopt some form of relief for war-torn Europe at the conclusion of the war. A Women's Advisory Committee of the LWML was appointed to work with Synod's Emergency Planning Council, a committee of Synod appointed to direct its program of postwar relief for Europe. Appointed to the LWML Advisory Committee were Mrs. Frederick Schuermann, chairman, Mrs. Odis Stellhorn, Mrs. Paul Beinke, and Miss Esther Fedderson.[78]

Little did anyone realize what a gigantic task the League had undertaken. In June 1945 the Executive Board went on record making the postwar project voted at the 1943 convention "the task of helping to relieve the physical destitution and the spiritual needs of Europe's orphaned and dislocated children." [79] The LWML committee was to ascertain from Synod's Emergency Planning Council the nature of the aid needed. Requests went out to all societies in the League for clothing (to be sewn or purchased) for children from infancy up to 12 years of age, and for bed linens, quilts, blankets, and medical kits.[80] But there was a long delay in shipping because of government regulations. Numerous inquiries were received; the women were getting impatient. "There were dark moments," wrote Mrs. Schuermann in April 1946, "when we wondered whether perhaps we had been too hasty in launching our project — we feared that our materials would lie unused because of Government regulations. But God in His mercy heard our prayers, and now the way is cleared, and we are prepared to ship." [81] Just a short time before, President Truman had issued a directive permitting clothing, food, and medical supplies to be sent to Poland, Finland, Czechoslovakia, Hungary, and the American zone in Germany.[82] By the time this phase of the League's project ended officially on Nov. 1, 1946 (it had begun in December 1945), the LWML had shipped 2,818 layettes; 1,311 clothing kits for boys; 2,611 clothing kits for girls; 1,191 articles of bedding; 27,110 articles of clothing; and 2,866 medical kits.[83] The printing of 10,000 prayer books was authorized at the 1947 convention.[84]

Meanwhile, after much delay and many difficulties, it was reported in July 1947 that orphanages were in operation in Paris, Berlin, Pforzheim, and the Heidelberg area as a result of the efforts of Synod's Emergency Planning Council. Arrangements had also been made to care for some orphans in Finland. It was urged that individual food and clothing packages be sent by Districts and individuals to children and to the personnel of the orphanages individually until large supplies could be shipped in.[85]

There were difficulties to be dealt with other than government regulations. In December 1946, shortly after government restrictions were lifted, two women from Zion Lutheran Church, Akron, Ohio, were busy preparing packages for mailing. They had 41 bundles ready by midafternoon but were concerned over the amount of postage these would require. The pastor had $19 in reserve for this purpose, but $59 was needed. Where would they get the difference? The pastor called the chairman of the church's poor fund, who agreed to loan the women the necessary money out of that fund, with the provision that it be repaid. He brought the money to the church, but while he was chatting with the pastor, a woman member of the congregation came and asked to see the pastor privately. She told him that several weeks before she had found some money and had not been able to locate the owner. She wanted to give it for some charitable purpose and suggested that it might be used for postage on packages to Europe if this were possible. Assured by the pastor that it was, she handed him two 20-dollar bills! [86]

By the time the project was discontinued officially by the League in 1949, the Financial Secretary reported that from June 1, 1947, to July 22, 1949, a total of $71,639.25 had been received for this project, of which $68,263.75 had been disbursed.[87] $32,000 had been allocated by the 1947 convention for this purpose to supplement the $18,000 which had already been designated, and, in addition, it voted that 10% of the mite-box collections received by the general League be made available for European relief.[88] The Executive Board had voted the day before the 1949 convention to authorize the chairman of the Postwar Planning Council to use the balance on hand for orphans and orphanages. The committee was retained "for guidance and counsel to District Presidents," who were encouraged to carry on the work on a District and local level.[89]

Monterrey, Mexico. The third project of the League, adopted in 1947, was a chapel for Monterrey, Mexico, in the amount of $30,000. Though some attempts had been made to begin mission work in Mexico late in the last century, nothing of any consequence had really been done until the Texas District commissioned the first native Mexican for work in Mexico City in 1940.[90] From there the work extended northward to Monterrey, a large industrial city. Santa Cruz (Holy Cross) Lutheran Church was dedicated on Nov. 12, 1950.[91] Problems related to getting the necessary permit to build and other unforeseen circumstances prevented the completion of the building earlier.[92] A training school to prepare native pastors was housed in the church for a time but was discontinued in 1958. A small clinic has been conducted in the rear of the church for some time and continues to serve with limited facilities. The work in Mexico has grown to 11 stations carried on in Spanish and an additional one conducted in English.

Honolulu, Hawaii. With the close of World War II and the occupation of Japan by American forces, the islands of the Pacific which had so recently been battle zones now became fertile fields for missionary activity. The church was made aware of this great challenge not only by the pleas of General MacArthur to churches of all faiths to send Christian missionaries into these areas but also by returning servicemen who had seen firsthand the great need to penetrate these areas with the Gospel. The two projects adopted by the LWML in 1949 reflected the desire of the women to cooperate with Synod in meeting this challenge.

One of the projects was $30,000 toward facilities for the congregation in Honolulu, Hawaii. Already during the war Chaplain Alvin Katt had been instrumental in persuading Synod to open a Lutheran Service Center in Honolulu in 1943. Services were conducted there by Rev. Virtus Gloe, who had been called as the service pastor for both military personnel and civilians who were employed in the many operations connected with the war effort.

In December 1944 Rev. Adolph R. Meyer was called to be the

first resident missionary in Hawaii, in fact in the whole Pacific area. At that time many of the islands of the Pacific were still battle zones. By the time the various arrangements had been made and government priorities received, it was June 1945 before Pastor Meyer and his family could leave for Hawaii. Government restrictions and limited accommodations resulted in his being assigned to one ship while the rest of the family were assigned to another. As a result, the family arrived in Honolulu several days before Pastor Meyer, on June 29, 1945, probably the first time in the history of the Missouri Synod that a missionary's wife and children preceded him to the field.

Several months later, Our Redeemer Lutheran Church was organized with a nucleus of interested civilians and servicemen. The congregation worshiped at first in the Lutheran Service Center. But with 500,000 people in the Islands (exclusive of service personnel), about half of whom were in Honolulu, it was evident that it was essential for the congregation to have a house of worship of its own. The mission opportunities were limitless since many of the people in the Hawaiian Islands had never heard the Gospel of Jesus Christ.

The congregation was fortunate in being able to rent a church building for a time for $200 a month. Here a school was begun in 1948 in addition to a Sunday school which had been conducted from the very beginning. The Women's Guild, which was organized in the summer of 1946, had immediately joined the LWML and participated actively in the European relief program.[93]

It was with great joy that the congregation learned of the LWML grant, which would help provide facilities for the congregation. The new church building was dedicated in September 1950[94] and included the first facilities of a permanent nature for the school as well. These school facilities have been increased considerably through the years to meet the increasing enrollment. The work in Hawaii has expanded so that in 1965 it reached out to include eight congregations on three islands in the Hawaiian group. There are parochial schools in three congregations in addition to Our Redeemer, the first congregation, and both in the congregations and in the schools most of the racial groups that make up the Island population are represented.

Tokyo, Japan. The other grant made by the LWML in 1949 was

Tokyo Lutheran Center

$35,000 for Tokyo, Japan. Here, too, our chaplains were active after the occupation began in helping to get the work of our church started among the Japanese people. Rev. William Danker, who was serving as a counselor for the Northern Illinois District LWML, was commissioned as the first missionary to Japan and arrived there in the fall of 1948.[95]

Here, too, it was very important that a building be acquired to put the work on a firm footing. The LWML grant helped to make possible the purchase of a building in Tokyo which became the Tokyo Lutheran Center. This building served as a hub for a variety of activities connected with the establishment of The Lutheran Church — Missouri Synod in Japan. Dedicated in 1951, the center contained facilities for "a Bible Institute for the training of Japanese church workers; professors' offices; a student dormitory program for young men from outlying areas studying in the colleges and universities of Tokyo; Japanese church services; Bible classes and Sunday schools; youth activities, including regular fellowship meetings and English classes at present [1953]; production of our Japanese Lutheran literature; special events, such as Sunday school teachers' conferences and talent festivals; the Japan Lutheran Hour headquarters . . . the administration and business offices of our mission; a Japanese language school for our own missionaries and for others who pay tuition; living quarters for missionary language students." The center also served as a place of worship for American servicemen in the area, for whom services were conducted by a Lutheran service pastor, Rev. Edwin Sohn.[96]

This was only the beginning. The far-reaching effects of the many activities for which the Tokyo Lutheran Center has served as a hub cannot be measured. Statistics do not tell a complete story, but they do show that the work in Japan has grown to the extent that by 1965 there were 37 stations being served by 32 American missionaries, 17 Japanese pastors, and other personnel.

Summary

When the LWML was organized in 1942, it was a small, somewhat timid group desirous of using the hitherto untapped resources of the women of the church for the promotion of the Kingdom. By the time the League held its convention at the close of the decade (1949), it had paid the debts which it had incurred to begin operations, had adopted five projects totaling $183,000, and above all, had experienced the joy of serving in the community of fellow Christians who had strengthened one another in their Christian concern and their motivation for such service.

Despite these blessings, the members of the LWML were also aware that they had only made a beginning. Mrs. Roehrs wrote in "The President's Page" (October 1949 *Quarterly*): "The growth of the Lutheran Women's Missionary League has been phenomenal. . . . But let us not rest on our laurels. . . . Less than half of the congregations [in Synod] have a Lutheran Women's Missionary League, and far less than half of the women are active in this great missionary movement. THERE IS MUCH WORK TO BE DONE BY THE GENERAL AND BY THE DISTRICT LEAGUES." [97]

Notes

VIII

1. *Proceedings,* LWML convention, Aug. 31—Sept. 1, 1943, p. 3. (Hereafter cited as LWML *Proceedings.*)

2. Letter from Mrs. O. F. Schmitt to Mrs. Geo. Nickels, May 4, 1944. File of Mrs. Schmitt.

3. Minutes, LWML Executive Board, June 19—20, 1945, p. 3.

4. Minutes, LWML Administrative Board, Nov. 10, 1943, p. 3; LWML *Proceedings,* July 18—19, 1947, pp. 4—5; LWML *Reports and Memorials,* 1947, p. 19.

5. Minutes, LWML Administrative Board, April 29, 1943, p. 3.

6. *Lutheran Woman's Quarterly,* July 1943, p. 3. (Hereafter cited as *LWQ.*)

7. LWML *Proceedings,* 1943, p. 14.

8. *LWQ,* Oct. 1943, p. 19.

9. Ibid., pp. 17—19.

10. Ibid., p. 19.

11. LWML *Proceedings,* 1943, p. 4.

12. Minutes, LWML Executive Board, Oct. 6, 1942, p. 2.

13. LWML *Proceedings,* 1943, p. 3.

14. Ibid., pp. 11, 12.

15. Ibid., p. 12.

16. LWML *Proceedings,* July 27—28, 1949, pp. 15—16.

17. LWML *Proceedings,* July 26—27, 1961, p. 28.

18. LWML *Proceedings,* 1947, p. 5.

19. LWML *Proceedings,* 1943, p. 14.

20. LWML *Proceedings,* 1947, p. 7.

21. Minutes, LWML Executive Board, July 24, 1951, p. 5.

22. LWML *Proceedings,* 1943, p. 14.

23. Ibid., p. 15.

24. Letter from Mrs. E. Muck to Mrs. O. F. Schmitt, Feb. 14, 1945. File of Mrs. Schmitt.

25. *LWQ,* April 1945, p. 13.

26. Minutes, LWML Executive Board, June 19—20, 1945, pp. 4, 6.

27. *LWQ,* Oct. 1946, p. 12.

28. *LWQ,* Oct. 1947, p. 3 (April and October 1947 *Quarterly* should have read "Second Regular Convention" — the 1943 convention was designated as the first *regular* convention).

29. *LWQ,* July 1947, p. 2.

30. *LWQ,* Jan. 1948, p. 19.

31. LWML *Proceedings,* 1947, pp. 4—5.

32. LWML *Proceedings,* 1949, p. 4.

33. Minutes, LWML Administrative Committee, Nov. 4, 1947, p. 2.

34. LWML *Proceedings,* 1949, p. 3. The Lutheran Woman's League, a charter member of the LWML, did not change its name to Lutheran Women's Missionary League until 1948.

162

35. Ibid., p. 4.

36. LWML *Proceedings,* 1947, p. 5.

37. LWML *Proceedings,* 1943, p. 1.

38. LWML *Proceedings,* 1947, p. 1.

39. LWML *Proceedings,* 1949, p. 1.

40. LWML *Proceedings,* 1943, p. 12; Minutes, LWML Executive Board, Aug. 30, 1943, p. 5.

41. Minutes, LWML Executive Board, June 19—20, 1945, p. 1.

42. Ibid., Nov. 12—13, 1946, p. 1.

43. LWML *Proceedings,* 1949, pp. 2—3.

44. Ibid., pp. 20—21.

45. *LWQ,* Oct. 1949, p. 9.

46. LWML *Proceedings,* 1949, p. 7.

47. Ibid., p. 6.

48. *LWQ,* July 1943, p. 11.

49. *Proceedings of the Twenty-First Convention of the English District of the Evangelical Lutheran Synod of Missouri, Ohio, and Other States,* June 15—16, 1943, p. 50.

50. Minutes, LWML Administrative Board, Nov. 10, 1943, p. 2.

51. Proceedings, LWML Executive Board, Nov. 12—13, 1946, pp. 3, 8. (Called "Proceedings" because this meeting substituted for the war-canceled 1945 convention.)

52. *LWQ,* Oct. 1948, pp. 13, 20.

53. *LWQ,* Oct. 1945, pp. 13—14.

54. LWML *Proceedings,* 1947, p. 7.

55. Ibid.

56. LWML *Proceedings,* 1949, p. 11.

57. Minutes, LWML Executive Board, Oct. 6, 1942, pp. 3—4.

58. Ibid., p. 4.

59. Minutes, LWML Literature Committee, Nov. 8—9, 1955, pp. 1—2.

60. LWML *Proceedings,* 1943, p. 6.

61. Ibid., p. 11.

62. Minutes, LWML Administrative Board, Nov. 10, 1943, p. 3.

63. As reported in Minutes, LWML Administrative Committee, Sept. 15, 1944, p. 1.

64. Minutes, LWML Administrative Board, Nov. 10, 1943, p. 3.

65. Letter from Mrs. O. F. Schmitt to Mrs. Geo. Nickels, Jan. 19, 1943. File of Mrs. Schmitt.

66. Disbursement vouchers, LWML, Feb. 14, 1943; Nov. 16, 1944; Feb. 25, 1946.

67. Minutes, LWML Literature Committee, Feb. 19, 1944, pp. 1—2.

68. Letter from Mrs. O. F. Schmitt to Mrs. H. W. Lembke, Nov. 25, 1944, file of Mrs. Schmitt; Minutes, LWML Administrative Committee, Sept. 15, 1944, p. 1.

69. Minutes, LWML Literature Committee, Nov. 11, 1944 (one page).

70. Minutes, LWML Executive Board, July 17, 1947, p. 3.

71. Minutes, LWML Literature Committee, June 12, 1948 (one page).

72. Ibid., Jan. 19, 1946 (one page).

73. LWML *Proceedings,* 1949, p. 3.

74. LWML *Proceedings,* July 7—8, 1942, p. 8.

75. LWML *Proceedings,* 1943, pp. 3, 12.

76. *LWQ,* Oct. 1945, p. 5.

77. *Statistical Yearbook,* The Lutheran Church — Missouri Synod, 1965, p. 114.

78. Minutes, LWML Administrative Board, Nov. 10, 1943, p. 3.

79. *LWQ,* Jan. 1946, p. 19.

80. Ibid., p. 20.

81. *LWQ,* April 1946, p. 9.

82. Ibid.

83. *LWQ,* July 1947, pp. 3—4.

84. LWML *Proceedings,* 1947, p. 9.

85. *LWQ,* July 1947, pp. 3—4.

86. Ibid., pp. 15—16.

87. LWML *Proceedings,* 1949, p. 8.

88. LWML *Proceedings,* 1947, pp. 8—9.

89. Minutes, LWML Executive Board, July 26, 1949, p. 3.

90. W. H. Bewie, "History of Spanish Missions in Texas," unprinted manuscript, p. 22.

91. *LWQ,* IX, No. 1 (Jan. 1951), p. 10.

92. Ibid., pp. 7—9.

93. *LWQ,* Oct. 1948, pp. 3—7.

94. *Lutheran Witness,* LXIX (Nov. 14, 1950), 371.

95. *Proceedings of the Forty-First Regular Convention of The Lutheran Church — Missouri Synod,* June 21—30, 1950, p. 467.

96. *LWQ,* XI, No. 2 (April 1953), pp. 6—7.

97. *LWQ,* Oct. 1949, p. 9.

IX
Spreading Branches
1950 — 1960

As ANOTHER DECADE DAWNED, war clouds again hung heavy over a war-weary world. In June of 1950 a civil war began in Korea which before long developed into a limited international conflict. Almost simultaneously with the action of the United Nations Security Council on June 27, calling upon member nations to assist the Republic of Korea, President Truman ordered American military forces into action against the invading Communist-equipped North Korean forces. While the war did not compare in scope with World War II, the resulting tensions were nevertheless reflected on the home front during the 3 years of its duration.

Cooperation in Synodical Endeavors

In addition to the misery created by the war in South Korea, widespread suffering existed in the entire Far East, as well as Europe, as an aftermath of World War II. At its convention in 1951, therefore, the Lutheran Women's Missionary League passed a resolution asking the Relief Committee, which had served so well in directing the League's relief program for Europe, to continue to function and to expand its activities to include the Far East. The committee was instructed to see that funds designated for Europe (there were still 23 Districts who were carrying on a program for European relief)[1] and those for the Far East were properly channeled to reach their intended destination. The committee was also directed to work with the Board of Foreign Missions of Synod and to inform the LWML Districts of any additional ways in which they could help in this emergency. Countries specifically mentioned to receive relief were China, Japan, India, Korea, and the Philippines.[2]

The program was adopted for a period of 2 years. At the end of that time (1953) the Missouri Synod reactivated its relief program by appointing a new board for this purpose and by calling an Executive Secretary. Clothing drives were begun and contributions solicited for the purchase of food and medicines. The LWML went on record at its 1953 convention encouraging all local LWML societies, as well as individuals, to give their full cooperation to the World Relief Program of the Synod.[3] It reiterated its desire to cooperate with the Synod in this effort by a similar resolution in 1956.[4] The Synod's World Relief Program has been an ongoing project ever since and has continued to receive the wholehearted support of the LWML.

Other programs of Synod during the '50s also received the cooperation of the LWML. The first of these, the "Conquest for Christ," was a $10,000,000 effort to provide much-needed buildings for expansion of the church's educational institutions. The LWML endorsed this program and pledged the assistance of its members individually to help the local congregations realize their goal.[5]

Another such effort, "Building for Christ," a $5,000,000 project to provide funds for various agencies of the church not included in the regular budget of the Synod, was not successful. It became part of the "Venture of Faith" several years later, in which the goal was $12,900,000. LWML members were encouraged in both instances to give their wholehearted support.[6]

The desire of the LWML to cooperate with the Synod was evident in areas other than financial endeavors. The long-neglected need for programs in adult education which would stimulate the adult membership to greater service in the Kingdom through adequate Bible study and other means was presented at the synodical convention in 1944. As a result, resolutions were adopted instructing the Synod's Board of Parish Education to provide promotional, study, and teaching materials for adults, and urging the board to have occasional joint meetings with the Synod's Board for Young People's Work, the Walther League, the Lutheran Laymen's League, the Lutheran Women's Missionary League, and other organizations to evaluate and coordinate the educational work which each organization was doing.[7]

The LWML in 1946 was represented at a meeting of what came to be known as the Coordinating Council.[8] Later that year Rev. Oscar E. Feucht, Secretary of Adult Education for Synod, outlined a plan to the Executive Board of the LWML in which he said "a uniform topic study might be conducted for effective group discussion, Bible study and parent education." [9]

The LWML continued to be represented in the above group. In 1957 the League took note of the help it had received through participation in the Council and endorsed the continuation of representation of the League on this committee. *Parish Activities,* a planned educational program for an entire year, for use by the various organizations in the congregation, was published annually by the Board for Parish Education of the Synod, beginning in 1947.[10] In 1955 *Parish Activities* was incorporated into a new publication of the Synod, *Advance* magazine, as its June issue.

Early in the '50s the Board of Parish Education launched a Bible Study Advance program to create a greater participation in Bible study by the members of the Missouri Synod on all levels. Again the LWML urged its members to join existing local Bible study groups and to help organize new classes in their congregations, particularly for women, both married and single.[11] Beginning in 1956, Bible study became a part of the LWML convention program. The Bible Study Advance Committee of the LWML realized that to be successful the program must be ongoing. It therefore suggested that LWML Districts and zones cooperate by having Bible study at District conventions and zone rallies.[12] The Bible Study Advance program was integrated with the Christian Growth program in 1956. However, a representative of the LWML was retained on the synodical Bible Study Advance Committee to act in an advisory capacity to the Districts.[13]

The LWML participated in another cooperative effort in the '50s. Representatives of the Walther League, the Lutheran Laymen's League, and the Lutheran Women's Missionary League met with the Board of Directors of Synod to form a Synodical Affairs Committee for the purpose of informing the laity of Synod's various activities. The result was the appointment of such a committee which included a representative from each of the three auxiliary organizations, plus a representative of the board of Directors of the Synod and of the Praesidium.[14] Mrs. Otto F. Stahlke, who had been chosen to represent the LWML in 1957,[15] reported at the expiration of her appointment in 1959, that 13,000 copies of the Synod News Bulletin were being sent out monthly (except July and August) to each congregation (one copy to the pastor and one to the stewardship chairman, where one was designated).[16] Approximately 2,000 of the 5,600 congregations in the Synod had local Synodical Affairs committees.[17]

Membership

The continuing growth and development of the Lutheran Women's Missionary League was evident in many ways. Mrs. Roehrs referred to this remarkable growth in her President's report to the 1951 convention. She pointed out, however, that approximately 30 percent of the congregational units of the Missouri Synod were not affiliated with the LWML.[18] By 1957, the 15th anniversary of its founding, the membership had grown to 4,246 societies in 37 Districts, with a combined membership of 175,567, including four Canadian Districts.[19] By the end of the decade, two years later, the membership numbered approximately 190,000 members in 4,428 congregational units.[20]

The League's growth was evident also in its financial picture. Since its beginning in 1942 with borrowed funds, the League had by 1947 allocated $88,262.33 for its projects. From 1947 to 1957 such allocations amounted to $565,000, and during the 1957—59 biennium $200,000 was allocated.[21] In addition, in 1959 the League had $125,000 on loan to The Lutheran Church — Missouri Synod Church Extension Fund, payable on demand, until projects for which the money had been designated reached the point where the funds were needed.[22] The $1,000 which the Synod had loaned the LWML at the beginning had turned out to be a good investment!

Attendance at the conventions of the League also gave evidence of increasing interest in the organization and its work. Twenty-eight delegates, representing 15 Districts, and about 100 visitors had attended the 1942 convention.[23] In 1959, 425 delegates, 50 District presidents and League officers, 111 pastors, and 1,107 guests were registered. In addition many more were present who did not register, bringing the total to approximately 2,000.[24]

Statistics are meaningless unless they reflect a growth which comes as the result of an expanding and challenging program. Such growth was evident in the program of the LWML during the '50s.

Literature Committee

The growing awareness of the missionary education objective of the League was pointed up by action to establish a Speakers' Bureau and a Book of the Quarter Club in the Districts. Because of varying needs of Districts and their component parts, a Central Speakers' Bureau was deemed inadvisable and costly. Districts were encouraged, however, to "systematize mission information and make speakers' lists available to all their zones and societies." They were advised to seek further information, if desired, from the Literature Committee of the LWML.[25]

Districts were also urged to give serious consideration to establishing a Book of the Quarter Club in their District as a means of providing an impetus to the reading of good books relating to the missionary objectives of the League. The Literature Committee was asked to suggest two books each quarter in the *Quarterly* for this purpose.[26] When Concordia Publishing House introduced its Concordia Book Club in 1951, the LWML integrated its Book of the Quarter Club with the CPH plan.[27]

Growth was also demonstrated by resolutions which took cognizance of the importance of acquainting the people of the community with the church through placement of religious books in public libraries. Local societies were urged to determine the situation in their community and, in addition to placing books in libraries, to pursue a program of tract distribution, both in their own congregations and in the community.[28] The League also publicized its program through a display at the convention of The Lutheran Church — Missouri Synod in 1956 at St. Paul, Minn.[29]

A filmstrip showing the League's projects was prepared for showing at the 1950 synodical convention and made available subsequently for distribution to local societies on a purchase or rental basis.[30] On recommendation of the Literature Committee, preparation of a new filmstrip was approved by the Executive Board in 1956.[31] Entitled "A Mighty Host," it presented the program of the LWML as well as its projects up to that time. It was ready for distribution in the fall of 1958.[32] The filmstrip was made available to Districts for a purchase price of $25 per copy, or on a rental basis through Synod's Audiovisual Aids Department.

An overture submitted by the Northwest District LWML in 1956 proposed the appointment of a Director of Public Relations for the international LWML, calling attention to the opportunities afforded through the press, radio, and television, as aids in bringing both the work of the League and the Gospel message to the attention of people.[33] The matter was referred to the Executive Board with authority to act as it saw fit.[34] It was not until 1964, however, that the position of Director of Public Relations was created by the Executive Committee on the recommendation of the Editorial Staff.[35]

A suggestion that the League have a "Day of Prayer" was considered by both the Administrative Committee and the Executive Board. A committee was appointed to consider the question further and to confer with Dr. J. W. Behnken, President of the Synod.[36] In response to numerous requests, a suggested order of Prayer Service was subsequently drawn up by the Literature Committee (Editorial Staff) and presented to the 1957 convention, where it was adopted as a guide in preparing local prayer services. It was suggested also that the Day of Prayer be held on the Tuesday following the first Sunday in Lent or any other day of that week.[37] The suggested order of service was offered to societies through the LWML office (January 1958 *Quarterly*).

There was also a growing awareness during the '50s of the need for materials to broaden the horizons of the women of the church so that they would be better equipped for their role of service to the church and for witnessing to their faith. Some Districts had experienced a greater degree of spiritual and numerical growth through the years than others, resulting from a greater awareness of the tremendous challenges which presented themselves. To assist such individuals and groups who felt the need for aids to develop a greater consciousness of their responsibilities in the Kingdom, the Literature Committee was authorized to prepare guidelines for use by all Districts. The Districts, furthermore, were encouraged to use these guides in setting up regular study groups in the local societies.[38]

The *Lutheran Woman's Quarterly* continued to be a powerful influence in bringing the work of the League to the attention of its members and by its articles and other helps to provide motivation for carrying out the objectives of the League. Not only did the circulation of the *Quarterly* continue to climb through the years (it had reached 229,000 by July 1959),[39] but it had increased in size to 24 pages in 1959. In addition, the LWML shared a page with the Walther League and the Lutheran Laymen's League in the *Lutheran Witness* beginning in January 1957.[40] This arrangement continued until 1962. The editor of the *Quarterly* served as a contributing editor on the staff of the *Lutheran Witness*.

Christian Growth

The Christian Growth program, which is now an integral part of the LWML and is taken for granted by most LWML members, did not really begin until 1954. While it is true that the founders of the LWML envisioned a mission education program, they were handicapped, as pointed out previously, by their inability to know just how to proceed to accomplish their stated goals. While many programs in mission education and spiritual development were carried out on the local level and also in a few Districts, there was no specific program of this nature on the international level except the regular quarterly topic studies and articles on missions in the *Lutheran Woman's Quarterly*. Even where such programs did exist there was a wide divergence in their type and quality.

The resolutions of The Lutheran Church — Missouri Synod in 1950 emphasizing the importance of training the laity served to focus the attention of the auxiliary organizations on this part of their program.[41] Action in the LWML, however, was not spontaneous. In fact, it was not until 1953 that the movement gained impetus as the result of an overture submitted by the Atlantic District LWML to the international convention. The convention acted by directing the Administrative Committee to appoint a committee for the training of the laity, to consist of four members of the LWML and one of its Counselors. The committee was to provide materials which would be available to all zones and Districts who desired to conduct a training program for women in the church.[42] A letter from New Jersey urged the League to sponsor a program, "Learn by Doing." This, together with a report of the program which the California and Nevada District was carrying on in its area, prompted the Administrative Committee in its November 1953 meeting to elect Mrs. Harold Brandt, then president of the California and Nevada District, to become the chairman of the "Leadership Training Program." Mrs. Brandt was authorized to select her own committee.[43] At the request of the President she chose three women from her geographical area.

A pilot project was held in Oakland, Calif., on Oct. 18 and 19, 1954, and was called the "Lutheran Women's Guidance Institute." The committee worked tirelessly to make this project possible. It conducted extensive correspondence with officers of the international LWML, with the Counselor who was appointed to the committee, Rev. Raymond T. Eissfeldt, and with synodical headquarters. Questionnaires and reports from District Presidents were studied and evaluated. In addition, interviews were held with the executive secretary of the international Walther League and pastors in various places who had had special experience in leadership training. (The Walther League had had a leadership training program for many years.) The committee also was in touch with the Lutheran Laymen's League and had reviewed its leadership training materials.[44]

Both Oklahoma and Northern Illinois had held 2-day seminars in August 1947.[45] Two additional districts had conducted Leadership Training programs prior to the appointment of the international committee. A "Laywoman's Seminar" sponsored by the St. Louis Zone of the Western District LWML had been held in St. Louis for 2 days in March 1952, and the Michigan District LWML sponsored the "First Guidance Conference of the Michigan District" in Detroit, June 24—25, 1953. Officers' conferences had been held in a number of Districts. Those of the Atlantic District and the Southern California District deserve special mention.[46]

The international committee borrowed ideas from all of these. However, according to Mrs. Brandt, "the Committee's most valuable source [for the choice of topics] was a Synodical publication . . . 'Enlisting and Training Kingdom Workers.' " This booklet, which had been issued by Synod's committee on lay training, provided the

Christ-centered motivation which was to become the heart of the LWML Christian Growth program.[47]

When the time came for the pilot institute in the fall of 1954, representatives of the California and Nevada, Southern California, Northwest (later divided into two Districts: Washington and Oregon), Utah-Idaho, and Colorado Districts were present.

It was not until after the institute had been held that the committee received a report of a similar meeting, sponsored by Synod, which had been held in Detroit in October 1949. It was called "Women Mission Workers' Training School." Its intention was to interest women in "full-time" mission work. It developed, however, that the 22 women who were present during the entire 11-day period, plus the four who were present part time, were not interested in becoming "full-time" workers but in securing additional training to equip them to become better mission workers in their respective congregations.[48] One of the women who attended later became president of the Michigan District LWML and cites the training she received at the "Training School" as an important influence in preparing her for her LWML offices. "Unfortunately," Dr. William Hillmer wrote Mrs. Brandt, "we were not able to follow through, chiefly because of lack of staff personnel here in the office." [49]

Less than a month after the pilot institute of the LWML had been held, Mrs. Brandt presented an enthusiastic report to the Executive Board. She stated that "the purpose of the Institute was to make the women of our church aware of the *need,* and to suggest *ways* of spiritualizing the activities of women's societies within the Lutheran Church." [50] The recommendation of the committee to have the LWML sponsor at least five to seven institutes the following spring, similar to the pilot project, was adopted by the board, who designated that Mrs. Brandt attend them as leader.[51] A resolution was also passed providing that each District appoint a Leadership Training Chairman.[52]

Eight institutes were conducted during 1955 at the following locations: Portland, Oreg.; Mission, Kans.; Chicago, Ill.; Moorhead, Minn.; Orange, Calif.; Austin, Tex.; North Tonawanda, N. Y.; and Cullman, Ala.[53]

The institutes met with enthusiastic response on the part of the women. There were some skeptics, particularly among the clergy, who wondered what this new outreach of the women would mean. It did not take long, however, for many of them to change their attitudes when they saw the institutes in action. Those women who attended one of the institutes were convinced that they could "never shrink back to their former dimensions." To Mrs. Brandt, who participated in all nine institutes, it was most gratifying to see that, while special regional characteristics were evident in some places, there was a "blessed sameness about the atmosphere everywhere, regardless of geographical location. There was an air of excitement for and a dedication to a very high cause: that of learning to serve more effectively as missionaries in the Lord's Kingdom." [54]

In Minnesota, where those attending the institute were largely from rural areas, there was some hesitance at first in carrying out the assignments because the women felt inadequate. However, by the end of the second day they were surprising both themselves and the pastors who were present by their "spontaneous response and eloquent witness." [55]

In another area a stirring testimony was given by a woman who had belonged to another Protestant denomination prior to becoming a Lutheran. She praised the program and encouraged the support of all such programs in the church. "I became a Lutheran," she said, "because I was impressed by the way this Church underscored the importance of knowing what you believe." [56]

By the end of 1956 76 2-day institutes, patterned after the pilot institute, had been held in 26 Districts. Nine of the remaining 11 Districts had conducted 1-day workshops with the same basic topics: "Deepening the Inner Spiritual Life"; "Personal Evangelism"; and "Training Kingdom Workers." [57]

Earlier in 1956, at the League's convention, Mrs. Preisinger, the President, had reported that "because of the gratifying results and the enthusiastic support of these Institutes, your Executive Board resolved to maintain a four-member Committee, known as the 'Christian Growth Committee', to serve in an advisory capacity to the Districts in organizing Leadership Training Institutes on a District and Zone level." [58] She also reported that the Bible Study Advance program was being integrated with the Christian Growth program and that Dis-

Mrs. Arthur Preisinger
President, 1953—1959

trict Christian Growth chairmen would be responsible for Bible Study Advance in their respective Districts.[59]

The 1956 convention took note of the fact that the eight regional institutes conducted by the League had had representatives of all 36 Districts and that all were currently in the process of conducting similar institutes on both District and zone levels. Since the program which had been used at the regional institutes was deemed adequate to serve the Districts for some time to come, the convention passed a resolution encouraging the Districts to continue with the 1955 program until fuller coverage had been reached on District and zone levels and had extended into the local congregation.[60]

The Christian Growth Program took on new dimensions with the scheduling of a Christian Growth workshop for all District Christian Growth chairmen on the day preceding the opening of the convention in 1957.[61] (A similar workshop was conducted in 1959.)[62] This was the first opportunity the District chairmen had had to meet as a body for an interchange of ideas and problems and to undergird the program by group planning.[63]

"From 'case histories' reported by almost every district," said Mrs. Brandt in her report to the 1957 convention, "it can be concluded that the Christ-centered emphasis of the League's Christian Growth program has had a most salutary effect not only on individual workers but on entire societies and groups of societies, perhaps even complete districts." [64]

Another forward step was taken with the acceptance of the recommendation of the Christian Growth Committee to hold a 3-hour workshop for District Presidents in connection with the Board of Directors meeting in November 1958.[65]

By the close of the decade the pattern had changed somewhat, though the purposes had not. Instead of 2-day institutes, the majority of meetings were now 1-day workshops. The spiritual emphasis had been carried into officers training sessions and to conventions and zone rallies, where a presentation by the Christian Growth committee had become the accepted procedure.

In evaluating the benefits which had accrued from the Christian Growth program up to 1959, the retiring chairman of the committee, Mrs. Earl C. Muck, said: "It is impossible to gauge just how many thousands of women have benefited by this program. We do know some societies have reorganized to involve more women; we do know more Bible study groups have been formed; we do know more women have sought more opportunities for personally doing mission and evangelism work; we do know the program has been instrumental in supplying what many members may have lacked, namely, a vital, living, active, working faith in Christ, who must motivate all our actions." [66]

Mission-Hospice Committee

The Committee for Housing Missionaries on Furlough, which had been appointed in 1947, found its assignment a very difficult one because of a scarcity of housing in all parts of the country; in fact, it was almost impossible for it to function satisfactorily.[67] As a result, a new committee was appointed by the Executive Board in 1950, with instructions to submit a new name for the committee.[68] The name was changed to Mission-Hospice Committee and its function from seeking housing for furloughing missionaries to welcoming and bidding farewell to missionaries at points of arrival or departure.[69]

The activities of this committee were enlarged as time went on. The program also varied somewhat from place to place. In all cases, efforts were made to show a Christian concern for returning or departing missionaries. The committee was assisted by District committees, who in some areas provided the missionaries with a small cash gift ($10) when they were en route to their field of labor. In other areas a small amount ($5.00) was given the missionaries for "tips." Wives of missionaries were sometimes presented a corsage, and children were given toys and books. Meals and other incidental expenses were also taken care of during the missionaries' stopover.[70]

As the program of the committee developed, other projects were added. Missionaries' children attending school in America were befriended by the committee through LWML contacts in the places where the young people were. Appreciation for this interest in the children of missionaries is demonstrated by a letter received from one of the missionaries who wrote: "I need not tell you that it warmed my heart as I read how you were prepared and willing to help just in the ways in which we so often need help and wish deep in our hearts for someone who would actually do the little things for our children that we know every father and mother would do for his own children." [71]

Another project, that of sending magazines to missionaries, was welcomed by the missionaries and elicited a hearty response on the part of LWML members. In 1957 about 2,000 members offered to send almost 4,000 magazines each month to missionaries.[72] Some of these were subscriptions, but most of them were magazines which members sent to the missionaries after they themselves had read them. The enthusiasm for this project waned during 1958 "until the Western District had an article about this project in its paper. Since 1956 until the present [1959] 4,730 magazines have been offered to be sent each month by 2,618 of our members." [73]

The committee was also privileged to render special services. A long-distance call from Tokyo sought assistance for a Japanese bride whose plans had been changed, thereby creating a problem in meeting her husband in America. Through the efforts of the Mission-Hospice Committee the bride was united with her husband without any difficulty.[74]

Missionaries were also assisted through LWML societies who supplied them with bed jackets for medical missions, bandages, and hospital utensils.[75]

Thus a project which had been initiated for the purpose of helping missionaries find housing while on furlough had by the end of the '50s developed into a project which extended its interest and concern for the missionaries' welfare in their respective fields of labor.

International LWML History

The LWML had not only had the vision to appoint a historian at the outset, but it realized the importance of keeping its members informed about the progress of the organization from time to time. It had therefore printed several editions of a history, called "Facts and Figures," in the first years of its existence, as already indicated. This custom was continued in the '50s. Two "Facts and Figures" booklets were produced during this time, one covering the period 1942—55, the other the period 1955—59.[76]

During this decade several revisions of the *Handbook* were also printed (1951, 1954, 1956). The first of these contained a revised "Brief Historical Sketch of the Lutheran Women's Missionary League." The historical sketch contained in the original *Handbook* had traced the development of the LWML from the initial effort to organize a national women's federation in 1929 to the organization of the Lutheran Woman's League, St. Louis, and the Central District Lutheran Women's Missionary Endeavor. The revised sketch did not refer to the above organizations but indicated that "missionary activity by the women of the Lutheran Church — Missouri Synod did not start with the organization of the Lutheran Women's Missionary League." It then made reference to the activities carried on by women of "various Districts" which ultimately culminated in the organization of the Lutheran Women's Missionary League in 1942.

Another change appearing in the 1951 edition of the *Handbook* was use of the term "international" in place of "general" in reference to the League at large. This change was the result of a request from the Colorado District. The recommendation of the Resolutions Committee was adopted. It stated that "since the term 'General' is not used at any place in the constitution, nor in the By-Laws, neither is the designation 'General' part of the name of the League, and so does not disturb the constitution in any way, we therefore recommend that in referring to our organization and in our Handbook, we be known as the International Lutheran Women's Missionary League." [77]

All three of the above *Handbooks* contained, in addition to the historical sketch, information about the way in which the League functioned, i. e., organization and purpose, officers, counselors, meetings and representation, finances, literature, and projects. They continued with a series of questions and answers about the League, followed by the official League song, "Lutheran Women, One and All."

A new feature was added to the 1956 edition. The convention had passed a resolution to accept the recommendation of the Northern Illinois District LWML to adopt the pledge it had had since its organization as the official pledge of the international LWML.[78] The pledge, written for the District by one of its Counselors, Rev. Harry Fricke, reads as follows:

"In fervent gratitude for the Savior's dying love and His blood-bought gift of redemption, we dedicate ourselves to Him with all that we are and have; and in obedience to His call for workers in the Harvest Fields, we pledge Him our willing service, wherever and whenever He hath need of us. We consecrate to our Savior our hands to work for Him, our feet to go on His errands, our voice to sing His praises, our lips to proclaim His redeeming love, our silver and our gold to extend His Kingdom, our will to do His Will, and every power of our life to the great task of bringing the lost and the erring into eternal fellowship with Him! Amen!"

The pledge is used, as stated by the overture of the Northern Illinois District, "as a renewed source of inspiration and consecration to greater service to the Lord." [79]

District Histories

While the LWML had seen the wisdom of keeping an up-to-date record of its history, the advisability of keeping such a record of the various Districts did not become apparent until 1951. At that time a resolution was adopted to "instruct all districts to 'prepare a complete and accurate history of their organizations and to transmit two copies thereof to the President of the League, whose duty it shall be, after approval by a special Historical Committee of three, to transmit one copy to the Concordia Historical Institute and entrust the other copy to the League's Historian.' " [80] The resolution also suggested that Districts bring their histories up to date every 2 years.[81] This procedure still prevails.

The Mite Box

The term "mite" box and the Lutheran Women's Missionary League have become synonymous. The term was not original with the LWML; "mite" boxes had been in use since the beginning of the last century, as pointed out earlier. Several times in the course of the LWML history overtures have been submitted for a change in name. The first of these was presented in 1951 by the Atlantic District LWML. It suggested that "the word 'Mite' denotes and suggests a small amount of money, usually a penny or nickel, thereby suggesting that we save our pennies for the Lord and give Him our left overs." The overture called attention to the fact that "the Bible teaches us to give the Lord the first fruits and the best of our income." It asked that the name be changed to "Mission Boxes" in keeping with the name and the objectives of the LWML.[82] The convention committee charged with consideration of this overture presented a resolution which stated that "the word MITE in the sense of something small, was deliberately chosen, because the League members should primarily give their offerings and first fruits through the God-appointed channel of the congregation, and the League as such, does want to gather up the left-overs. From the beginning of the organization, we have emphasized that we are not primarily a collecting agency, but an educational and inspirational organization." [83] The committee's recommendation to retain the term "mite" box was accepted.[84] The idea of the "leftovers" being gathered by the women's organization was stressed at the beginning to assure those who opposed such an organization that their program would not be detrimental to the Synod's program.

It is noteworthy that, when a "collecting device" was spoken of at the first board meeting of the League in October 1942, there was no reference made to a "mite" box. Furthermore, references to this device, after its adoption, both in the correspondence of Mrs. Schmitt and on the vouchers she wrote for the payment of printing these devices, are to "mission offering" boxes. Mrs. Schmitt also referred to these devices as "mission offering" boxes in her report to the 1943 convention. On the other hand, the first issue of the *Lutheran Woman's Quarterly* announced that "attractive mite boxes are now available." It would seem, then, that both terms were used, depending on the individuals. In some of the Districts that existed prior to the organization of the LWML, such a collecting device had been called a "mite" box, and where those people recorded anything about the mission offering box they automatically referred to it as the "mite" box. So far as we have been able to determine, the term was never officially adopted in the early years of the LWML but came to be regarded as such through a common use of the term by its members. The design of the "mite" box has not changed; it still bears the words "My Mission Offering."

Conventions

Strange as it may seem, both the 1945 and the 1955 conventions had to be canceled. Announcement of the cancellation of the 1955 convention, scheduled for New Orleans, was made in the *Lutheran Woman's Quarterly*. It stated that "local customs of segregation make it impossible for the New Orleans Zone fully to entertain the international LWML in a manner characteristic of this organization." [85]

Dr. J. W. Behnken, President of the Missouri Synod, explained the decision of the New Orleans Zone to withdraw its invitation. This was the first time in the history of the LWML, he said, that there would be Negro delegates to an LWML convention. The Supreme Court decision to desegregate the schools had been handed down since the last convention of the LWML. Dr. Behnken suggested that this undoubtedly emphasized the problem.[86] The New Orleans Zone had already made extensive plans and preparations before the problem became apparent, and the decision to withdraw its invitation was not an easy one under the circumstances.

Mrs. Arthur Preisinger refers to this as the "most difficult decision that had to be made during my term as president." Reflecting on the situation, she says: "I shall never forget the many serious meetings held with Synodical officials, our international Counselors, the New Orleans Convention Committee, and our Board of Directors before the final decision was reached. Also the letters, phone calls, and telegrams, which ran into the hundreds, received from every part of the nation, from Pastors, laymen, LWML members, and many other interested parties, some advocating cancellation, others urging us to proceed with the Convention as scheduled. Those days were dark and trying days for me, and I spent many a sleepless night, wrestling in prayer, asking the good Lord to guide me in the paths that would tend toward the welfare of our dear LWML and redound to His glory, but also, at the same time, not offend any Leaguers or other deeply concerned individuals." [87]

This problem reflected the changing scene in America which was just beginning to take shape. Under the circumstances, those responsible had no recourse but to cancel the convention. As a result, the convention was rescheduled for 1956 in Denver as a delegate convention. Another convention was held in 1957 to resume the prescribed schedule for holding conventions.

Affiliation of Slovak Societies

Several times during the '50s, as previously, inquiries were received from societies affiliated with the Slovak Evangelical Lutheran Church (an affiliate of the Missouri Synod in the Synodical Conference) about the possibility of becoming members of the LWML. A resolution adopted in 1951 declared that the League is bound by the Constitution, which limits membership to members of the Missouri Synod.[88] When an inquiry was received in 1953, a resolution was adopted expressing a desire to admit societies of the Slovak Synod in the LWML, provided that the application of such groups for membership would have the endorsement of their synodical officials. The resolution also called for a revision of the League Constitution to make such affiliation possible, if approval for such change could be obtained from the officials of the Missouri Synod.[89] The Executive Board expressed itself the following year as favoring the affiliation of the groups, but no definite action was taken.[90]

When another request for membership was received in 1959 from a society of the Slovak Synod, the Corresponding Secretary was requested to write the President of the Slovak Synod, and a committee of three was appointed to study the matter.[91] The committee subsequently reported that the Slovak Synod "had not yet adopted a definite policy regarding the LWML and that they were considering the formation of a women's missionary society within their synod." The President of the Slovak Synod indicated that in the meantime he would be happy to act on requests of individual societies for membership in the LWML.[92] The committee reported further that the interim policy of the LWML would be to accept societies of the Synod of Evangelical Lutheran Churches (formerly Slovak Evangelical Lutheran Church) into membership upon their formal application accompanied by a letter of approval from the president of their Synod. No change in the Bylaws was contemplated at that time, however.[93]

Constitution

The demands of a growing organization made additional amendments to the Constitution necessary during the '50s. The first of these was made in 1951. Included in the changes were the stipulation that credentials of delegates to the general conventions be in the hands of the Secretary 6 weeks before the convention instead of 4 weeks, as required previously.[94] The restriction to two projects at any one time by the League was changed to eliminate any specific number.[95] However, this was changed again to read three projects when further amendments were made in 1953.[96] The article on "Projects" was further amended in 1953 by the addition of a paragraph providing that individual members, societies, or Districts may propose projects to the international League, provided they have the approval of the Executive Board of the LWML in the District in which they originate and also the Executive Board of the District in which the project is to be carried out.[97]

A major step forward came in 1954 with the decision for a complete revision of the Constitution and Bylaws.[98] Of special significance in this connection was the action taken in 1956 accepting the recommendation of the Executive Board to execute an application for articles of incorporation for the LWML.[99] Incorporation was deemed advisable to relieve individual officers and members of personal liability. Incorporation as a nonprofit organization would also exempt League funds from taxation. The incorporation was com-

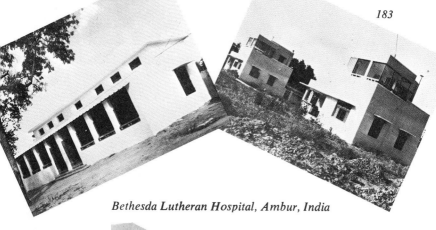

Bethesda Lutheran Hospital, Ambur, India

*Angela Rehwinkel, R. N.,
at dedicatory plaque*

pleted in the State of Missouri on Nov. 29, 1956.[100] The revised Constitution and Bylaws, including the articles of incorporation, were adopted at the 1957 convention.[101]

Projects

The growth of the League was reflected not only in its membership and its program but also in the projects which it adopted. Up to the time of the 1959 convention a total of $853,262.33 had been allocated for various mission projects, of which almost 80% had been voted during the '50s. An additional $215,000 was voted in 1959.

Bethesda Hospital, Ambur, India. Two projects were chosen for the 1951—53 biennium. One of these, Bethesda Hospital, Ambur, India, received a grant of $70,000. The story of medical missions in India, so far as the Missouri Synod is concerned, is synonymous with the story of Miss Angela Rehwinkel, who from the time of her arrival in India as a registered nurse in 1921 was the mainstay of the work at Bethesda Hospital in Ambur for many years. Though medical mission work had been carried on prior to Miss Rehwinkel's arrival, her long and dedicated service made a noteworthy contribution to the work at Ambur. The LWML took note of this service in 1951 by passing the following resolution:

"WHEREAS, Miss Angela Rehwinkel, a registered nurse, is entering upon her thirtieth year of service in the Bethesda Lutheran Hospital in Ambur, India; and

"WHEREAS, under her wise and efficient management Bethesda Lutheran Hospital has developed from a meager tent to the present pleasing array of hospital buildings giving 70,000 treatments a year to the native population; and

"WHEREAS, The example of Nurse Rehwinkel has been a constant source of inspiration to her fellow workers in India and to others who have followed her career, therefore be it

"RESOLVED, That we recognize gratefully the unselfish service of Miss Angela Rehwinkel as an outstanding example of faith expressing itself in works of Christian mercy; and be it further

"RESOLVED, That we authorize the Administrative Committee to prepare a suitable scroll to be presented to Miss Rehwinkel when she returns to this country on furlough in 1952." [102]

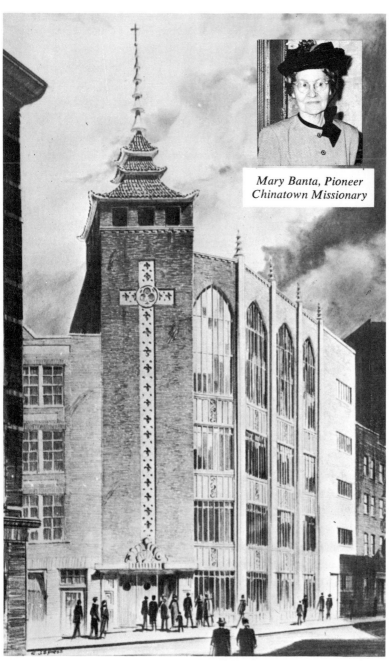

Mary Banta, Pioneer Chinatown Missionary

True Light Lutheran Church, New York City

Miss Rehwinkel's furlough was delayed, however, and the presentation of a plaque (instead of a scroll) was made on April 19, 1953, in St. John's Church, Kendallville, Ind.[103]

The $70,000 voted by the LWML was to help provide not only much-needed buildings but also improvements in the facilities of Bethesda Hospital at Ambur.[104] The new and expanded hospital was dedicated on Jan. 28, 1955. A plaque in honor of Miss Rehwinkel's 33 years of service in India and acknowledging the LWML gift of $70,000 was placed on the front of the building.[105] Miss Rehwinkel retired in 1958 after 37 years of devoted service. Bethesda Hospital continues to be a living symbol of her concern and that of her sisters in Christ for the physical as well as the spiritual ills of men everywhere.

True Light Lutheran Church, New York. The other project for the 1951—53 biennium reflects the consecrated efforts of another woman, Miss Mary Banta. Miss Banta opened the first Sunday school in Chinatown on New York's lower East Side in 1904 under the auspices of another Protestant denomination. In 1935 the Atlantic District of the Missouri Synod was invited by the Chinese Christians to take over the mission work among them. Miss Banta continued her consecrated service for many years after the Atlantic District accepted the invitation. The $75,000 grant of the LWML [106] helped to solve the problem of a church building for True Light Lutheran Church, which in 1962 had the largest membership among all Chinese Protestant churches in America.[107]

In 1964 101 infants, children, and adults were baptized at True Light. Five of its "sons" have become Lutheran pastors, another is a graduate of Concordia Teachers College, River Forest, Ill., and one young woman graduated from the Deaconess School in Valparaiso. Two additional young men are preparing for the ministry at the present time (April 1966). In addition to Rev. Ernest J. Kunsch, the present pastor of True Light, there is now a Chinese pastor on its staff. Its 30th anniversary, observed on April 3, 1966, was marked by services in both English and Chinese and by a parade through the streets of Chinatown.[108]

"Little Mexico," Los Angeles. Of the three projects chosen at the Portland, Oreg., convention for the 1953—55 biennium, one was

Santa Cruz Lutheran Church, "Little Mexico," Los Angeles

the direct result of the efforts of women, and another was designated to assist women. The story of "Little Mexico" in Los Angeles is the story of Christian faith in action. Through the efforts of a concerned Christian woman, Alice Fiene, the need for bringing the Gospel to the Mexican residents of Los Angeles was explained to a group of 20 Lutheran young women whom Miss Fiene had invited to a party in the spring of 1938. She expressed a desire to begin mission work among the Mexicans. As a result, these young women formed a mission society which met weekly for several years to carry out their project. In the fall of 1938 they canvassed the Mexican slum area without any interest or encouragement on the part of the Mexicans. The next Sunday they canvassed a section of Mexicans whose circum-

Deaconess Hall, Valparaiso University Campus

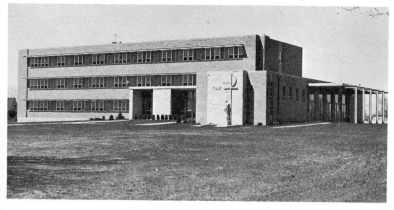

stances were better than in the previous area. The result was the establishment of a Sunday school. For 3 years the women assumed the entire responsibility for the mission, including the financial obligations and planning of the services. Pastor David Stirdivant, who became the first permanent pastor of the mission, says of the efforts of these women: "Had it not been for the constant God-given interest of the Mission Society, this work would have been terminated many a time." [109]

When the need for adequate worship and educational facilities became apparent, the Southern California District LWML petitioned the international LWML for a grant to help make this possible. "The petition," says Mrs. Geo. E. Theiss, President of the Southern California District of the LWML at that time, "was undergirded by a district-wide prayer campaign. This proved a fine spiritual experience for the women of our District." [110] It also brought results, for the LWML included this project in its grants in the amount of $60,000. The chapel of La Santa Cruz Lutheran Church was dedicated on May 19, 1957.[111]

Deaconess Chapter House, Valparaiso, Ind. The LWML responded to the needs of the school for the training of deaconesses at Valparaiso, Ind., by voting $60,000 for a Chapter House as another of its projects for the 1953—55 biennium.[112] Deaconess Hall, a three-story building on the campus of Valparaiso University, accommodates 74 students. It provides a home away from home for young women training for special service both at home and abroad in ministering to the physical and spiritual needs of people. "Through the facilities of Deaconess Hall," says Deaconess Clara Strelow, "more deaconesses are being trained and sent forth with the Gospel message. . . . Eternity alone will reveal the far-reaching results of the seed sown by the deaconesses, supported and sent forth through the aid of this LWML project." [113]

Retreat Homes for Missionaries. The third project adopted for the 1953—55 biennium provided retreat homes for missionaries in the Philippines, Japan, Brazil, and Argentina. $15,000 was allocated to each of these with the provision that the Mission Boards be allowed a reasonable latitude in adjusting these allocations.[114] Vacation homes have been put to good use by missionaries in Japan, Argentina,

---

Vacation Home for Missionaries, Argentina

*University Lutheran Church and Student Center
Toronto, Ont., Canada*

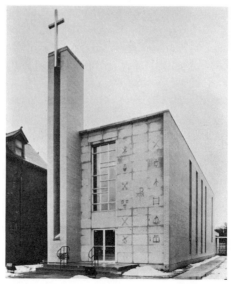

and the Philippines. The Brazil District did not find it possible to use the $20,000 appropriated for this purpose. The money was returned to the LWML and channeled to another project, in honor of Miss Olive Gruen, in Taiwan (see next chapter for details).[115]

Lutheran Student Center, Toronto, Canada. Projects adopted by the LWML at Denver in 1956 offer a study in contrasts. A total of seven overtures were presented requesting assistance in providing a Lutheran Student Center at the University of Toronto, in Canada. These overtures pointed out that the University of Toronto is the largest university in the British Empire, that the LWML had not undertaken a major student-service project, that it had not adopted a project on Canadian soil, and that the University of Toronto presented a mighty challenge in the mission program of The Lutheran Church — Missouri Synod. They also pointed out that the Synod had provided a full-time campus pastor but that for his work to be effective it was necessary to have a chapel and student center.[116] $70,000 was voted for this purpose.[117]

School, Zacapa, Guatemala. From the big metropolitan and cultural center of Toronto we go to Zacapa, a town of about 20,000, rural in character, 100 miles northeast of Guatemala City. Mission work was begun there by our church in 1947. Here there was little culture and, for the most part, very primitive living conditions. The $5,000 grant from the LWML made possible a four-room adobe school, which was built in 1957 largely by the members of the mission themselves. Few people in Zacapa had ever heard about the Savior and His love for them. By 1957 a real transformation had taken place. Children who did not know the meaning of discipline now, through the transforming power of the Gospel, could take what they had learned back to their homes.[118] In 1966 the school had three full-time and several part-time teachers, all accredited by the government. It has about 100 students enrolled in six grades, which is the standard elementary plan in Guatemala. The school is accredited by the government and is the best school by far in Zacapa, the railroad and government center of the area. The local congregation administers the school through its own school board.[119]

Chapel, Viña del Mar, Chile. The $5,000 appropriated by the LWML for the school at Zacapa, together with a $20,000 grant,

Zacapa, Guatemala, School

constituted one project. The latter amount was for a chapel at Viña del Mar, Chile, where work was begun in 1954, when Rev. Juan G. Berndt was sent there by the Mission Board in Argentina. After surveying the situation, studying the conditions and people, Pastor Berndt began his work with a summer vacation Bible school which had an enrollment of twenty-seven children, in Recreo Alto. This was considered a good enrollment under the circumstances. The opening of a Sunday school and the holding of regular church services followed. In another section of the city where Rev. Jose Avendaño, a native pastor, was working, there was promise of a good future. It was here that the LWML voted in 1956 to place $20,000 for a combination chapel, parsonage, and school. At the time the chapel was dedicated on Dec. 25, 1958, there was an enrollment of 80 in the Sunday school, a communicant membership of 30, and 75 baptized souls in the congregation. About 500 persons attended the dedication, including the mayor of the town.[120] In 1965 the congregation numbered 33 communicants, 92 souls. There were 30 children in the school and 50 in the Sunday school.[121]

Chapel, Havana, Cuba. The third project adopted in 1956 was an appropriation of $50,000 for a chapel in Havana, Cuba. The Missouri Synod had been conducting mission work for many years on the Isle of Pines, Cuba. The Lord turned adversity into advantage in 1946 when a devastating hurricane drove many of these people to Havana, where services were begun. Redeemer (originally Holy Trinity) Church in Havana was the recipient of the LWML grant, which made possible the construction of the building which houses a chapel on the upper level and a parish hall below.

Since the emergence of the Castro regime the American missionaries (there were two ordained pastors and two vicars) were compelled to leave the country. Rev. Ernest Carl, a national pastor, continues to serve on the Isle of Pines, but the work otherwise is carried on by lay evangelists who are striving valiantly to keep the flame of the Gospel alive and vital in the lives of those who are willing to come under its influence. They are supported in their efforts by the Spanish Lutheran Hour, which can be heard throughout Cuba.[122]

Highland Lutheran School, New Guinea. When the LWML met in 1957, projects totaling $200,000 were adopted. Two of these were to promote the cause of missions in areas far removed from the affluent society and the accompanying economic prosperity which we enjoy in America. Unlike some other countries, where American or private schools are available for the education of the children of missionaries, New Guinea had nothing like this. "It is an absolutely virgin field as far as all educational efforts go," wrote Dr. O. H. Schmidt, Executive Secretary of the Board of Foreign Missions.[123] In view of the primitive circumstances in New Guinea, where the Missouri Synod had begun to work only a relatively few years before, it was necessary to send young men as missionaries. Consequently there were a number of small children for whom schooling had to be provided.[124] The LWML answered this need by appropriating

$60,000 for this purpose.[125] The grant made possible the school and dormitories with the necessary equipment, a teacher's residence, and the installation of a diesel electric power plant.[126] In 1962 (2 years after the school was dedicated) it had grown to the point where a second teacher had to be added to the staff.[127]

Africa Project. Dr. Karl Kurth, Executive Secretary of the Missionary Board of the Lutheran Synodical Conference, presented the pressing need in another part of the world. Certain projects, he wrote, "are vital and essential toward the building of a strong Lutheran Zion in Nigeria, West Africa." They included a Bible institute to train lay evangelists, chapels in Ogoja Province, where it was hoped work would begin soon, and a chapel in connection with the medical mission work being carried on in Eket.[128] Pastor Kurth's requests were augmented by memorials from several Districts of the LWML and the Executive Committee of the Lutheran Church in Nigeria.[129] In all, $55,000 was appropriated for this project, to be divided as follows: Bible institute for Nigeria, $25,000; chapels for Ogoja Province, $15,000; a chapel for Eket, Nigeria, $15,000.[130]

Girls' Dormitory, Selma, Ala. The third project adopted at the 1957 convention of the LWML was for the erection of a girls' dormitory at the Lutheran Academy at Selma, Ala., in the amount of $85,000.[131] (This story will be treated in detail in the next chapter.)

1959—61 Projects. The projects adopted in 1959 were all for educational purposes: a high school for Hanno, Japan, $60,000; a combination administration building and dormitory for a coeducational high school in Teofilo Otoni, Brazil, $75,000; and a seminary in Manila, Philippine Islands, $80,000.[132] These projects, all executed during the '60s, will also be discussed more fully in the following chapter.

Honorable Discharge

The big forward strides which the Lutheran Women's Missionary League made during the '50s gives evidence of the increasing awareness of its leaders of the purpose for which it existed. While this mighty army of Kingdom workers marched on, some of its valued veterans had to step out of the ranks. Despite their withdrawal, the foundations which they helped to lay have made their influence felt down to the present time.

On June 10, 1950, the Lord removed the first President of the LWML, Mrs. Otto F. Schmitt, to join the ranks of the saints. Her successor, Mrs. Roehrs, elected in 1947, paid this tribute to her: "She gave unselfishly of herself, her time, and her talents. We who were associated with her in the work of the League knew Mrs. Schmitt as an enthusiastic, sincere, and consecrated child of God. Always friendly, humble, helpful, she was an example to all of us of the devoted Christian worker." [133]

The Pastoral Counselors who played such a large part in molding the structure and program of the LWML through its formative years now stepped out of the ranks, too. Rev. R. H. C. Meyer, who had served with Rev. Walter C. Birkner on the synodically appointed committee to organize a national women's federation, was called to his eternal rest in 1958. (His term as Counselor had expired in 1949.) Pastor Birkner's term expired in 1951 and that of Pastor Fedder in 1953.

Summary

Looking back over the blessings which the LWML enjoyed during the '50s, one is compelled to acknowledge them with deep gratitude and at the same time heed the admonition of the 1959 convention motto: "Labour with MORE Love." Addressing that convention on this theme, Rev. Walter O. Rathke said in part:

"The Lord Jesus Christ laboured with love for us. He could not have laboured with more love for us because He laboured for us with all the love He had. . . . No one who has by faith accepted this love is ever the same again. . . . You go to the cross. . . . It is there that the Spirit will inspire and impel you to labour with *more* love for Jesus." [134]

Notes

IX

1. *Proceedings,* LWML convention, July 25—26, 1951, p. 5. (Hereafter cited as LWML *Proceedings.*)

2. Ibid., p. 14.

3. LWML *Proceedings,* July 28—29, 1953, p. 20.

4. LWML *Proceedings,* April 20—21, 1956, p. 8.

5. LWML *Proceedings,* 1951, p. 5.

6. *Lutheran Woman's Quarterly,* XIII, No.: 1 (Jan. 1955), p. 8; XIV, No. 1 (Jan. 1956), pp. 6—7 (hereafter cited as *LWQ*); LWML *Proceedings,* 1956, p. 3.

7. *Proceedings of the Thirty-Ninth Regular Convention of the Ev. Lutheran Synod of Missouri, Ohio, and Other States,* June 21—29, 1944, pp. 115—136.

8. Proceedings, LWML Executive Board. Nov. 12—13, 1946, p. 3.

9. Ibid., p. 8.

10. LWML *Proceedings,* July 31—Aug. 1, 1957, p. 11.

11. LWML *Proceedings,* 1953, p. 19.

12. LWML *Proceedings,* 1956, p. 11.

13. President's Report, LWML convention, April 20—21, 1956, unpublished manuscript, p. 4.

14. *Reports and Memorials,* LWML convention, 1959, p. 36. (Hereafter cited as LWML *Reports and Memorials,* with year of convention.)

15. LWML *Proceedings,* 1957, p. 4.

16. LWML *Reports and Memorials,* 1959, p. 36.

17. LWML *Proceedings,* July 22—23, 1959, p. 14.

18. LWML *Proceedings,* 1951, p. 2.

19. LWML *Proceedings,* 1957, p. 3.

20. LWML *Proceedings,* 1959, p. 5.

21. LWML *Proceedings,* 1953, p. 2; 1957, pp. 3, 12, 13, 16; 1959, p. 5.

22. LWML *Proceedings,* 1959, p. 7.

23. LWML *Proceedings,* July 7—8, 1942, p. 9; *The Lutheran Woman,* IV (Sept. 1942), 20.

24. LWML *Proceedings,* 1959, p. 18.

25. LWML *Proceedings,* 1951, pp. 13—14.

26. Ibid., pp. 14—15.

27. Minutes, LWML Executive Committee, Nov. 15, 1951, p. 3.

28. LWML *Proceedings,* 1951, p. 16.

29. LWML *Proceedings,* 1956, p. 12.

30. Minutes, LWML Executive Board, Nov. 28—30, 1950, p. 1; Minutes, LWML Literature Committee, June 24, 1950 (one page only).

31. Minutes, LWML Literature Committee, Nov. 27, 1956, p. 3; Minutes, LWML Executive Board, Nov. 28—29, 1956, p. 2.

32. Minutes, LWML Literature Committee, Nov. 10, 1958, pp. 1, 3.

33. LWML *Reports and Memorials,* 1956, pp. 51—52.

34. LWML *Proceedings,* 1956, p. 8.

35. Minutes, LWML Executive Committee, Nov. 9—12, 1964, p. 9.

36. LWML *Proceedings,* 1956, p. 12.

37. LWML *Proceedings,* 1957, p. 11.

38. LWML *Proceedings,* 1959, p. 13.

39. Ibid., p. 5.

40. Minutes, LWML Executive Board, Nov. 28—29, 1956, p. 1; Minutes, LWML Literature Committee, July 29, 1957, p. 2.

41. *Proceedings of the Forty-First Regular Convention of The Lutheran Church — Missouri Synod,* June 21—30, 1950, pp. 392—395.

42. LWML *Proceedings,* 1953, p. 11.

43. Minutes, LWML Administrative Board, Nov. 12, 1953, p. 2.

44. Mrs. Harold Brandt, "History of LWML Christian Growth program 1954—57" (unprinted manuscript prepared for the author's use), pp. 1—5.

45. *LWQ*, Jan. 1948, p. 20.

46. Brandt.

47. Ibid.

48. Letter from Mrs. Harold Brandt to Mrs. A. R. Meyer, July 6, 1966, p. 2.

49. See note 44.

50. Minutes, LWML Executive Board, Nov. 11—12, 1954, p. 2.

51. Ibid., p. 3.

52. Ibid.

53. President's Report, LWML convention, April 20—21, 1956, p. 3.

54. Letter from Mrs. Harold Brandt to Mrs. A. R. Meyer, July 6, 1966, p. 2.

55. Ibid.

56. Ibid.

57. LWML *Reports and Memorials*, 1957, p. 20.

58. President's Report, LWML convention, April 20—21, 1956, p. 4.

59. Ibid.

60. LWML *Proceedings*, 1956, p. 10.

61. LWML *Reports and Memorials*, 1957, pp. 20—21.

62. *LWQ*, XVII, No. 4 (Oct. 1959), p. 9.

63. LWML *Reports and Memorials*, 1957, pp. 20—21.

64. Ibid.

65. Minutes, LWML Executive Board, July 30, 1957, p. 4.

66. LWML *Reports and Memorials*, 1959, p. 33.

67. Minutes, LWML Executive Board, Nov. 28—30, 1950, p. 2.

68. Ibid.

69. LWML *Reports and Memorials*, 1951, p. 18.

70. LWML *Reports and Memorials*, 1959, pp. 34—35.

71. LWML *Reports and Memorials*, 1957, p. 22.

72. Ibid.

73. LWML *Reports and Memorials*, 1959, p. 35.

74. Ibid.

75. Ibid.

76. LWML *Reports and Memorials*, 1956, p. 20; *LWQ*, XVIII, No. 3 (July 1960), p. 13.

77. LWML *Proceedings*, 1951, pp. 20—21.

78. LWML *Proceedings*, 1956, p. 8.

79. LWML *Reports and Memorials*, 1956, pp. 49—50.

80. LWML *Proceedings*, 1951, p. 15.

81. Ibid.

82. LWML *Reports and Memorials*, 1951, p. 50.

83. LWML *Proceedings*, 1951, p. 15.

84. Ibid.

85. *LWQ*, XIII, No. 3 (July 1955), p. 9.

86. *LWQ*, XIII, No. 4 (Oct. 1955), pp. 9, 11, 22.

87. Questionnaire completed by Mrs. Preisinger for the author's use, Oct. 1, 1966.

88. LWML *Proceedings*, 1951, p. 21.

89. LWML *Proceedings*, 1953, p. 10.

90. Minutes, LWML Executive Board, Nov. 11—12, 1954, p. 2.

91. Ibid., July 21, 1959, p. 3.

92. LWML *Reports and Memorials*, 1961, p. 34.

93. Ibid.

94. LWML *Proceedings*, 1951, p. 4.

95. Ibid., p. 20.

96. LWML *Proceedings*, 1953, pp. 9—10.

97. Ibid., p. 13; LWML Constitution, 1954, p. 4.

98. LWML *Proceedings*, 1956, p. 3.

99. Ibid., p. 5.

100. Minutes, LWML Executive Board, Nov. 28—29, 1956, p. 8.

101. LWML *Proceedings*, 1957, pp. 8—9.

102. LWML *Proceedings*, 1951, p. 18; see also *LWQ*, X, No. 1 (Jan. 1952), pp. 7—10.

103. *LWQ*, XI, No. 3 (July 1953), p. 6.

104. *LWQ*, X, No. 1 (Jan. 1952), pp. 7—10.

105. *LWQ*, XIII, No. 4 (Oct. 1955), p. 11.

106. LWML *Proceedings*, 1951, p. 20.

107. *LWQ*, XX, No. 3 (July 1962), p. 14.

108. Letter from Rev. Ernest J. Kunsch to Mrs. O. E. Feucht, April 14, 1966.

109. *Lutheran Witness*, LXXIII (April 13, 1954), 122.

110. Questionnaire returned by Mrs. Geo. Theiss to the author.

111. *LWQ*, XV, No. 4 (Oct. 1957), p. 9.

112. LWML *Proceedings*, 1953, p. 18.

113. *LWQ*, XVIII, No. 2 (April 1960), pp. 3—4, 30.

114. LWML *Proceedings*, 1953, p. 6.

115. *LWQ*, XX, No. 3 (July 1962), p. 15.

116. LWML *Reports and Memorials*, 1956, pp. 42—46.

117. LWML *Proceedings*, 1956, pp. 13—14.

118. *LWQ*, XX, No. 3 (July 1962), p. 15.

119. From an interview with Rev. Leonard Stahlke.

120. Information on file in LWML office.

121. *Statistical Yearbook*, The Lutheran Church — Missouri Synod, 1965, p. 173.

122. *LWQ*, XX, No. 3 (July 1962), p. 15.

123. LWML *Reports and Memorials*, 1957, pp. 38—39.

124. Ibid.

125. LWML *Proceedings*, 1957, pp. 12, 16.

126. Letter from Dr. H. A. Mayer to Mrs. Erna Feucht, Feb. 9, 1960.

127. Memorandum from Dr. H. H. Koppelmann re LWML projects (LWML file); *LWQ*, XVIII, No. 4 (Oct. 1960), pp. 8, 14.

128. LWML *Reports and Memorials*, 1957, pp. 42—43.

129. Ibid., pp. 44—47.

130. LWML *Proceedings*, 1957, pp. 13, 16.

131. Ibid.

132. LWML *Proceedings*, 1959, p. 16.

133. *LWQ*, VIII, No. 4 (Oct. 1950), p. 15.

134. LWML *Proceedings*, 1959, p. 3.

X
The Fruit Ripens
1960 — 1967

THE DOORS OF A NEW DECADE opened to unfold a view such as the world has never seen before. The population explosion, due in large measure to advances in medical technology, is unprecedented in world history. Manned space flights and other accomplishments related to the space program were undreamed of only a few short years ago. The emerging nations, with the problems they encounter in their new role, have also given a new dimension to the world picture. All this, together with racial unrest and strife in our own country, points up, on the one hand, the tremendous blessings of this age in which we are living and, on the other hand, the responsibilities and opportunities which these blessings impose.

The church could not help being caught up in the rapidly changing world scene. The ecumenical movement, which had long struggled for recognition, was given impetus by Vatican II. As a result, the church has been engaging in a self-analysis and reevaluation of its program and practices to meet the challenges which confront it. Social problems are receiving attention on a scale unmatched before.

Organizations within the church have likewise been compelled to rethink their objectives and effect changes in their programs. The role of women, subject as it has always been to the cultural climate of the times, has taken on new dimensions, too. The new emphasis on the role of the laity, including women, in the Roman Catholic Church is also having its effect on women in Protestantism. Of special significance in this connection is the appointment of the

Mrs. Walter N. Hoppe
President, 1959—1963

first woman in history to the curia, the Rome-based central administration of the Roman Catholic Church.[1] Women's organizations, along with their church bodies, are readjusting their programs to make them relevant to the changing emphases.

The Survey

The Lutheran Women's Missionary League recognized the need to evaluate its program even before the beginning of the present decade. In 1955 the Executive Board decided "that a committee of five members be appointed to conduct a survey and to make a report on the Christian growth of the League at the 15th anniversary convention in 1957."[2] No such study of women's work in the church had ever been undertaken before in The Lutheran Church — Missouri Synod. The enormity of the task necessitated an extension beyond the original date for its completion, first to 1959 and then to 1961.[3]

The survey was carried out in two phases: (1) a questionnaire on women's work was mailed to all pastors on Feb. 14, 1958; and (2) a questionnaire was mailed to the 400 zones of the League in the spring of 1960.[4] Prof. David S. Schuller, a member of the faculty of Concordia Seminary, St. Louis, and Dr. Oscar E. Feucht, Secretary of Adult Education of the Missouri Synod, reviewed and analyzed the replies submitted on the questionnaire.[5] The findings, together with Prof. Schuller's recommendations and those of the Survey Committee, were published by the LWML in 1961 as *Women's Work in The Lutheran Church — Missouri Synod: A Survey Report.*

Findings. While space does not permit a lengthy discourse on the findings, several seem to be particularly significant.

The response of the pastors indicated that "the real influence of lay women within the church remains pretty much of a 'frozen credit,' only partially utilized in meeting the unique challenges of our modern day." [6]

Though there has always been a strong emphasis on the use of the "mite" box, and though it remains in wide use, the survey showed that "the personal spiritual meaning of the endeavor escapes the majority of women. Ideally, the mite is to be a daily symbolic giving back to God a token of thanks for His gifts to us." [7]

Despite the efforts which had been made by the League to supply program helps of various kinds, pastors still expressed a desire for all kinds of materials, as they had early in the history of the LWML, "particularly in the form of mission topics, worship suggestions for meetings, and family-life educational materials." Their desire for other types of materials was almost equally strong.[8]

Of special significance is that, in spite of the strong emphasis on the missionary character of the League from its very beginning, "one of the clearest findings of the entire study was the fact that there apparently is no correlation between conducting mission topics and doing mission work!" Furthermore, "the most commonly reported service projects did not involve mission work on a personal or local level." [9]

The response of the women indicated that while "they come together because they enjoy one another's fellowship," they are also serious about being an organization which is church-related and has spiritual goals, including Bible study. They expressed a concern over the lack of trained leadership and the difficulty in enlisting other women in the church to join their organization. They wanted their organization to be one that offers an opportunity for women to be creative. They expressed a desire for their programs to relate to the problems and emphases of the times, and they realized that to be effective such programs would require long-range planning.[10]

Proposals. On the basis of Professor Schuller's conclusions, the Survey Committee made a number of recommendations to the 1961 convention of the League relative to meeting the needs in the various areas of its program. The recommendations suggested by the committee and approved by the convention provided (1) that every society make a self-study in the light of the findings; (2) that every member of the League assist in evaluating its program on the basis of the expressed needs; (3) that the Executive Committee, the Board of Directors, the Editorial Staff of the *Quarterly,* and the committees of the League, particularly the Christian Growth Committee, develop more adequate methods and materials for use on all levels; and (4) that a special committee be appointed to study the structure of the organization and its administrative procedures with the view to making the necessary adjustments to supply the needs as stated.[11]

Implementation. In keeping with the proposals of the Survey Committee, a Survey Study Committee was elected by the Executive Committee in October 1961.[12] Each member of the committee was assigned certain areas in which intensive studies were made by comparing the structure, programs, membership, etc., of other national church women's organizations with those of the Lutheran Women's Missionary League, keeping in mind the suggestions made in the survey. After considering the results of their research, the committee reported that it "is firm in its agreement that the principal objectives of the League, *missionary education, missionary inspiration, and missionary service,* to develop and maintain a greater mission consciousness among the women of Synod, are still pertinent and should remain intact." [13] While calling attention to the strengths of the League, the committee also saw the need for certain changes for the future growth and progress of the organization.

Mrs. Gilbert O. Hankel
President, 1963—1967

Nine recommendations were made by the committee. Four of these were adopted in 1963: those regarding an LWML *Handbook,* Materials Committee, Extension of Membership, and Study of the Financial System.[14] The remainder, because of their far-reaching effects, were referred to the Executive Committee and the Board of Directors for additional study.[15] Without a doubt the survey and the resulting action has had a greater influence on the operation of the organization than anything else in its history. It is a real credit to the leaders of the LWML that the need for such an evaluation was apparent to them and, particularly, that they did something about it.

Handbook. One of the recommendations of the Survey Study Committee adopted by the League was that a new *Handbook* be prepared for publication without delay, "to provide motivation, guidance, and training in the areas of LWML aims and objectives, procedures, service, organizational structure, and program building." It recommended that such a *Handbook* be used both personally and in group study to improve the League on all levels.[16]

The new *Handbook,* prepared by a committee appointed by the Executive Committee, was mailed to all member societies in January 1965.[17] The Directives Committee, which had been appointed in 1960,[18] was dissolved with the resolution to publish a *Handbook,* and its work was incorporated into that of the *Handbook* Committee.[19]

Editorial Staff. The recommendation of the Survey Study Committee to establish a Materials Committee was also adopted. This committee was to examine all materials, such as devotional and Bible study materials, study outlines, playlets, etc., for their value in relation to the total program of the League before being released for publication.[20] But in view of the fact that this involved another proposal of the Survey Study Committee: to revise the structure of the League, and since this was still under consideration, the Materials Committee was incorporated into the editorial staff of the *Quarterly.* The Mission Education editor, together with the Counselor to the editorial staff, were directed to review all such materials.[21]

As the League expanded both numerically and in the scope of its program, changes were made in the *Quarterly* to meet the resulting needs. Beginning with the January 1960 issue, the size of the *Quarterly* was increased from 24 to 32 pages. A new cover design was introduced in 1963.[22] With the change from a designation by month (January, April, July, and October) to a designation by seasons, beginning with the fall issue in 1966, the size was increased again, this time to 40 pages. The publication schedule was also revised at that time so that each issue of the *Quarterly* would appear a month earlier than previously.[23] At the same time another innovation found its way into the *Quarterly.* For the first time since it began publication in January 1943, three monthly topics appeared instead of one quarterly topic. This was a long sought-after goal of many who through the years had been holding monthly meetings for which they wanted such helps. This also accounts for the fact that at the time of the survey so many pastors expressed a desire for more such materials.

Along with the increase in size in 1966 an increase in the subscription price was also affected. Bulk mailings (10 or more copies to one address) were increased from 6¼ cents per copy, or

25 cents a year, to 7½ cents per copy, or 30 cents a year. Individual subscription rates remained at 10 cents per copy, or 40 cents a year.[24]

An index covering the period from 1943 to 1962 was published early in 1964.[25] This is being brought up to date at the present time.

Extending the Membership. The Survey Study Committee took note of the "frozen assets" in the church, i.e., the unused talents of women. It recommended that every effort be made to gear the program on the local level to the needs of all groups, including young mothers, homemakers, professional and working women, and young confirmands, and that such groups be invited to participate in the activities of the League on all levels.[26]

These proposals of the Survey Study Committee were implemented by a resolution in 1965 urging every individual member of the LWML to recruit additional members by means of increased participation in Bible study, by a better use of the *Quarterly,* and by education in the "proper use of the mite box." It also encouraged every society to devise ways of involving more women in the congregation in Kingdom work.[27]

The fact that the membership of the Lutheran Women's Missionary League includes only about one third of the women members of The Lutheran Church — Missouri Synod [28] points up the fact that the League is far from having reached its potential and that an all-out effort must be made on the part of every member if the LWML is to rise to the stature of being the women's auxiliary of the church.

Finances. The fourth proposal of the Survey Study Committee to be adopted in 1963 recommended a thorough study of the League's financial structure. It recognized the need for the adoption of a budget to guide and systematize the financial expenditures of the League and the necessity of studying all aspects of its financial program, including the gathering and division of funds, the selection of projects, and the allocation of funds. Yet it did not feel competent in this area and suggested that such a study be made by those qualified in finances.[29]

The committee also suggested a study of the name and use of the mite box. Not only was this portion of the resolution deleted, but a memorial submitted 2 years later (1965) requesting a change in name from "Mite" box to "Thankoffering" box was likewise defeated.[30] It seems strange that, while "impassioned speakers rose to defend the traditional significance of the name," [31] the survey several years previous had shown that the personal spiritual meaning of the mite box was not achieved.[32] Furthermore, the financial statement of the League for the year ending May 31, 1966, shows mission offering receipts of $147,356.40 [33] from a membership of 213,000, representing a per-capita contribution for the year of $ .69 to meet a goal of $290,000 in projects voted for the biennium.[34] These figures represent 25% of the total mite box offerings gathered — the other 75% is retained by the Districts. The average contributed for both Districts and international projects was $2.76.[35]

At the 1965 convention a resolution was passed which took note of the need for expanding the work of missions on all levels and the fact that many "urgent mission projects proposed for the LWML will have to be rejected for lack of funds." It stated further that though blessings have been enjoyed in abundant measure the per-capita contributions for the 1963—65 biennium had actually decreased from $2.32 to $2.24. The resolution called for a fuller realization of the personal responsibility in meeting the needs and encouraged each member to raise her sights and give sacrificially as the Lord has blessed her.[36]

In keeping with the suggestion of the Survey Study Committee a special committee was appointed to study the financial structure of the League. It prepared a work program in which it attempted to allocate sufficient funds for the operation of the League for the 1965—67 biennium. This work program (budget) was adopted by the Board of Directors after approval by the Executive Committee.[37]

Revision of Bylaws. Revisions in the Bylaws, which were the direct result of the findings of the Survey Study Committee and other factors connected with the increasing needs of a growing organization, are too numerous to spell out. A number of amendments were adopted in 1965.[38] At the same time a complete revision of the Bylaws was authorized in compliance with the suggestion of the Survey Study Committee and necessitated by plans for structural changes in the League. These are to be presented for consideration at the 1967 convention.[39]

Cooperation in Synodical Endeavors

The Lutheran Women's Missionary League continues to support synodically sponsored programs. The Venture of Faith, referred to earlier, was undergirded by the Faith Forward program, adopted by the Synod in 1962 in an effort to strengthen the spiritual life of its members.[40] The League passed a resolution in 1963 encouraging the entire organization on District, zone, and local levels to give full support to this effort.[41] Such support was spearheaded by a Bible study thrust of the League at large and through its Day of Prayer service.[42]

Several years earlier the Parish Education Department of the Synod had initiated a program called "Train Two," a training program for Bible class teachers. The League encouraged its members to promote this effort by personal interest and participation and by recommending it for use in their congregations.[43]

In addition to supporting such special synodical efforts, the Lutheran Women's Missionary League has assisted the Synod in other projects through the local societies and through individuals. One of these efforts is the program of Braille transcription, which makes such materials as Sunday school lessons available in Braille for use by the blind.[44]

Because of its missionary objectives the Lutheran Women's Missionary League has been represented at meetings of the Synod's Department of Missions.[45] It has also been represented at meetings of other synodical agencies, such as the Coordinating Council of the Synod (referred to previously), the Lutheran Medical Mission Association, and the synodical Stewardship Conference. Currently the LWML President has been appointed by the Synod President to membership on the committee preparing for the observance of the 450th anniversary of the Reformation.[46]

Although the Synod had authorized the organization of a national women's federation in 1941, it was not until 1962 that it gave the organization official recognition. A resolution, which become a part of the Synod's Bylaws and as such was included in its *Handbook,* stated that "Synod recognize the work of the Lutheran Women's Missionary League as the women's organization within the Synod and advises all women's organizations within the Synod to affiliate with the Lutheran Women's Missionary League." It also gave such recognition at that time to the Lutheran Laymen's League,[47] which had been organized in 1917. The Walther League had been given official recognition in the *Handbook* earlier.

Though the League has cooperated with the Synod through the years, even closer cooperation is anticipated in the future. A 1965 synodical resolution urged the auxiliary organizations to function as "free-standing institutions, self-determining in their internal affairs." At the same time the resolution called for the appointment by the President of the Synod of representatives to serve as counselors to the governing bodies of the auxiliary organizations to insure that the work of auxiliary organizations be in harmony with and subordinate to the work of the Synod.[48]

Christian Growth

The Christian Growth program of the Lutheran Women's Missionary League continues to be a vital factor in the developing and expanding program of the organization. Its leadership from the beginning has been alert to the needs and has continued to meet them in keeping with the changing scene.

The enthusiasm with which the program has been received gives evidence that such a program was much sought after. Christian Growth workshops on the zone level were reported in 1961 to have been held in 33 of the 35 existing Districts; the other two held one workshop each on the District level.[49] By that time also the Christian Growth chairmen in almost all Districts were given voice, if not vote, on the District boards.[50]

A Christian Growth workshop for all District Christian Growth chairmen on the day prior to the opening of the League convention was begun in 1957 and continued until 1965. Such a workshop with the emphasis on evangelism was held in 1965 in San Diego. It marked a "first" in that 255 of those registered made house-to-house calls for 14 congregations in the San Diego area on the day of the workshop. They completed 1,931 calls which yielded 658 prospects for membership in the Lord's kingdom.[51] Another "first" will be accomplished when the League meets in Washington, D. C., in 1967. The Christian Growth workshop then will not be limited to

Christian Growth chairmen but will be incorporated into the daily program of the convention.[52]

The growing awareness on the part of the church of its responsibility to help meet the social needs of its fellowman served as the motivation for the theme of the Christian Growth workshop for District Presidents, District Christian Growth chairmen, and Christian Growth counselors in St. Louis on Oct. 25, 1966. (Workshops for District Presidents had been held separately until then.) [53] The theme "God's People Prepared for Action" had as its aim: "That *I* may be sensitized, motivated, activated and personally involved in *my* Mission and Ministry to the social problems confronting *my* community and the world — in the name of Christ, *my* Savior." [54] This workshop supplanted regional workshops which had been held previously. Leaders attending this workshop are to conduct similar workshops in their areas.[55]

The observance of a Day of Prayer has likewise been carried on each year under the auspices of the Christian Growth Committee. Beginning in 1964 a suggested order of service for the Day of Prayer was incorporated into the January issue of the *Quarterly*.[56] In addition many original services are being written by women.[57]

During the 1963—65 biennium special emphasis was given to the promotion of an intensified Bible study program. A subcommittee under the Christian Growth Committee was appointed in November 1963 for this purpose. The committee adopted plans to provide one new Bible study each which was especially adapted for use by women's groups. The first of these, "So Live in Him," based on Paul's letter to the Colossians, was distributed for use in 1965. It had been prepared by Miss Oletta Wald for The American Lutheran Church Women, who had given the LWML permission to reproduce it. This was followed by a study on the Book of Amos and a study on Philippians.[58]

Mission Hospice Committee

The Mission Hospice Committee continues to serve the missionaries en route to and from their respective fields, although the frequent use of air transportation reduces the time missionaries are required to stop over. All but 10 of the Districts have a Hospice Chairman. In these the District President assumes the responsibility.

Most of the activity is to be found on the east and west coasts. Seventy-seven missionaries and families were reported to have been assisted in one way or another in the year prior to the 1965 convention of the LWML, in the California and Nevada District (including its Hawaii zone), the Oregon District (including Alaska), and the Atlantic District. Since many of the returning missionaries are based in the St. Louis area during their furloughs, the Western District Committee engages in quite a bit of activity, too. The six-member committee has assisted in various ways.[59]

A new area of service presented itself to the committee with the erection of a mission house in St. Louis to house furloughing missionaries, for which the LWML had voted $125,000 (see "projects"). This did not include furnishings, however. A pilot project was introduced by the Mission Hospice Committee in two Districts (Northern Nebraska and Western) by way of a "money-gift shower" to assist in furnishing the mission house.[60] A check for $5,038.27, representing the amount received for this purpose, was presented to Dr. William Hillmer at the time of the dedication of the mission house in October 1966.[61]

Another avenue of service was called to the committee's attention. The many foreign students who are studying in our country, both Christian and non-Christian, offer a real opportunity for Christian witness and service. A resolution adopted by the League in 1965 encouraged members to extend Christian hospitality and genuine concern for such students attending colleges and universities in their area.[62]

Mission Service Committee

Changing world conditions impelled the LWML Board of Directors in 1961 to authorize the President to appoint a committee "to study and develop directives for mission service."[63] Its primary purpose was to determine what needs of the missionaries in overseas missions could be filled by women's groups. It found, however, that in most cases excessive customs duties and stringent import regulations made this impractical.[64] As a result, the committee turned its attention to such service projects as could be carried on in local communities. Where specific requests were received from missionaries, however, the committee asked that the matter be cleared with it first because of changing conditions. A large variety of items were sent to Hong Kong, Japan and New Guinea.[65]

The befriending of specific missionaries, a project which had previously been a responsibility of the Mission Hospice Committee, has been assumed by the Mission Service Committee. Under its direction many societies are assuming the cost of duplicating and mailing out letters of missionaries to American addresses supplied by the missionaries. Where possible, the committee also helps to provide some of the needs of missionaries in their field of labor. The sending of magazines to missionaries, begun under the Mission Hospice Committee, is still carried out.[66]

Mission service projects were, of course, carried out long before such a committee on the national level came into existence. Individual women and women's groups have extended their love and concern for their fellowman in one way or another long before the Lutheran Women's Missionary League came into existence. An outstanding example of such service is demonstrated by two women in the Alberta and British Columbia District who for the past 15 years have visited an average of 900 patients a year in hospitals.[67] The Mission Service Committee is eager to assist local societies in witnessing effectively in their communities through projects such as this and also others which provide opportunity to witness for Christ through a concern for both the physical and the spiritual needs of individuals.[68]

Conventions

Conventions of the League are always a highlight in its program because of the Christian fellowship enjoyed by those attending and particularly because of the enthusiasm which they generate to go home and try to carry out the many resolutions which are adopted. Attendance at conventions shows a continuing and growing interest on the part of both women and pastors.

Perhaps at no other time in the League's history was its missionary objective demonstrated more forcefully than at the 1963 convention in Kansas City, Mo., when 66 persons participated in a Parade of Missionaries. While the assembly sang the hymn "Jesus Shall Reign Where'er the Sun Does His Successive Journeys Run," the 66 individuals (missionaries and their families and others representing missionaries), dressed in the native garb of the country whose placard they carried, entered the convention hall in procession. This spectacle, coupled with a stirring address by Missionary Erwin L. Spruth of New Guinea which followed, gave real meaning to the convention theme: "The Harvest Is Great." All served as a fitting reminder, not to be forgotten, of the tremendous opportunities the world offers for proclaiming the love of God in Christ. It is significant, too, that the total registration at this convention was one of the largest in League history — 2,618.[69]

Equalization of Travel Costs

The resolution passed in 1959 authorizing the appointment of a committee to work out a plan of equalization of delegates' travel costs to the 1961 convention of the international LWML on a trial basis was carried out by a committee of three women and a pastoral counselor. The plan agreed upon provided that the cost be determined on the basis of the coach fare to the convention site from a centrally located town in each District selected by the District President. Districts whose travel cost per delegate would be higher than the determined equalized cost would be reimbursed so as to bring the figure down to the equalized rate. Districts whose actual travel cost would be less than the equalized rate would pay the established equalized rate.[70] Through the cooperation of the Districts the computation of the equalization was completed by mid-March prior to the convention, and checks were mailed to the delegates in ample time before the convention.[71]

The plan, by which the cost had been figured on the basis of the number of delegates allowed rather than on the number of delegates attending the convention, met with approval and was adopted by the 1961 convention as a permanent procedure.[72] The committee appointed to handle this matter for the 1965 convention figured the fares on the basis of the round trip fare from the convention city to the central point rather than the reverse order so as to equalize local tax and tariff.[73]

Projects

One evidence of the growth of the Lutheran Women's Missionary League is the increasing number of projects adopted, the amounts of

Taiwan (Formosa) Educational Buildings, Olive Gruen Memorial

Missionary Olive Gruen

the projects, and their diversity. This is particularly evident in the present decade.

Educational Buildings, Taiwan. The $20,000 allocated in 1953 for rest homes in Brazil could not, because of circumstances, be used for this purpose. It was therefore reallocated in 1960 "for the ten educational buildings of the Taiwan (Formosa) project in gratitude to God for 40 years of service by Miss Olive Gruen." [74] Miss Gruen had spent 30 years on the mainland of China as a teacher, and when it became impossible for missionaries to remain there, she went to Taiwan,[75] where she did yeoman's work in establishing the work of

Rosa Young Dormitory for Girls,
Alabama Lutheran Academy, Selma, Ala.

Dr. Rosa Young

The Lutheran Church — Missouri Synod there. The LWML grant was set aside as a special Education Building Fund from which loans were made to congregations for adding an educational unit to their existing plant. By the middle of 1965 such loans had been made to three congregations, and educational buildings were in the planning stage at three more. "If it were not for the Olive Gruen Memorial Fund these churches would not have their educational buildings and the others would have to wait a long time before their dreams could come true," wrote Mr. R. W. Henningfield, business manager of the church's mission operation in Taiwan.[76]

Girls' Dormitory, Selma, Ala. Another project had to be postponed. The dormitory facilities at Alabama Lutheran Academy and College, Selma, Ala., a high school and junior college, for which the LWML voted $85,000 in 1957, suffered years of unavoidable delay resulting in part from a rift and the ultimate withdrawal of the Wisconsin Synod from the Synodical Conference, of which The Lutheran Church — Missouri Synod is a part. The work at Selma had been sponsored jointly, and until this matter was resolved, no building could take place. Finally, after the Missouri Synod acquired the school and other difficulties regarding location had been settled, building was begun.[77] The dormitory, a two-story brick-veneer structure, provides facilities for 68 young women and the matron and is part of a $297,699 building project. A dining hall, plus built-in furnishings and equipment, accounts for the difference between the LWML grant and the total cost of the buildings.[78] The dormitory, named after Rosa Young, was dedicated on May 16, 1965.[79] Miss Young, first Negro Lutheran in Alabama, had been a Christian day school teacher for her race for more than 40 years. She also served on the faculty at Selma from 1947 for a number of years.[80] The dormitory stands as a fitting tribute to one who gave unselfishly of herself, through many hardships, to serve her people and her Lord.

High School, Hanno, Japan. The three projects adopted in 1959, all for educational purposes, were widely separated geographically. The $60,000 voted for the building of a new structure for the high school in Hanno, Japan, answered a real need. Most of the existing buildings were very old and in a bad state of repair, in fact they had deteriorated beyond repair.[81] The new building was dedicated on April 15, 1961, 10 years after the school's founding. It is "one of the most modern and attractive buildings in this area. In fact, it is one of three buildings in Hanno that rise above two stories," according to Rev. Albert Carow, the religious adviser to the school.[82] The building contains seven classrooms, a large faculty room, a broadcasting room, and modern lavatories on each floor. The new building enabled Holy Hope High School to take care of an enrollment of 460 students when its school year began on April 18, just 3 days after its dedication.[83]

It was pointed out at the time the project was adopted that the $60,000 grant would be sufficient for only one of the three necessary units. But further development and expansion of the plant was to be the responsibility of the school and the congregation which developed as a result of the school.[84]

Motivated by the LWML gift, parents of the high school students, though 95% non-Christian, planned and financed a $140,000 addition (dedicated in April 1964) with the help of Holy Hope teachers and alumni and the Hanno city and prefectural governments.[85] Recently the board of directors of the high school made extensive plans for continued expansion of the Hanno school, and "your project," writes Rev. Richard Meyer, "undoubtedly played an important role in encouraging the staff, faculty and parents of students enrolled in the school in their enthusiastic support of the school." [86]

Seminary, Philippines. The importance of training young men to minister to people of their own national origin is becoming more and more apparent. This need was recognized in the Philippines as elsewhere. A seminary was begun in Quezon City, a suburb of Manila, in 1955 with all five of the Missouri Synod missionaries in Manila teaching in addition to their other duties. This arrangement however, was found to be unsatisfactory. As a result, three of the missionaries were assigned to the teaching; the others devoted their full time to working among the people. Classes were conducted first in the home of one of the missionaries, then in rented quarters above stores.[87]

The need for adequate facilities was called to the attention of the League, whose grant of $80,000 made possible the purchase of an estate on the outer edge of the resort city of Baguio, in the mountains of North Luzon. The estate had three furnished residences on it that could easily be converted to classroom and dormitory use.[88] The 1961 class was the last to graduate from the temporary quarters. Though results have not been outstanding when measured by present enrollments in our own country, the seminary is making every effort to train young Filipinos to bring the Gospel to their own people. Our seminaries in America also had very meager beginnings. The growing trend of nationalism all over the world makes this a most important endeavor. "As the church [the Philippine church] becomes conscious of her share in bringing Christ to those within her locality," writes Rev. Thomas P. Batong, "no doubt she will also become mature enough to feel that need around her. The young church can carry out her responsibility through what she can offer: training young men to go and reach out into neighboring countries." [89]

High School, Teofilo Otoni, Brazil. The third project adopted in 1959, in the amount of $75,000, was for a high school in Teofilo

Hospital, Wandoor, India

Otoni, Brazil. A part-time elementary school, teaching only religion and German, had been started there by the pastor. Ultimately this endeavor grew into a full-fledged parochial school. Because it drew children from quite a distance, the parsonage became a "dormitory." Educational facilities had been almost nonexistent in the interior of Brazil. But this situation changed so that by the latter part of the 1950s it became a "must" for everyone to get a high school education.[90]

The congregation at Teofilo Otoni also felt this need. Though there were other high schools in the area, the closest Protestant high school was more than 300 miles away. A church building program, however, prevented the congregation from carrying out such a project. A Lutheran high school, it was felt, would not only provide a Christian education but also be a means of winning souls for Christ.[91]

Though the grant was made in 1959, various problems necessitating unavoidable delays prevented the completion of this project until very recently.[92] The site which was finally acquired is situated near the Brasilia-Belém highway. Five rooms will be equipped for classes for the present and five used as dormitories (60 beds). Simple and modern in design, the structure cost $60,000, leaving $15,000 for furnishings and supplies.[93]

Medical Missions (Wandoor, India; Ogoja Province, Nigeria). Five projects totaling $240,000 were voted by the League in 1961. Medical missions received $72,000 of this amount for use in Wandoor, India, and the Ogoja Province in Nigeria. The development of a medical program in Wandoor was deemed important because it would provide a means of reaching the Muslim people and because there was no hospital in the area. The program was to be carried out in three phases.[94] Begun as a dispensary in a rented building in the bazaar, the medical phase of the Christian witness in Wandoor labored with an inexperienced staff in addition to woefully inadequate facilities. Despite this, 17,175 patients had been treated by the end of the first year. One tiny room, which had to be reserved for maternity cases, was all that was available for inpatient service. Other treatments had to be limited to outpatient care.[95]

The first and second stages of the development of the Wandoor facilities were completed in November 1964 at a total cost of $71,243, of which the LWML supplied $58,000. The hospital itself was dedicated on May 15, 1963.[96] An additional $40,000 grant in 1963 made the third stage of the program possible. The grant, together with limited budgeted grants and other gifts, made possible the expansion of the former dispensary into a small hospital equipped with good laboratory, X-ray, and operating facilities. In addition to the hospital, the medical program in Wandoor includes extensive home treatment for tuberculosis and a family-oriented public-health program.[97]

Of the $72,000 allocated for medical missions in 1961, $14,000 was set aside for a dispensary in the Ogoja Province of Nigeria. This was built and in use by 1963. It is the beginning of a larger program which will include a bush hospital and several maternity centers in the area.[98] Present facilities (1966) consist of an outpatient clinic with laboratory and pharmacy, in addition to staff residences. A public health and health education program is in the early stages, and provisions are being made for an inpatient ward of 20 beds. An additional grant of $30,000 in 1965 will provide surgical, laboratory, X-ray, diagnostic, and nursing equipment.[99]

Nigerians are being trained for various roles in the team of medical workers. Some have been sent away to train as doctors and nurses. "Proper Christian personnel who are dedicated and well-trained are very important," writes Rev. E. W. Bunkowske, "but without the medicines and the kind of equipment that God has given to us, their work would not be as effective as it could be. It is for this reason that the LWML has given money for additional hospital equipment at Yahe. This money will outfit the rural health and preventive medicine teams that will spread out across Ogoja Province. It will help to equip a new diagnostic building at the medical center which will make it possible for the medical staff to diagnose more accurately the many strange and unheard of diseases that are rampant here in Ogoja Province. Right at this point this additional equipment is extremely vital in the extension of the medical program to its fullest potential. . . . Once again the LWML has been God's tool of salvation in a real moment of need." [100]

Here, as elsewhere, one of the biggest hindrances to carrying out an effective program of medical missions is the inability to recruit and retain qualified medical personnel in our country who are willing to give a small portion of their lives to the cause of bringing healing of body and soul to those in faraway lands who need both very sorely.

Literature Program. The printed page has long been used by the church to spread God's message of love and salvation. Thomas De Quincy once said, "All that is literature seeks to communicate power." [101] Nowhere is this more apropos than in the area of religion. Unfortunately, most of the literature which the Missouri Synod had produced for the mission fields had been materials geared to strengthening the faith of those already familiar with the Gospel. Conscious of the need to reach those who had not yet become Christians, the mission boards petitioned the convention of the Missouri Synod in 1959 to authorize the creation of a committee for Literacy and Literature (Lit-Lit Committee for short). The request of the committee which was appointed for a grant from the LWML to help implement this program met with affirmative response. $70,000 was voted for this purpose.[102]

in making a study of the best use of literature. As a result, by 1963

Guidelines were prepared by the committee to assist missionaries most mission fields had special literature committees to direct the various aspects of a well-planned literature program. This includes the recruiting and training of national writers, editing, printing, and distributing their materials, and following them up. By 1963 small printing establishments had been set up in two places.[103]

The impact of this program is demonstrated by one instance, in Korea. Rev. Paul Bartling wrote: "Within forty-five minutes 25,000 copies of the LWML grant-supported newspaper tract were distributed to every home, shack, teahouse, shop, and industry in the Chungku district of Seoul, climaxing a month-long evangelistic program of Immanuel Congregation." [104]

The final check for this project was remitted by the LWML in April 1964. Literature in one form or another had found its way into countries around the world.[105] "My Word," said the Lord, "shall not return unto Me void" (Is. 55:11). Eternity alone will reveal the number of souls who learned about their Savior through the literature program.

Chapels, Ghana. Work was begun by the Synodical Conference in Ghana, one of the new independent countries in Africa, late in the '50s. Efforts were concentrated in two areas: Accra, the capital city, and Tema, a short distance away. For the work to become established there, it was imperative that assistance be given to help make the first chapel possible.[106] The LWML granted $20,000 for this purpose in 1961.[107] The young church, however, requested that it be permitted to use the grant as a loan fund so that it could claim the house of worship as its own. This request was granted. When a congregation, therefore, accumulated 10% of the cost of a chapel in its building fund, it could apply for a loan for the remainder.[108]

Tema, which only a few years before had been a village of several hundred people, had grown to a city of 40,000 by 1962.[109] By 1963 Tema had acquired a building site, and plans for a chapel were underway. At the same time two additional congregations had been established in and around Accra.[110] The remaining half of the LWML grant was remitted in 1964.[111]

Radio Transceivers, New Guinea. Two projects adopted in 1961 involved communications. While the Lit-Lit program was an effort to communicate with non-Christians, the other project involved communication between Christians, specifically Christian missionaries. The outreach of Missouri Synod missionaries in New Guinea into new areas which could not be reached by jeep, and only one of which had an airstrip, posed the problem of communicating with fellow missionaries or with the mission doctor to advise about treatment when natives brought their sick to the missionary for healing. The problem was solved through an LWML grant of $10,800 which provided communication by means of radio transceivers.[112]

Chapel, Montreal. The final project adopted by the League in 1961 takes us from the highlands of New Guinea to the big metropolitan center of Montreal in Canada. Interestingly enough, Christ Memorial Lutheran Church came into existence as the result of a woman organizing a Sunday school for her children and others in the neighborhood. Several attempts had been made to have a suitable church building, but the cost was prohibitive.[113]

Montreal, with a population of 2 million, representing many European countries in addition to the predominantly French segment, presented a tremendous challenge. Despite the handicap of inadequate facilities the congregation managed to grow. The dream of these faithful people was realized with the granting of $67,200 for a site.[114] Christ Memorial Lutheran Church, the only English congregation of the Missouri Synod in Canada's largest city, was completed in 1963.[115]

Rural Alabama Redevelopment. Rosa Young, who had figured in a project earlier, was again responsible, at least indirectly, for another project of the LWML. Dr. Young (she had been awarded the honorary degree of Litt. D. by Concordia Seminary, Springfield, Ill., in 1961) [116] had been instrumental in establishing no less than 25 rural Lutheran schools and more than two dozen small church-school units in central rural Alabama. Despite the changing American scene all around, from the primitive to the ultramodern in facilities, the economic status of these Negro congregations did not permit them to improve their facilities. Conditions were so primitive and facilities so dilapidated that it is almost impossible to envision. In addition, many of these people moved to other parts of the country where there was better opportunity for work. With this reduced membership the plight of these people was even more hopeless — or so it seemed. The answer to the problem came with the decision to amalgamate into five congregations and the resolution of the LWML to assist by allocating $75,000 to provide land and the construction of a foundation for the churches. The balance of the necessary funds will be provided by the Missouri Synod on a long-term low-interest loan basis.[117]

The first of the new units was dedicated at Arlington, Ala., on Jan. 3, 1965. It consists of a church building seating about 250, three classrooms, a parsonage, and an apartment for three lady teachers. In addition, several other projects were underway at that time. The entire $75,000 had been remitted at the time of the 1965 convention, and it was anticipated that the entire program would be completed by 1966.[118]

Mission House, St. Louis. Suitable living accommodations for furloughing missionaries had long been a necessity. The old mission house in St. Louis, which had once been the residence of Dr. Francis Pieper, a member of the faculty of Concordia Seminary for many years and also its president, had been purchased during the latter part of the 19th century. While it had served well in its day, it had long outlived its usefulness. Poor wiring, deteriorating structure, and woefully inadequate facilities, such as closets, cabinets, and laundry facilities, made it something to be ashamed of for the housing of furloughing missionaries. The Synod had purchased a six-family apartment building in addition to this old structure, but it alone was not adequate to take care of the number of missionaries requiring housing.

The $125,000 allocated by the League in 1963 for the construction of a new facility for furloughing missionaries therefore filled a real need. After some delays in starting and then additional delay on account of strikes during construction, the new mission house was finally dedicated on Oct. 27, 1966, during the meeting of the LWML Board of Directors in St. Louis. At that time the remainder of the unpaid balance of $28,968.91 was turned over to Dr. William Hillmer, the Synod's Executive Secretary for the Board of Missions.[119] The new facility contains four apartments which are so arranged that they can accommodate both large and small families. This tribute to the missionaries, which demonstrates the concern of the members

Furlough Home for Missionaries, St. Louis, Mo.

Former Furlough Home
Old "Dr. Pieper Residence"

of the LWML for them, is something of which the League can be justly proud.

Foreign Mission Chapel Fund. In addition to the foregoing projects, $25,000 was allocated in 1963 for a Foreign Mission Chapel Fund which would enable congregations in foreign countries to borrow from the fund for the erection of churches. In addition to making such structures possible, it also places a responsibility on the groups to do their share in providing worship facilities. It also makes it possible for many different groups to have the use of these funds as they are repaid by others. Requests for such funds totaled more than $75,000 at the time the grant was made.[120] By 1965 30 building projects were underway, and it was anticipated that by the comple-

Original chapel replaced through LWML grant

Foreign Mission Chapel, India

tion of the project some 50 village congregations will have received help for new or refurnished facilities.[121]

Leprosy Treatment Program. Once again, as the representatives of the LWML met in convention in 1965, the amount for the projects which they adopted increased. From a beginning of $15,000 for its first project in 1943, the amount voted in 1965 rose to a total of $290,000, evidence not only of increased membership but of an increased awareness of, and a readiness to accept, the almost limit-less challenges which presented themselves.

One of these projects, amounting to $85,000, was for leprosy treatment programs in connection with Bethesda Hospital, Ambur,

India; Immanuel Hospital at Mambisanda, New Guinea, and Emanuel Medical Center at Yahe, Nigeria. (An additional $30,000 voted at this time for other facilities at Yahe was referred to above.) Leprosy continues to be one of the greatest problems confronting our medical missionaries in these areas.[122] Though leprosy is now a curable disease, thanks to medical progress, most of the 15 million persons so afflicted do not know this, nor do those who are not afflicted. As a result, lepers are still ostracized and are often unable to secure a means of livelihood. This stigma also prevents those who are afflicted from seeking help. The leprosy control program is one of seeking out the cases, treating them, following up the treatment, educating the public about leprosy, and evaluating the data gathered.[123]

Though not as prevalent in New Guinea as in the other two areas, leprosy has received little systematic work there for its cure. Dr. Paul Brand, world-famous orthopedic surgeon and missionary, describes the picture of leprosy in New Guinea as it presented itself to him. He says: "The mental picture is still with me of leprosy patients literally walking their feet right off the end of their legs, and finally using the end of the leg bone to walk on while the remnant of the foot is still attached to the inside of it." [124]

Our Immanuel Hospital in Mambisanda, New Guinea, will cooperate with the Australian branch of the British Leprosy Mission by providing a ward for leprosy patients and a treatment room with necessary physiotherapy equipment. In addition, nurses engaged in part-time leprosy work are to be made available for special training, and a qualified physiotherapist and occupational therapist will need to be added to our medical staff. $30,000 has been set aside for this program.[125]

In Africa severe budget restrictions and other problems have heretofore prevented the treatment of leprosy on even a small scale. Now, through the LWML grant, it will be possible to send staff for specialized training to a training center known as ALERT, located at Addis Ababa. $15,000 has been designated for this.[126]

Bethesda Hospital, Ambur, India, is far ahead of the other two areas as a result of previous grants. With the present grant a physiotherapy department with two small postoperative wards will be constructed and equipped. It will also be possible to give the present staff special postgraduate training at the Karigiri Leprosy Research Center, and necessary diagnostic and surgical instruments can be purchased.

Coupled with the physical benefits received by the leprosy patients at Bethesda is the spiritual care which they receive.[127] The program of vocational rehabilitation is equally important, and it is hoped that an experienced social worker or occupational therapist can be acquired to head this part of the program. $40,000 is assigned to this area.[128] What a tremendous blessing this LWML grant!

Jeeps for Brazil. The Jeeps for Brazil project, for which $30,000 was allocated, presents quite a different picture. It is almost inconceivable to the average American that pastors to the south of us in Brazil serve anywhere from two to 20 congregations or preaching places scattered over a wide area.[129]

In 1947 a revolving fund for buying jeeps was established by the Brazil District Mission Board. Primitive road conditions in Brazil make jeeps the most satisfactory means of transportation. Previously pastors had to serve their mission stations on horseback. Despite the fact that a fund had been established for buying jeeps, the need increased as the number of missions increased and as the price of jeeps increased.[130] The LWML grant will meet a real need in making the work of the missionaries in Brazil more effective.

Messengers of Christ. The need for producing the Scriptures in the language of the people is evidenced by the fact that there are 2,000 tribes in the world without a single word of Scripture because their language has never been reduced to writing. This prompted the LWML to grant $10,000 to recruit and train workers as linguists. Messengers of Christ, a voluntary organization within the Missouri Synod, was founded just for this purpose. It indicated that it would work in close cooperation with the Mission Departments of the Synod in this effort. Training for those recruited for this purpose would be provided by Wycliffe Bible Translators, an international scientific linguistic agency whose services are available to any denomination.[131]

Rev. Morris Watkins, for 6 years a missionary to Nigeria, together with other pastors and laymen, founded Messengers of Christ, Inc., in May 1964. Pastor Watkins had experienced problems and frustrations in trying to convey the Gospel message effectively with-

Dormitory, Modern III Girls School, Nung Udoe, Nigeria

out the written word in the language of the people to whom he ministered. "At the present rate of Bible translation," wrote Pastor Watkins, "it will take 150 years to complete the work for all Bibleless tribes. But, by calling upon our laymen to help meet this challenge, every tribe can have the wonderful message of God's redeeming love in its own language in this generation!" [132] With the possibility of hitherto open doors being closed to Westerners, it is all the more important that the written Gospel be put into the hands of the people so that the national church can continue even if the missionaries are forced to leave.[133]

Wycliffe Bible Translators, Inc. Closely allied with the project of the Messengers of Christ is that of the Wycliffe Bible Translators, Inc., which received one of the other grants made by the League in 1965. $100,000, the largest of the 1965 grants, was appropriated for a Linguistic Training Center at Enugu, Nigeria.[134] At the invitation of the Missouri Synod, Wycliffe Bible Translators, Inc., began work in Ghana, Africa, in 1962 and in three regions in Nigeria in 1964. It has been offered valuable land in Enugu, adjacent to the Enugu campus, for a translation center. The Missouri Synod expects to establish mission headquarters in Enugu. The Bible translation center will provide housing for five permanent staff members, serving as consultants, and up to 12 teams of translators. It will also provide a dining room, library, and office building.[135]

Modern III Girls School, Africa. The final grant made in 1965 provided $35,000 for a Modern III Girls School at Nung Udoe, also in Africa.[136] The only school for girls operated by the Missouri Synod was the Modern II school at Nung Udoe, which was opened in 1959 as a 2-year secondary school. It used the facilities of the former elementary school. The increasing interest in further education for girls, coupled with the rising standards of education, made these facilities inadequate. The grant will make possible facilities for an additional year of training and of admission of 60 new students each year instead of 30, as previously. The new cement-block dormitory, to accommodate 180 students, will be a great improvement over the old building, constructed of deteriorating mud block coated with plaster. The new 3-year course will enable graduates to enter teachers' training or nurses' training. Such education as offered in this school is vital to the proclamation and expansion of the Gospel message in Nigeria.[137]

25th Anniversary

That the LWML would complete 25 years of existence at the time of its 1967 convention was noted by the following resolution adopted in 1965:

"WHEREAS, The year 1967 is the 25th anniversary year of the Lutheran Women's Missionary League; therefore be it

"Resolved, That the Executive Committee take note of this anniversary in the planning of the 1967 convention." [138]

The Executive Committee took steps to implement this resolution in several ways. Through the President and Secretary it issued a proclamation declaring the month of July 1967 as a period of remembrance for the manifold blessings enjoyed by the League during the 25 years of its existence. The proclamation also encouraged each society "to promote further recognition of these blessings in some special manner through appropriate program planning." [139]

A visual record of the 25th-anniversary convention was authorized by the Board of Directors in the form of a filmstrip with audio presentation.[140] A similar filmstrip had been prepared of the 1965 convention.[141]

A 25th-anniversary thankoffering, in which all members of the

Executive Committee, 1967: (Seated left to right) Miss Louise Krueger, Miss Hella Hillger, Mrs. Henry Tuchenhagen, Miss Ruby Rutkowsky, Mrs. Warren Hartman, Mrs. W. C. Nieman, Mrs. Gilbert Hankel, Rev. Edgar Kaiser. (Standing) Rev. Andrew Sabo, Rev. John Zimmermann.

LWML will be given an opportunity to take part, was also authorized. Envelopes for this purpose are to be distributed to members through the District Presidents.[142]

Finally, the Executive Committee authorized the publication of a book for the 25th anniversary on the history of the Lutheran Women's Missionary League and commissioned Mrs. Adolph R. Meyer of Warrensburg, Mo., to write it. The book is to take the place of a "Facts and Figures" booklet, such as had been published previously (the last one appeared in 1960 and covered the 1955—59 period).[143] A short history had been compiled by the League's historian, Mrs. Albert Pollex, in 1960. It was produced in mimeographed form and distributed on a limited basis. No extensive history has been prepared prior to the present time.

Worldwide Influence of LWML

NOTE: *Information for the following section has all been gleaned from letters received by the author from individuals in the countries discussed.*

The influence of the Lutheran Women's Missionary League has been felt around the world not only through its projects but also through the efforts of missionaries and missionaries' wives to carry on a program for women in the church. The extent to which such a program is carried on and the nature of the program are determined largely by the circumstances which exist in a given area. Unfortunately, space does not permit a detailed account of the activities of women in other countries. Yet a brief glance at some of the situations should prove stimulating.

South America. In the two principal countries of South America where our church has been carrying on its work for many years — Argentina and Brazil, there is a vast difference in the work done among women of these two countries. In Argentina circumstances are such that very little has been done at all until recently, and even now the situation is comparable to that which existed in our own country a century ago. Though many of the pastors have tried for some time to initiate women's organizations, they have not made much progress because of the predominantly German background of the membership, the instability of congregations due to a shifting population, and other circumstances. A small beginning has now been made, however.

The educational program of these local societies consists of a talk by the pastor. In a few societies there is Bible study. Since only about 25 percent of the pastors are able to use the English language, they cannot utilize materials printed in English that would help them to improve their program. Organized women's work in Argentina has not yet reached beyond the local level. If it does in the future, the initiative will have to come from the pastors; the women will not make any effort in this direction.

By contrast, in Brazil, the Lutheran Women's League of Brazil will observe its 10th anniversary in 1967. Its membership of over 2,000 represents six organized districts. Its objectives are similar to those of the LWML in that the projects of the League are such for which no provision has been made in the synodical budget. Its first project provided for the translation of mission tracts into Portuguese. The League uses the official LWML song, "Lutheran Women, One and All" which was translated by Rev. George Mueller. It has adopted the official pledge of the LWML. A collection device to take the place of our "mite" box has been used in the form of a muslin draw-string bag with a cross and the intials of the congregation embroidered on it. The Lutheran Women's League of Brazil has made a good beginning and under God's blessing ought to continue to grow.

Guatemala. No women's organizations have been started in Guate-mala. Cultural and economic conditions are responsible, at least in part. Women on the lower economic levels must work and are therefore not able to meet during the day. Since the supper hour is customarily observed from 7:00 to 9:00 P. M., evening meetings are of necessity excluded. Women in the upper economic levels do not seem to be interested in a church organization — they have various cultural groups that meet during the day.

India. Local ladies' societies were organized in both the Ambur and the Trivandrum Districts in India before the Lutheran Women's Missionary League came into existence. The first local ladies' society in the Nagercoil District was organized in 1947. Societies were or-ganized on a district basis in the Ambur District in 1954 and in the Nagercoil District in 1951. Trivandrum has had district conventions from time to time but has no district organization at present.

The function of these organizations has been to stimulate Chris-tian growth and to offer Christian fellowship to the women of the congregations. Bible study always precedes the business meeting. All societies have visiting committees, who visit shut-ins, members who are lax in their church attendance, and also the homes of non-Christians. Some societies have also contributed to the mission ex-pansion program of the India Evangelical Lutheran Church. Future plans call for a greater involvement of nonmembers who show some interest in Christianity. Though definite plans for this program are still in the formative stage, the desire of the women of India to make their mission outreach a vital part of their program is quite evident.

Hong Kong. The program of the LWML has definitely set the pattern for women's work in Hong Kong, where there are 16 ladies' aids. Retreats have drawn as many as 200 women. Though the women are very capable, they need guidance, which is supplied by the missionaries' wives. The women meet twice a month for a family devotion in the home of one of the members, and women from the neighborhood are invited to attend.

Though plans have been discussed for projects, nothing definite has been done, largely because the multitudinous duties of the mission staff have made this impossible.

Japan. The situation in Japan presents a strange picture to the Westerner. Very few married women are members of our congregations; this is because the older people still cling to their non-Christian religions. The membership of the churches is consequently made up largely of young people. However, despite the fact that there are no women's organizations, or very few, there are women's groups composed of nonmembers of the church. The explanation lies in the church's emphasis on evangelism, which involves the community through Bible study, the teaching of crafts, and Western cooking. The missionaries' wives direct this program.

In Tokyo there are three organized women's groups whose main objectives are Christian growth and Christian fellowship. Most often the women in a family are the only ones who are Christians, and Christian fellowship is of vital importance to sustain their faith. Meetings for both men and women are held once a year for a whole area for the purpose of fellowship. Some travel 6 to 8 hours by train to attend these meetings.

"The goal of the Japanese Church," says Lois (Mrs. Richard) Meyer, "is to become autonomous by 1969, a bold step for which the groundwork is being carefully laid at the present time. As this young church, anxious to meet the demands for its own leadership, grows and matures, it is certain that the consecrated program of the LWML and its strength within the church will be an example and inspiration for the Lutheran women of Japan in the future as they seek to serve their Lord."

Korea. Since the Missouri Synod has been doing mission work in Korea only since 1958, the women's organization is conducted along very simple lines. Special monthly meetings were begun in 1962 for Bible study and Christian doctrine. The project during the last 2 years has been the raising of scholarships for middle and high school students from the two Lutheran congregations. This is of special significance in a land where families will do without adequate food in order to make it possible for their children to get an education. Once a year the Korean women meet with the Western Lutheran women, who are also organized, for Bible study and a service. Last year part of the worship was conducted in Korean and part in English.

Taiwan (Formosa). In Taiwan, as in other places, the emphasis of the women's groups, still comparatively small in number, is on Bible study and mission activity. Women open their homes for Bible study and bring lists of prospects whom they have met. A joint prayer is spoken for the prospects, and discussions are held on methods of personal evangelism.

Philippines. Because of the numerous dialects in the Philippines and because the culture of the Philippines places the emphasis on the local "kinship" group, it is difficult in most cases for members of the church to develop any concern outside their own families, communities, and congregations. As a result, it has not been possible to organize the women into any large-scale women's society. Most of the lowlands congregations do have a ladies' society in one form or another. In addition to these, the missionaries' wives have a loosely knit organization of their own whose main function is to prepare packets to be sent to the United States in answer to inquiries about the work of the church in the Philippines.

New Guinea. The Christians of New Guinea have been a sterling example in Christian responsibility. The women are no exception. Societies were organized about 3 years ago on the local level. There are now two circuits with circuit organizations, representing 12 stations in one circuit and approximately the same number in the other. A separate group for evangelists' wives (all nationals) from 17 congregations makes up another group. Bible study, conducted at each meeting, is led by one of the women, by a missionary, or by a missionary's wife. Business meetings are held to determine projects, which include service programs on the local level, and a program of evangelism.

Of special interest to LWML members is that Mrs. Lois Kroenke, a former District LWML President, currently serving with her husband in New Guinea, has been requested by the committee on evangelism to organize a program suited to the Enga women.

Great Britain. The Lutheran Women's League of Great Britain, begun in 1959 with five organized guilds, today has 10 such guilds with a membership of approximately 100 women. Its objectives are almost identical with those of the LWML. Its projects, for both foreign and home missions, are supported by mite-box offerings. It holds conventions, retreats, and rallies annually. Its projects are chosen at the convention.

Australia. Though local women's groups existed in the Lutheran churches in Australia since the beginning of the century, the larger organization began with the formation of women's leagues in several Districts 28 years ago. Other Australian Districts have formed organizations since. Each District has developed a program of active support for its District and the church at large. Projects include both home and foreign missions.

In 1962 an Australia-wide organization was formed. The first convention was held in March 1965. Organizational structure is very similar to that of the LWML.

Prospect and Retrospect

It is fitting to pause as the first quarter century of the Lutheran Women's Missionary League's history comes to a close and to acknowledge with humility the tremendous blessings which the Lord has bestowed on this organization. At the same time lost opportunities, the lack of consecration, an unwillingness to sacrifice, which at times have hampered the progress of the Lord's work in one way or another, cannot be overlooked. Coleridge said: "If men could learn from history, what lessons it might teach us! But passion and party blind our eyes and the light which experience gives is a lantern on the stern, which shines only on the waves behind us!" [144]

The past is gone — the future lies before us. It would be presumptuous on our part to try to predict what course the Lutheran Women's Missionary League will take in the years ahead. Several things, however, seem to point to the direction in which it is going.

Though a national women's organization was long in coming in the Missouri Synod, it has made great strides in both its program and its projects. Its efforts to provide the means by which its members could grow spiritually are commendable. It has had the courage to take a long, hard look at its organization and its program and to make sweeping changes in order that its operation might be more effective. It has also looked at other denominational women's groups and assimilated some of their strengths, so that today its program is equal to some and superior to others in meeting the challenges of the times.

The Lutheran Women's Missionary League has done more. It has been quick to capture the spirit of the church as such today, and of its parent body, The Lutheran Church — Missouri Synod in particular, which also has made a thorough study of its program and practices. As a result of its survey, the Missouri Synod reaffirmed its belief in the Biblical concept of the church's mission — its unchanging mission — that of communicating the love of God in Christ to all men everywhere in a way that is effective in the kind of world in which we live.

If the Lutheran Women's Missionary League is to continue to fulfill its mission in the 20th-century space age, it, too, will challenge each one of its members to become personally involved in a Christian concern for the physical as well as the spiritual needs of all sorts and conditions of men everywhere. If this concept of the term "mission" is maintained, then the members of the Lutheran Women's Missionary League will continue to be what their counterparts have been throughout all ages — women on a mission — Christ's mission — to the whole man, to the whole society, in the whole world.

SOLI DEO GLORIA!

Notes

X

1. Kansas City *Star,* Jan. 11, 1967, p. 12A.

2. *Women's Work in The Lutheran Church — Missouri Synod: A Survey Report* (St. Louis: Lutheran Women's Missionary League, 1961), Introduction. (Hereafter cited as *Women's Work.*)

3. *Proceedings,* LWML convention, July 31—Aug. 1, 1957, p. 6; July 22 to 23, 1959, pp. 14—15. (Hereafter cited as LWML *Proceedings.*)

4. *Women's Work,* Introduction.

5. *Lutheran Woman's Quarterly,* XIX, No. 2 (April 1961), pp. 9—10. (Hereafter cited as *LWQ.*)

6. *Women's Work,* p. 27.

7. Ibid., p. 28.

8. Ibid.

9. Ibid., pp. 27—28.

10. Ibid., p. 48.

11. LWML *Proceedings,* July 26—27, 1961, pp. 26—27.

12. Minutes, LWML Executive Committee, Oct. 18—19, 1961, pp. 5—6.

13. LWML *Proceedings,* July 17—18, 1963, p. 33.

14. Ibid., p. 38.

15. Ibid.

16. Ibid., pp. 34—35, 38.

17. *Reports and Memorials,* LWML convention, 1965, p. 39. (Hereafter cited as LWML *Reports and Memorials,* with year of convention.)

18. Minutes, LWML Board of Directors, Nov. 17—18, 1960, p. 4.

19. LWML *Proceedings,* July 21—22, 1965, p. 13.

20. LWML *Proceedings,* 1963, pp. 35—36, 38.

21. LWML *Proceedings,* 1965, p. 15.

22. LWML *Proceedings,* 1963, p. 22.

23. Minutes, LWML Executive Committee, Nov. 10—12, 1965, p. 4.

24. LWML *Proceedings,* 1965, p. 24.

25. LWML *Reports and Memorials,* 1965, p. 19.

26. LWML *Proceedings,* 1963, p. 36.

27. LWML *Proceedings,* 1965, p. 34.

28. Ibid., p. 15.

29. LWML *Proceedings,* 1963, pp. 36, 38.

30. LWML *Proceedings,* 1965, p. 40.

31. *LWQ,* XXIII, No. 4 (Oct. 1965), p. 5.

32. *Women's Work,* p. 28.

33. *LWQ,* XXIV, No. 4 (Fall 1966), p. 32.

34. *LWQ,* XXV, No. 1 (Winter 1966), p. 38.

35. Ibid.

36. LWML *Proceedings,* 1965, p. 22.

37. Ibid., p. 14.

38. Ibid., pp. 28—33.

39. Ibid., pp. 23, 33.

40. *LWQ,* XXII, No. 2 (April 1964), p. 3.

41. LWML *Proceedings,* 1963, p. 42.

42. LWML *Proceedings,* 1965, p. 34; *LWQ,* XXII, No. 2 (April 1964), p. 5.

43. LWML *Proceedings,* 1961, p. 32.

44. *LWQ,* XX, No. 4 (Oct. 1962), pp. 4—6.

45. *LWQ,* XXIII, No. 2 (April 1965), p. 6.

46. LWML *Proceedings,* 1961, pp. 10—11; Minutes, LWML Board of Directors, Oct. 26, 1966, p. 4.

47. *Proceedings of the Forty-Fifth Regular Convention of The Lutheran Church — Missouri Synod,* June 20—29, 1962, pp. 134—135.

48. *Proceedings of the Forty-Sixth Regular Convention of The Lutheran Church — Missouri Synod,* June 16—26, 1965, pp. 122, 211.

49. LWML *Reports and Memorials,* 1961, p. 31.

50. Ibid.

51. LWML *Proceedings,* 1965, p. 27.

52. *LWQ,* XXIV, No. 4 (Fall 1966), p. 12.

53. LWML *Reports and Memorials,* 1961, p. 32; 1965, p. 34.

54. *LWQ,* XXIV, No. 4 (Fall 1966), p. 8.

55. *LWQ,* XXIV, No. 3 (July 1966), p. 9.

56. Minutes, LWML Executive Committee, Nov. 4—5, 1963, p. 2.

57. LWML *Reports and Memorials,* 1961, p. 32.

58. LWML *Reports and Memorials,* 1965, pp. 32—33.

59. Ibid., pp. 35—36.

60. *LWQ,* XXIV, No. 4 (Fall 1966), p. 36.

61. *LWQ,* XXV, No. 1 (Winter 1966), p. 21.

62. LWML *Reports and Memorials,* 1966, p. 36; LWML *Proceedings,* 1965, p. 33.

63. Minutes, LWML Board of Directors, July 25, 1961, p. 9.

64. LWML *Reports and Memorials,* 1963, p. 34.

65. Ibid.

66. LWML *Reports and Memorials,* 1965, pp. 36—37.

67. Questionnaire returned by Mrs. Harold Witte to the author.

68. LWML *Reports and Memorials,* 1965, p. 36.

69. LWML *Proceedings,* 1963, pp. 17, 45.

70. *LWQ,* XIX, No. 1 (Jan. 1961), p. 24.

71. *LWQ,* XIX, No. 3 (July 1961), p. 30.

72. LWML *Proceedings,* 1961, p. 28.

73. LWML *Reports and Memorials,* 1965, pp. 37—38.

74. LWML *Proceedings,* 1961, p. 23.

75. *LWQ,* XVIII, No. 2 (April 1960), p. 14.

76. Letter from Mr. R. W. Henningfield to Mrs. O. E. Feucht, June 9, 1965.

77. LWML *Proceedings,* 1963, p. 14; *LWQ,* XXIII, No. 1 (Jan. 1965), pp. 14—15.

78. *LWQ,* XXIII, No. 1 (Jan. 1965), pp. 14—15.

79. *LWQ,* XXIII, No. 4 (Oct. 1965), p. 17.

80. *LWQ,* XVI, No. 3 (July 1958), pp. 7—9.

81. *LWQ,* XVIII, No. 1 (Jan. 1960), p. 10.

82. *LWQ,* XIX, No. 3 (July 1961), p. 4.

83. Ibid.

84. LWML *Reports and Memorials,* 1959, p. 39.

85. *LWQ,* XXII, No. 3 (July 1964), p. 15.

86. Letter from Rev. Richard Meyer to the author, Aug. 17, 1966.

87. *LWQ,* XVIII, No. 1 (Jan. 1960), pp. 7—8.

88. *LWQ,* XIX, No. 3 (July 1961), p. 5.

89. *LWQ,* XXI, No. 3 (July 1963), p. 11.

90. *LWQ,* XVIII, No. 1 (Jan. 1960), pp. 5—6.

91. Ibid.

92. LWML *Proceedings,* 1963, pp. 14—15.

93. *LWQ,* XXIV, No. 4 (Fall 1966), p. 13.

94. LWML *Reports and Memorials,* 1961, p. 40.

95. *LWQ,* XX, No. 1 (Jan. 1962), pp. 3, 30.

96. LWML *Proceedings,* 1963, p. 15.

97. LWML *Proceedings,* 1965, pp. 21—22.

98. LWML *Proceedings,* 1963, p. 15.

99. *LWQ,* XXIV, No. 1 (Jan. 1966), p. 7.

100. Letter from Rev. E. W. Bunkowske to the author, Oct. 19, 1966.

101. Thomas De Quincey, "Letters to a Young Man" (Letter iii), as quoted in *The Oxford Dictionary of Quotations,* 2d ed. (London: Oxford U. Press, 1955), 172:25.

102. LWML *Proceedings,* 1961, pp. 32—33.

103. LWML *Proceedings,* 1963, p. 15.

104. *LWQ,* XXI, No. 2 (April 1963), p. 8.

105. *LWQ,* XXII, No. 3 (July 1964), p. 24.

106. LWML *Reports and Memorials,* 1961, p. 38.

107. LWML *Proceedings,* 1961, pp. 32—33.

108. LWML *Proceedings,* 1963, p. 15.

109. *LWQ,* XX, No. 1 (Jan. 1962), p. 5.

110. *LWQ,* XXI, No. 2 (April 1963), p. 13.

111. *LWQ,* XXII, No. 4 (Oct. 1964), p. 9.

112. *LWQ,* XX, No. 1 (Jan. 1962), p. 12.

113. LWML *Reports and Memorials,* 1961, p. 39.

114. *LWQ,* XX, No. 1 (Jan. 1962), pp. 6, 30; LWML *Proceedings,* 1961, pp. 32—33.

115. *LWQ,* XXI, No. 4 (Oct. 1963), p. 8.

116. *LWQ,* XIX, No. 3 (July 1961), p. 15.

117. *LWQ,* XXII, No. 1 (Jan. 1964), pp. 10—11.

118. LWML *Proceedings,* 1965, p. 21.

119. *LWQ,* XXV, No. 1 (Winter 1966), p. 21.

120. LWML *Reports and Memorials,* 1963, p. 37.

121. LWML *Proceedings,* 1965, p. 21.

122. LWML *Reports and Memorials,* 1965, p. 40.

123. *LWQ,* XXIV, No. 1 (Jan. 1966), p. 9.

124. *LWQ,* XXIV, No. 4 (Fall 1966), pp. 3—4.

125. Ibid., p. 4.

126. Ibid., pp. 4—5.

127. Ibid., p. 5.

128. Ibid.

129. LWML *Reports and Memorials,* 1965, p. 41.

130. *LWQ,* XXIV, No. 1 (Jan. 1966), p. 8.

131. LWML *Reports and Memorials,* 1965, p. 42; LWML *Proceedings,* 1965, pp. 34—35.

132. *LWQ,* XXIV, No. 1 (Jan. 1966), p. 4.

133. Ibid., pp. 4—5.

134. LWML *Proceedings,* 1965, pp. 34—35.

135. *LWQ*, XXIV, No. 1 (Jan. 1966), p. 5.

136. LWML *Reports and Memorials,* 1965, p. 41.

137. *LWQ*, XXIV, No. 1 (Jan. 1966), pp. 6—7.

138. LWML *Proceedings,* 1965, p. 40.

139. *LWQ*, XXIV, No. 3 (July 1966), p. 11.

140. Minutes, LWML Board of Directors, Oct. 27, 1966, p. 17.

141. LWML *Proceedings,* 1965, pp. 17—18.

142. Minutes, LWML Board of Directors, Oct. 27, 1966, p. 17.

143. Minutes, LWML Executive Committee, Nov. 10—12, 1965, p. 8.

144. Samuel T. Coleridge, "T. Allsop's Recollections," quoted in *Oxford Dictionary of Quotations,* 152:24.

Selected Bibliography

Books

Bliss, Kathleen. *The Service and Status of Women in the Churches.* London: SCM Press Ltd., 1952.

Bodensieck, Julius, ed. *The Encyclopedia of the Lutheran Church.* Minneapolis: Augsburg, 1965.

Brummitt, Stella Wyatt. *Looking Backward — Thinking Forward.* Cincinnati: Woman's Home Missionary Society (Methodist Episcopal Church), 1930.

Daniélou, Jean Fr. *The Ministry of Women in the Early Church.* London: Faith Press, 1961.

Diehl, Nona M. *Lutheran Women Around the World.* Philadelphia: Board of Publication, Lutheran Church in America, 1963.

———. *U. L. C. W. Heritage and History 1879—1959.* Philadelphia: United Lutheran Church Women, 1961.

Emery, Julia C. *A Century of Endeavor — 1821—1921.* New York: Department of Missions (Protestant Episcopal Church in the U. S. A.), 1921.

Fuerbringer, Ludwig. *Persons and Events.* St. Louis: Concordia, 1947.

History of Central District Lutheran Women's Missionary Endeavor 1928 to 1942 and Lutheran Women's Missionary League 1943—1964. n. p., 1966.

Hunt, Alma. *History of Woman's Missionary Union (Baptist).* Nashville: Convention Press, 1964.

Lehmann, Katharine. *And the Women Also.* Columbus: Women's Missionary Federation of the American Lutheran Church, 1952.

Lueker, Erwin L., ed. *Lutheran Cyclopedia.* St. Louis: Concordia, 1954.

Lutheran Women's Work in Greater St. Louis. n. p., 1938.

Luthers Werke, Briefwechsel IV. Weimar: Hermann Böhlaus Nachfolger, 1933.

Manual of Practical Church Work. New York: Lutheran Press, 1938.

Mathis, Marie, and Elaine Dickson. *The Woman's Missionary Union Program of a Church.* Nashville: Convention Press, 1966.

Mayer, F. E. *The Religious Bodies of America.* St. Louis: Concordia, 1954.

Meyer, Carl S., ed. *Moving Frontiers.* St. Louis: Concordia, 1964.

1965 Report of the Board of Missions of the Methodist Church, Twenty-Sixth Annual Meeting, Jan. 16—21, 1966. Cincinnati: Board of Missions, The Methodist Church, 1966.

Olson, Oscar N., and Geo. W. Wickstrom. *A Century of Life and Growth — Lutheran Augustana Synod 1848—1948.* Rock Island, Ill.: Augustana Book Concern, 1948.

Peterson, Mrs. Peter, ed. *These Fifty Years — 1892—1942.* Chicago: Women's Missionary Society of Augustana Synod, 1942.

Prohl, Russell C. *Woman in the Church.* Grand Rapids, Mich.: Wm. C. Eerdmans, 1957.

Reishus, Martha. *Hearts and Hands Uplifted: A History of the Women's Missionary Federation of the Evangelical Lutheran Church.* Minneapolis: Augsburg, 1958.

Revised Interim Report of a Study on the Life and Work of Women in the Church. Geneva: World Council of Churches, 1948.

Smith, Ruth Juram. *Their Sound Goes Forth.* Philadelphia: United Lutheran Church Women, 1959.

Stellhorn, August C. *Schools of The Lutheran Church — Missouri Synod.* St. Louis: Concordia, 1963.

Walther League Manual. Chicago: The Walther League, 1935.

Warnke, Mabel. *Partners the World Around.* St. Louis: Concordia, 1966.

Weiherman, Wm. F., ed. *Fifty Years of Service to Lutheran Youth — 1893 to 1943.* Chicago: n. p., 1943.

Weiser, Frederick S. *Love's Response: A Story of Lutheran Deaconesses in America.* Philadelphia: Board of Publication, United Lutheran Church in America, 1962.

Winsborough, Hallie Paxson — as told to Rosa Gibbons. *Yesteryears.* Atlanta: Assembly Committee of Woman's Work, 1937.

Woman's Missionary Society Manual. Birmingham: Woman's Missionary Union, 1964.

Women's Work in The Lutheran Church — Missouri Synod: A Survey Report. St. Louis: Lutheran Women's Missionary League, 1961.

Periodicals

Die Abendschule, LVII, No. 22B, May 18, 1911.

American Lutheran, V, April 1922; XX, April 1937.

Concordia Theological Monthly, I, May 1930; IX, Jan. 1938.

Eternity, XVII, Feb. 1966.

The Harvest Call, I, Sept. 1938 — V, June 1943.

Lutheran Laymen's League Bulletin, I, Jan. 1, 1930 — II, March 1, 1931.

Lutheran Witness, XII, July 21, 1893 — LXXIII, April 13, 1954.

Lutheran Witness Reporter, II, June 5, 1966.

The Lutheran Woman, March 1939—Dec. 1942.

Lutheran Woman's Quarterly, Jan. 1943 — XXV, Winter 1966.

Der Lutheraner, XXII, Feb. 15, 1866; June 1, 1866; XXVIII, Feb. 1, 1872.

The Methodist Woman, XXV, Jan. 1964; XXVI, Sept. 1965.

St. Louis Lutheran, XXI, July 30, 1966.

Theological Quarterly, XXIV, Jan. 1921; April 1921.

Walther League Messenger — Vereinsbote, XXV, June-July 1917.

Western District Lutheran, IX, June 1933; Sept. 1933.

Convention Proceedings

Central District, Ev. Lutheran Synod of Missouri, Ohio, and Other States, 1928.

English District, Ev. Lutheran Synod of Missouri, Ohio, and Other States, 1943.

Ev. Lutheran Synod of Missouri, Ohio, and Other States, 1920; 1923; 1926 (English editions); 1938; 1941; 1944.

The Lutheran Church — Missouri Synod, 1950; 1962; 1965.

Lutheran Women's Missionary League, 1942—1965.

Appendix

Compiled by Erna C. Feucht

International Officers
International Conventions
Statistics — Membership and Financial
Districts — Organization Dates, Presidents
Mission Projects — International, District

INTERNATIONAL OFFICERS

President

1942—47	Mrs. Otto F. Schmitt
1947—53	Mrs. Sadie Fulk Roehrs
1953—59	Mrs. Arthur Preisinger
1959—63	Mrs. Walter N. Hoppe
1963—67	Mrs. Gilbert O. Hankel

First Vice-President

1942—47	Mrs. H. W. Lembke
1947—53	Mrs. Arthur Preisinger
1953—59	Mrs. Walter N. Hoppe
1959—63	Mrs. Harold Brandt
1963—67	Mrs. Warren P. Hartman

Second Vice-President

1942—47	Miss Gertrude H. Ressmeyer
1947—53	Mrs. H. Max Hunter
1953—57	Mrs. Wm. Fischer
1957—61	Mrs. Albert F. Pollex
1961—65	Mrs. Lucie Hahn
1965—	Miss Ruby Rutkowsky

Recording Secretary

1942—47	Mrs. Walter Widmann
1947—51	Mrs. R. H. C. Meyer
1951—57	Mrs. F. A. Eggert
1957—61	Mrs. Herbert Oberle
1961—65	Mrs. Wilbert Rosin
1965—	Mrs. W. C. Nieman

Corresponding Secretary

1942—49	Mrs. Raymond Roehrkasse
1949—53	Mrs. Frederick J. Schuermann
1953—59	Mrs. Merrill Gerstner (married John Luecke in 1954)
1959—63	Mrs. Gilbert O. Hankel
1963—67	Mrs. Henry Tuchenhagen

Financial Secretary

1942—43	Mrs. B. J. Theimer
1943—49	Mrs. C. A. Hass
1949—53	Mrs. Earl Boucher
1953—59	Mrs. L. S. Kenyon
1959—63	Mrs. A. H. Prueter
1963—67	Miss Hella W. Hillger

Treasurer

1942—49	Mrs. A. H. Meitler
1949—56	Miss Hilda Trarbach
1956—61	Mrs. E. C. Lehman
1961—65	Mrs. E. A. Kramer
1965—	Miss Louise Krueger

	Counselors	1951—54	Rev. Hubert G. Brueggemann
1942	Rev. Walter Birkner		
	Rev. J. Deckmann	1953—59	Rev. Ray Eissfeldt
	Rev. Oscar Fedder	1955—61	Rev. Theo. Gerken
	Rev. R. H. C. Meyer	1955—61	Rev. Herman Sieving
	Rev. A. H. Semmann	1959—63	Rev. Alwin Rubin
1943—49	Rev. R. H. C. Meyer	1961—65	Rev. Paul Lessmann
1943—51	Rev. Oscar Fedder	1961—67	Rev. John Zimmermann
1943—53	Rev. Walter Birkner	1963—	Rev. Andrew Sabo
1949—55	Rev. Martin Mayer	1965—	Rev. Edgar Kaiser

INTERNATIONAL CONVENTIONS

1942   **July 7 and 8**   **Chicago, Illinois**
Organizing Convention
Host: St. Stephen's Church
28 Delegates Representing 15 Districts
Total Attendance About 100

1943   **Aug. 31 and Sept. 1**   **Fort Wayne, Indiana**
First Regular Convention
Host: Central District LWML
Headquarters: Concordia College
77 Delegates Representing 19 Districts
Total Attendance About 300
Motto: *Serve the Lord with Gladness*

1945   No convention because of war restrictions

1947   **July 18 and 19**   **Chicago, Illinois**
Second Regular Convention
Host: Northern Illinois District LWML
Headquarters: Continental Hotel
214 Delegates Representing 29 Districts
886 Registered Guests   Total Attendance 1,100
Motto: *Serve the Lord with Gladness*

1949   **July 27 and 28**   **Cleveland, Ohio**
Third Regular Convention
Host: LWML of Greater Cleveland
(Central and English Districts)
Headquarters: Hotel Cleveland
257 Delegates Representing 31 Districts
528 Registered Guests   Total Attendance 785
Motto: *Thy Kingdom Come*

1951   **July 25 and 26**   **New York, New York**
Fourth Biennial Convention
Host: Atlantic District LWML
Headquarters: Hotel Commodore
278 Delegates Representing 34 Districts
1,112 Registered Guests   Total Attendance 1,390
Motto: *For Such a Time as This*

1953   **July 28 and 29**   **Portland, Oregon**
Fifth Biennial Convention
Host: Northwest District LWML
Headquarters: Civic Auditorium
276 Delegates Representing 35 Districts
1,100 Registered Guests   Total Attendance 1,376
Motto: *Saved to Serve*

1955   No convention

1956   **April 20 and 21**   **Denver, Colorado**
Sixth Biennial Convention
(Delegate Convention)
Host: Colorado District LWML
Headquarters: Shirley-Savoy Hotel
319 Delegates Representing 36 Districts
322 Registered Guests   Total Attendance 641
Motto: *Occupy Till I Come*

1957   **July 31 and Aug. 1**   **Minneapolis, Minnesota**
Seventh Biennial Convention
Host: Minnesota District LWML
Headquarters: Leamington Hotel
398 Delegates Representing 37 Districts
2,803 Registered Guests   Total Attendance 3,201
Motto: *Talk Ye of All His Wondrous Works*

1959   **July 22 and 23**   **Toronto, Ontario, Canada**
Eighth Biennial Convention
Host: Ontario District LWML
Headquarters: Royal York Hotel
475 Delegates Representing 37 Districts
1,218 Registered Guests   Total Attendance 1,693
Motto: *Labour with More Love*

1961   **July 26 and 27**   **Pittsburgh, Pennsylvania**

Ninth Biennial Convention

Host: Pittsburgh Area LWML Societies
(Eastern and English Districts)
Headquarters: Hilton Hotel
524 Delegates Representing 37 Districts
1,496 Registered Guests   Total Attendance 2,020

Motto: *Living with My Lord*

1963   **July 17 and 18**   **Kansas City, Missouri**

Tenth Biennial Convention

Host: Kansas District LWML
Headquarters: Municipal Auditorium
545 Delegates Representing 37 Districts
2,067 Registered Guests   Total Attendance 2,618

Motto: *The Harvest Is Great*

1965   **July 20 and 21**   **San Diego, California**

Eleventh Biennial Convention

Host: Southern California District LWML
Headquarters: San Diego Community Concourse
566 Delegates Representing 39 Districts
1,060 Registered Guests   Total Attendance 1,626

Motto: *The Lord Is My Light*

STATISTICS
Membership

As published in *Reports and Memorials*

Year	Members	Societies	Districts
1942	——	—	15
1943	39,890	—	19
1945	——	—	25
1947	87,008	2,091	29
1949	103,972	2,505	31
1951	126,416	3,024	33
1953	139,097	3,404	35
1955 ('56)	152,193	3,822	36
1957	169,575	4,212	37
1959	189,939	4,428	37
1961	199,833	4,721	37
1963	207,396	4,918	37
1965	212,350	5,121	39
1967 (Jan. 1)	214,699	5,338	39

Financial

Mission Offerings include 25% mite-box gifts received from Districts, international convention offerings, and special gifts for missions.

Year	Mission Offerings	Project Grants
1942—43	$ 2,412.90	
(Oct.—Aug.)		
1943—44	8,120.30	$ 15,000.00
(Aug.—May)		
1944—45	15,039.45	
(May—May)		
1945—46	22,727.27	
1946—47	27,969.99	
1947—48	37,032.66	73,262.33
1948—49	35,900.30	30,000.00
1949—50	43,257.02	65,000.00
1950—51	49,620.49	
1951—52	52,709.52	145,000.00
1952—53	65,559.70	
1953—54	68,485.04	180,000.00
1954—55	74,113.51	
1955—56	78,004.11	145,000.00
1956—57	84,609.73	
1957—58	102,178.24	200,000.00
1958—59	95,161.35	
1959—60	109,841.73	215,000.00
1960—61	117,808.35	
1961—62	125,119.52	240,000.00
1962—63	123,714.84	
1963—64	136,637.76	265,000.00
1964—65	135,784.56	
1965—66	132,586.06	290,000.00
1966—67	160,463.60	
	$1,904,858.00	$1,863,262.33
Total Mission Offerings 1942—67	$1,904,858.00	
Total Project Grants 1942—67	$1,863,262.33	

DISTRICTS

Organization Dates

The names of the 39 Districts now constituting the Lutheran Women's Missionary League are in regular type. The names of former Districts or of Districts that have been renamed are in italic type.

The 19 present and former Districts that were charter members of the Lutheran Women's Missionary League are marked with an asterisk (*).

Alberta and British Columbia   July 4, 1951

*Atlantic   May 20, 1942

*California and Nevada   May 28, 1942

  Area organizations of women had held joint annual Districtwide conventions beginning Oct. 19, 1938.

Carolina   Sept. 20—21, 1958
    Renamed from Southeastern (Carolinas and Georgia).

Central   May 27, 1942
    Previous District organization: Lutheran Women's Missionary
    Endeavor, June 27, 1928. — Divided into Indiana and Ohio,
    July 15—17, 1964.

Central Illinois   May 19, 1946
    Previous District organization: Women's Missionary Endeavor,
    Oct. 6—11, 1940.

Chesapeake   Oct. 18—19, 1952
    Renamed from Southeastern (Northern Branch).

Colorado   May 28, 1942

Eastern   March 9, 1944

English   Jan. 14, 1944

Florida-Georgia   Oct. 25, 1948
    Previously Southern, Florida Branch, Sept. 30, 1945.

Gulf States   Nov. 8—9, 1949
    Previously Southern, Gulf States Branch, Feb. 3, 1944.

Idaho   June 6, 1948
    Previously in Washington-Oregon-Idaho. — Became Utah-Idaho,
    June 9, 1950.

Indiana   July 15—17, 1964
    Previously in Central.

*Iowa East   May 20, 1942

Iowa West   May 15, 1946

*Kansas   May 16, 1943
    Previous District organization: Lutheran Women's League of
    Kansas, March 30, 1930.

Laurentian   May 15, 1950

Louisiana   Oct. 29—30, 1949
    Previously Southern, Louisiana Branch, May 30, 1944.

Manitoba-Saskatchewan   Oct. 12, 1953

Michigan   Oct. 22, 1944

Minnesota   May 19, 1942
    Divided into Minnesota North and Minnesota South, June 4,
    1964.

Minnesota North   June 4, 1964
    Previously in Minnesota.

Minnesota South   June 4, 1964
    Previously in Minnesota.

*Montana   Sept. 30, 1942

    Previous District organization: North Dakota-Montana Lutheran Women's Missionary Endeavor, June 23—29, 1937.

*North Dakota   June 7, 1942

    Previous District organization: North Dakota-Montana Lutheran Women's Missionary Endeavor, June 23—29, 1937.

North Wisconsin   Sept. 20, 1944

*Northern Illinois   Nov. 5, 1943

    Previous District organization: Lutheran Women's Mission Endeavor of Northern Illinois, May 5, 1938.

*Northern Nebraska   Nov. 19, 1941

Northwest   May 3—4, 1952

    Renamed from Oregon-Washington. — Divided into Oregon and Washington, May 17, 1956.

Ohio   July 15—17, 1964

    Previously in Central.

*Oklahoma   Oct. 11, 1942

    Previous District organization: Lutheran Women's League of Oklahoma, March 11, 1928.

Ontario   Oct. 15, 1950

Oregon   May 17, 1956

    Previously in Northwest.

Oregon-Washington   May 10—11, 1948

    Renamed from Oregon-Washington-Idaho when Idaho societies were released to form Idaho. — Renamed Northwest, May 3—4, 1952.

**Oregon-Washington-Idaho*   April 29, 1942

    Renamed Oregon-Washington, May 10—11, 1948.

*South Dakota   May 10, 1942

South Wisconsin   Nov. 21, 1946

**Southeastern (Carolinas and Georgia)*   Oct. 18, 1942

    Previous District organization: Lutheran Women's League in the Southeastern Conference, April 24, 1938. — Renamed Carolina, Sept. 20—21, 1958.

**Southeastern (Northern Branch)*   June 14, 1942

    Renamed Chesapeake, Oct. 18—19, 1952.

Southern   Nov. 10—12, 1944

    Southern organized with three "branches": Louisiana, Gulf States, and Florida, each of which later formed a separate District.

Southern California   Jan. 20, 1946

*Southern Illinois   Jan. 20, 1943

Southern Nebraska   Oct. 22, 1942
> Previous District organization: Lutheran Women's League of the Southern Nebraska District, Oct. 16, 1940.

Texas   June 10,1942

Utah-Idaho   June 9, 1950
> Previously Idaho.

Washington   May 17, 1956
> Previously in Oregon-Washington.

Western   Dec. 9, 1941
> Previous District organization: Lutheran Women's League, March 18, 1932.

District Presidents

Alberta and British Columbia

1951—56 Mrs. Harold Witte	1960—64 Mrs. Frederick A. Schole
1956—60 Mrs. Reinhold Henning	1964— Mrs. Walter F. Schoepp

Atlantic

1942—46 Mrs. Herman Hecker	1954—58 Mrs. Ernest B. Priebe
1946—50 Mrs. Louis T. Buchheimer	1958—62 Mrs. Lucie Hahn
1950—54 Mrs. Florence Bosse	1962—66 Mrs. August Biermann
	1966— Mrs. Ernest Hanschin

California and Nevada

1943—44 Mrs. C. F. Wessel	1958—60 Mrs. Floyd Schelby
1944—48 Mrs. H. W. Lembke	1960—62 Mrs. Waltraut Wilson
1948—52 Mrs. T. L. Frank	1962—66 Mrs. Paige L. Keiser
1952—56 Mrs. Harold Brandt	1966— Mrs. Richard Matousek
1956—58 Mrs. Oscar Wilson	

Carolina

1958—60 Mrs. Louise B. Pence	1964— Mrs. George Marschall
1960—64 Mrs. H. Frank Hollar	

Central

1942—46 Mrs. Sadie Fulk Roehrs	1958—62 Miss Olga Kaiser
1946—50 Mrs. Walter N. Hoppe	1962—64 Mrs. Herman Krueckeberg
1950—54 Mrs. Emil D. Frank	
1954—58 Mrs. C. W. Gruenhagen	

Central Illinois

1946—49 Mrs. Earl Boucher	1957—61 Mrs. Wilbert Kaspar
1949—51 Mrs. Orville Asper	1961—64 Mrs. Raymond Eissfeldt
1951—55 Mrs. Edwin Semelka	1964— Mrs. Otto Stahlke
1955—57 Mrs. Alvin Bluhm	

Chesapeake

1952—54 Mrs. Eric Johanson	1960—62 Miss Florine Nolde
1954—56 Mrs. Lee Eirich	1962—66 Mrs. Edward Cockrell
1956—60 Mrs. Henry Kroll	1966— Mrs. William Schaefer

Colorado

1942—44 Mrs. Fred Scherzer	1953—56 Mrs. Gilbert O. Hankel
1944—46 Mrs. H. Max Hunter	1956—58 Mrs. P. Alfred Abelt
1946—47 Mrs. Fred J. Zobel	1958—62 Mrs. Oscar Fischer
1947—50 Mrs. Earlyon Brass	1962—66 Mrs. A. E. Swanson
1950—53 Mrs. Fred J. Zobel	1966— Mrs. Martin W. Pollock

Eastern

1944—50 Mrs. Walter Thorman	1958—62 Miss Hella W. Hillger
1950—54 Mrs. Henry Schroeder	1962—66 Mrs. Alfred Hope
1954—58 Mrs. Karl Kriesel	1966— Mrs. Adolph Steinke

English

1944—46 Mrs. Edward G. Kasch	1954—58 Mrs. Elwood Zuelsdorf
1946—48 Mrs. Bert G. Allen	1958—62 Mrs. Dan Ludwig
1948—52 Mrs. Robert Jack	1962—66 Mrs. Martin Eggers
1952—54 Mrs. Francis E. Boyd	1966— Mrs. George Hampe

Florida-Georgia

1948—50 Mrs. F. H. Zucker	1956—58 Mrs. John Senkarik
1950—52 Mrs. Wm. Hofman	1958—62 Mrs. Esther Fischer
1952—54 Mrs. Otis Lundquist	1962— Mrs. Ted Berk
1954—56 Mrs. Esther Fischer	

Gulf States

1949—52 Mrs. A. B. Thomas	1960—64 Mrs. Wm. Kennell
1952—54 Mrs. Henry G. Miller	1964— Mrs. George Engel
1954—60 Mrs. Franz Schenk	

Idaho

1948—50 Mrs. A. F. Beawer

Indiana

1964—66 Mrs. Herman Krueckeberg	1966— Mrs. Chester Norton

Iowa East

1942—46 Mrs. Walter Widmann	1954—58 Mrs. Elmer Tiedemann
1946—48 Mrs. Carl Conway	1958—62 Mrs. Ed. Guetzko
1948—50 Mrs. R. C. Gerlach	1962—66 Mrs. Harold Affeldt
1950—54 Mrs. Arthur Tibben	1966— Mrs. Verle Francik

Iowa West

1946—50 Mrs. Earl Schoenrock	1962—66 Mrs. Waldemar Fegebank
1950—54 Mrs. Ralph Krenzin	1966— Mrs. Alfred Sump
1954—58 Mrs. Albert J. Roepe	
1958—62 Mrs. L. M. Patterson	

Kansas

1943—46	Mrs. C. A. Hass	1952—54	Mrs. Verle Bowers
1946—48	Mrs. L. H. Mehl	1954—60	Mrs. F. A. Eggert
1948—50	Mrs. Ray Boger	1960—64	Mrs. William Noller
1950—52	Mrs. Henry Buck	1964—	Mrs. Raymond Briggeman

Laurentian

1951—54	Mrs. Herbert Zadow	1960—64	Mrs. John Korcok
1954—56	Mrs. Chas. Kritsch	1964—Nov.	Miss Ida Mau
1956—60	Mrs. E. H. Polster	1964—	Mrs. Gerald Marion

Louisiana

1950—52	Mrs. Wm. Borcherding	1960—64	Miss Hazel G. Gadmer
1952—56	Miss Norma Stoll	1964—	Mrs. Edmond B. Burns
1956—60	Mrs. Frank Kothe		

Manitoba and Saskatchewan

1953—56	Mrs. V. Hergesheimer	1960—64	Mrs. D. C. Appelt
1956—60	Mrs. John McHugh	1964—	Mrs. Marvin Naber

Michigan

1944—48	Mrs. Louis Schwinger	1956—60	Mrs. Harold J. Rammler
1948—49	Mrs. Victor Felten	1960—64	Mrs. E. F. Wiese
1949—52	Mrs. J. H. Rieck	1964—	Mrs. Walter Gienapp
1952—56	Mrs. Richard Deierlein		

Minnesota

1944—46	Mrs. J. H. Deckman	1952—56	Mrs. Albert Plagens
1946—50	Mrs. L. G. Gallman	1956—60	Miss Della Wolf
1950—52	Mrs. E. A. Dicke	1960—64	Mrs. Wm. Buege
1952—	Mrs. H. H. Mesenbring (acting)		

Minnnesota North

1964—   Mrs. Edgar Bode

Minnesota South

1964—   Mrs. Wm. Morris

Montana

1942—44	Mrs. Wm. Bethke	1956—60	Mrs. Leo Konopatzke
1944—46	Mrs. V. J. Schultz	1960—62	Mrs. Ray Blohm
1946—48	Mrs. Richard Brandt	1962—66	Mrs. Gladys Wohler
1948—52	Mrs. R. E. Gumpf	1966—	Mrs. George Rummel
1952—56	Mrs. Frank Lewis		

North Dakota

1942—46	Mrs. A. G. Kellam	1956—60	Mrs. Fred Fiechtner
1946—50	Mrs. F. E. Brauer	1960—64	Mrs. J. H. Ruettell
1950—52	Mrs. H. J. Eininger	1964—	Mrs. C. R. Montz
1952—56	Mrs. H. H. Weiss		

North Wisconsin

1944—46	Mrs. Conrad Teschke	1958—62	Mrs. Robert Kroenke
1946—50	Mrs. Lloyd Goetz	1962—66	Mrs. Arnold Schoepke
1950—52	Mrs. Robert Rossow	1966—	Mrs. Raymond J.
1952—56	Mrs. Fred Goetz		Schmidt
1956—58	Mrs. T. H. Hartman		

Northern Illinois

1942—44	Mrs. E. T. Schumm	1954—58	Mrs. Bernard Klemm
1944—48	Mrs. Arthur Preisinger	1958—62	Mrs. T. H. Barkow
1948—50	Mrs. E. H. Ruprecht	1962—66	Mrs. F. Arthur Karst
1950—54	Mrs. Albert Maurer	1966—	Mrs. E. W. Parlee

Northern Nebraska

1942—46	Mrs. Theo. Mueller	1958—62	Mrs. Henry
1946—50	Mrs. A. H. Guettler		Tuchenhagen
1950—54	Miss Ruth Ebmeier	1962—66	Mrs. Warren Raabe
1954—58	Mrs. C. B. Drake	1966—	Mrs. Harold Rabbass

Northwest

1952—54	Mrs. Wm. H. Fischer	1954—56	Mrs. Gerhard Molden

Ohio

1964—	Mrs. Ross Barnes

Oklahoma

1942—44	Mrs. E. T. Schmidtke	1954—56	Mrs. Homer Benkendorf
1944—46	Mrs. A. J. Brase	1956—60	Mrs. H. E. Kehr
1946—48	Mrs. C. W. Luekens	1960—64	Miss Jaunita Weber
1948—52	Mrs. Miles Klima	1964—	Mrs. L. E. Henkel
1952—54	Mrs. H. O. Lockensgard		

Ontario

1949—52	Mrs. H. J. Neeb	1960—64	Mrs. Harry Berlet
1952—56	Mrs. A. F. Pollex	1964—	Miss Edna Schierholtz
1956—60	Mrs. H. W. Mehling		

Oregon

1956—60	Mrs. Walter Kahle	1964—	Mrs. A. D. Moore
1960—64	Mrs. Richard Moeller		

Oregon-Washington

1948—50	Mrs. W. W. Buttenhoff	1950—52	Mrs. Wm. H. Fischer

Oregon-Washington-Idaho

1944—46	Mrs. George Nickels	1946—48	Mrs. W. W. Buttenhoff

South Dakota

1942—43	Mrs. A. H. Meitler	1954—56	Mrs. Ed. Proehl
1943—44	Mrs. A. L. Ellwein	1956—60	Mrs. L. B. Mueller
1944—48	Mrs. J. H. Jungemann	1960—62	Mrs. Ed. Dite
1948—52	Mrs. A. L. Ellwein	1962—66	Mrs. C. F. Schmidt
1952—54	Mrs. Victor Hammer	1966—	Mrs. Josephine Carman

South Wisconsin

1946—47	Mrs. E. W. Schultz	1956—60	Mrs. Albert F.
1947—50	Mrs. E. W. Kienow		Schroeder
1950—56	Mrs. H. L. Stone	1960—64	Mrs. Carl J. Erdmann
		1964—	Miss Esther Schoessow

Southeastern (Carolinas and Georgia)

1938—	Mrs. L. B. Buchheimer	1948—50	Mrs. Howard Davis
1938—39	Mrs. F. A. Freed	1950—52	Mrs. Wm. von
1939—41	Mrs. C. O. Smith		Spreckelsen
1941—43	Mrs. F. A. Freed	1952—54	Mrs. James L. Summers
1943—45	Mrs. Vernon Eckerd	1954—55	Mrs. Martin Rupprecht
1945—48	Mrs. George P. Smith	1955—58	Mrs. Howard Davis

Southeastern (Northern Branch)

1942—44	Mrs. Theo. W.	1946—50	Mrs. Theodore Ernst
	Kaltenkamp	1950—52	Mrs. Eric Johanson
1944—46	Mrs. F. A. Freed		

Southern

1944—46	Mrs. Merrill Gerstner	1948—50	Mrs. Wm. Borcherding
1946—48	Mrs. Henry G. Miller		

Southern California

1946—50	Mrs. T. H. Joeckel	1956—60	Mrs. Walter J.
1950—52	Mrs. Arthur Holmberg		Rosenbrock
1952—56	Mrs. George E. Theiss	1960—64	Mrs. Samuel W. Turner
		1964—	Mrs. Richard S. Kelly

Southern Illinois

1943—46	Mrs. A. W. Saxenmeyer	1958—62	Mrs. Edward F.
1946—50	Mrs. Wm. C. Boese		Schoenleber
1950—54	Mrs. Martin Simon	1962—66	Mrs. Edmond Eden
1954—58	Mrs. Fred Droste	1966—	Mrs. O. L. Donner

Southern Nebraska

1942—44	Mrs. M. C. Duensing	1952—56	Mrs. Herbert Oberle
1944—48	Mrs. L. Lentz	1956—60	Mrs. H. E. Lammel
1948—52	Mrs. Raymond	1960—64	Mrs. Rudy Munderloh
	Roehrkasse	1964—	Mrs. Edwin Hahn

Texas

1942—43	Mrs. A. E. Bruns	1952—56	Mrs. W. B. Oswald
1943—45	Mrs. Walter E. Dorre	1956—Dec.	Mrs. Walter Wilkinson
1945—46	Miss Toni Kraatz	1956—58	Mrs. Leroy Tschatschula
1946—48	Mrs. E. C. Kobs	1958—60	Mrs. E. A. Kramer
1948—50	Mrs. A. O. Rast	1960—64	Mrs. J. M. Garrett
1950—52	Mrs. Carl Blasig	1964—	Mrs. Walter Kaltwasser

Utah-Idaho

1950—54 Mrs. Walter Conrad	1962—66 Mrs. H. W. Kammerlohr
1954—58 Mrs. Arthur Kaster	1966— Mrs. Louis Reinke
1958—62 Mrs. Herbert Zafft	

Washington

1956—58 Mrs. Gerhard Molden	1962—66 Mrs. Victor Rengstorf
1958—62 Mrs. Warren P. Hartman	1966— Mrs. Norval Roberts

Western

1932—40 Mrs. Otto F. Schmitt	1954—58 Mrs. Arthur H. Prueter
1940—46 Mrs. Henry L. Schulz	1958—62 Mrs. Paul Walkenhorst
1946—48 Mrs. Paul Streufert	1962—66 Mrs. Albert Schulz
1948—52 Mrs. Oscar Brauer	1966— Mrs. Frank Ritzen
1952—54 Mrs. Richard Delventhal	

MISSION PROJECTS

International Projects

All international projects are supported by 25 percent of District mite-box funds, special mission gifts, and convention offerings. Projects are selected by delegate vote in international conventions. These are:

1943—45	Christ Church for Deaf, Cleveland, Ohio		$	15,000.00
1945—49	To Orphans and Orphanages in Europe			
	For Religious Literature	$10,000.00		
	For Equipment	50,000.00		
	For Special Needs	13,262.33		
				73,262.33
1947—49	Santa Cruz, Monterrey, Mexico			30,000.00
1949—51	Lutheran Center, Tokyo, Japan	$35,000.00		
	Our Redeemer, Honolulu, Hawaii	30,000.00		
				65,000.00
1951—53	Bethesda Hospital, Ambur, India	$70,000.00		
	True Light Chinese Church, New York City	75,000.00		
				145,000.00
1953—55	Missionary Retreat Homes			
	Japan	$15,000.00		
	Philippines	15,000.00		
	S. America			
	Argentina		$10,000	
	Brazil		20,000*	
			30,000.00	

	La Santa Cruz, "Little Mexico," Los Angeles, Calif.	60,000.00	
	Deaconess Chapter House, Valparaiso, Ind.	60,000.00	
			180,000.00
1956—57	University Chapel and Student Center, Toronto, Ont., Canada	$70,000.00	
	School, Zacapa, Guatemala	5,000.00	
	Chapel, Parsonage, School, Viña del Mar, Chile	20,000.00	
	Redeemer, Havana, Cuba	50,000.00	
			145,000.00
1957—59	Highland School, New Guinea	$60,000.00	
	Rosa Young Dormitory for Girls, Selma, Ala.	85,000.00	
	Africa Project †		
	Bible Institutes, Ogoja	25,000.00	
	Chapels, Ogoja Province	15,000.00	
	Chapel, Hospital, Eket	15,000.00	
			200,000.00
1959—61	High School, Hanno, Japan	$60,000.00	
	Seminary, Philippines	80,000.00	
	Coeducational High School, Administration Bldg., Dormitory, Teofilo Otoni, Brazil	75,000.00	
			215,000.00
1961	* Reallocated ($20,000, Brazil) to Educational Buildings, Taiwan, as Olive Gruen Memorial		
1961—63	Medical Missions — Hospitals		
	Wandoor, India	$58,000.00	
	Yahe, Ogoja, Nigeria	14,000.00	
	Chapels, Ghana, Africa	20,000.00	
	Radio Transceivers, New Guinea	10,800.00	

Literature for Missions

India, Literature	$ 9,238.00	
India, Printing Press	15,600.00	
Ceylon, Sermonets	3,000.00	
Ceylon, 900,000 Tracts in Singalese	3,888.00	
Central America, Offset Press, VariTyper, Rent, and Help	9,290.00	
Concordia Tract Mission for Printing of Sunday School Pictures, Philippines and Hong Kong	6,890.00	
England, Six Tracts	420.00	

Japan, 3,000 each of Four Pamphlets	2,055.00		
Korea, Literature	7,169.00		
Korea, Braille Magazine	2,000.00		
Middle East Library — Set of Luther	750.00		
Nigeria, Luther Sets in Four Libraries	1,200.00		
Finnish Literature	2,500.00		
John of Beverley Work-book for Deaf	4,000.00		
New Guinea, Sunday School Leaflet Pictures for Old and New Testament for Bible History in Pidgin English	2,000.00		
		70,000.00	
Church Site, Montreal, Que., Can.		67,200.00	
			240,000.00

1963—65	Rural Chapels, Alabama	$75,000.00	
	Wandoor, India, Hospital, Third Unit	40,000	
	India, Chapels	25,000.00	
	Missionaries' Furlough Home, St. Louis	125,000.00	
			265,000.00

1965—67	Jeeps, Brazil	$30,000.00	
	Modern III Girls School, Nung Udoe, Nigeria	35,000.00	
	Medical Equipment, Yahe, Nigeria, Hospital	30,000.00	
	Nigeria Linguistic Center, Enugu, Nigeria — Wycliffe Bible Translators	100,000.00	
	Messengers of Christ, Recruitment for Linguistic Training	10,000.00	
	Leprosy Treatment at Hospitals, India, Nigeria, New Guinea	85,000.00	
			290,000.00

1943—67	Total Mission Grants, International	$1,863,262.33

1966 † ELM House (Boarding Home for Missionaries' Children), Jos, Nigeria, Bought with $22,400. Balance of 1957—59 Africa Project

DISTRICT PROJECTS

District grants are made to home missions, foreign missions, scholarships, or any other missionary cause from special gifts for missions in addition to the 75 percent of mite-box offerings retained by the District after 25 percent has been remitted to the international treasury. Following is an account of completed District projects since organization of the LWML Districts:

ALBERTA AND BRITISH COLUMBIA DISTRICT

1952—54	Furnishings, Bethlehem, Edmonton, Alta.	$ 1,100.00
1954—56	Zion, Rimbey, Alta.	851.00
	Trinity, Lulu Island, B. C.	851.00
1956—58	Mission, Hinton, Alta.	1,588.10
1958—60	Church Furnishings, Dawson Creek, B. C.	2,039.11
1960—62	Prince of Peace, Chinese, Vancouver, B. C.	1,774.82
	Chapel and Center for Deaf, Edmonton, Alta.	1,774.82
1962—64	Furnishings, Chapel and Center for Deaf, Edmonton, Alta.	1,907.06
	Lutheran School Association, Edmonton, Alta.	1,907.06
1964—66	Concordia College Ministerial Student Assistance Fund	1,800.00
	Site Purchase, Trinity Church for Deaf, Vancouver, B. C.	2,000.00
1966—68	Tuition for Two Chinese Medical Mission Students	1,000.00
	Concordia College Ministerial Student Assistance Fund	800.00
	Furnishings, Trinity Church for Deaf, Vancouver, B. C.	2,000.00
	Tape Recording Equipment for Courtenay, Campbell River Area, B. C.	500.00

Total **$21,892.97**

ATLANTIC DISTRICT

1943	Chapel and Lounge Furnishings, Lutheran Service Center, N. Y. C.	$ 1,195.00
1944	Army and Navy Service Center	5,228.00
1945	True Light Chinese Mission, N. Y. C.	2,530.00
	Trailer for Mission Work in New England States	2,530.00
1946	True Light Chinese Mission, N. Y. C.	2,784.00
	Trailer Mission	2,784.00
	European Relief (50% of Mite-Box Offerings)	5,741.00
1947	Chapel for Deaf, Jackson Heights, N. Y.	4,229.00
	War Orphans and European Relief	1,973.00
1948	Deaf Mission, Jackson Heights, N. Y.	3,800.00
	War Orphans and European Relief	2,332.00
	True Light Chinese Mission, N. Y. C.	636.00
1949	True Light Chinese Mission, N. Y. C.	605.00
	War Orphans	120.00
	1948 Projects	1,871.00
1950	True Light Chinese Mission, N. Y. C.	5,354.00
	War Orphans and European Relief	361.00
1951	True Light Chinese Mission, N. Y. C.	1,092.00
	Friends of the Deaf, Mill Neck Manor, N. Y.	5,354.00
	Deaconess Work at Valparaiso (Ind.) U.	1,000.00
1952	Friends of the Deaf, Mill Neck Manor, N. Y.	6,930.00
1953	Friends of the Deaf, Mill Neck Manor, N. Y.	7,747.00
1954	Friends of the Deaf, Mill Neck Manor, N. Y.	7,035.00
	American Lutheran Publicity Bureau	1,000.00

1955	Friends of the Deaf, Mill Neck Manor, N. Y.	8,482.00
	Works of Mercy, Boston, Mass.	1,000.00
1956	Wartburg Home for Aged, Brooklyn, N. Y.	5,495.00
	Trinity, Locust Manor, N. Y.	3,665.00
1957	Chapel, Hanover, N. H.	6,008.00
	St. Matthew's for Deaf, Newark, N. J.	6,008.00
1958	St. Matthew's for Deaf, Newark, N. J.	5,822.00
	American Lutheran Publicity Bureau	5,822.00
1959	Student Chapel, Bethany, Troy, N. Y.	6,240.00
	Lutheran Braille Workers	6,240.00
1960	Works of Mercy, West Roxbury, Mass.	6,881.32
	Redeemer, Plattsburgh, N. Y.	6,881.32
1961	Trinity, 9th St., N. Y. C.	7,272.04
	U. of Conn. Chapel, Storrs, Conn.	7,272.04
1962	Publication of Second Series, John of Beverley Workbooks for Deaf	7,984.09
	St. Mark's, Brooklyn, N. Y.	7,984.09
1963	Chapel, U. of Mass., Amherst, Mass.	8,078.70
	Scholarships, Medical Missions (India)	8,078.70
1964	Visual and Audiovisual Materials for Work Among Deaf in New England	9,254.29
	Lutheran Exhibit, New York World's Fair	9,254.29
1965	Spanish Mission Work, Atlantic District	7,939.38
	New Guinea Medical Missions	7,939.38
1966	Prince of Peace Volunteers, Atlantic District	8,616.75
	Spanish Mission Work, Atlantic District	8,616.75
1967	Lutheran Braille Workers, Inc.	*6,323.84
	Brownsville Mission, Brooklyn, N. Y.	*6,323.84

Total   **$253,713.82**

* To Jan. 31, 1967

CALIFORNIA AND NEVADA DISTRICT

1944	California Concordia College	$ 514.41
1945	Chapel for Deaf, Oakland, Calif.	1,000.00
1946	Chinese Mission, Bay Area	151.23
1947	Negro Mission, San Francisco	500.00
	Lutheran Deaconess Association	187.05
1948	Negro Mission, San Francisco	1,000.00
1949	Town and Country, Sacramento	1,000.00
	California Concordia College	110.00
1950	Japanese Missionary in Chinatown Mission	1,000.00
	California Concordia College	500.00
1951	Japanese Missions	1,191.23
	California Concordia College	1,145.61
1952	Good Shepherd Home of the West	1,310.37
	California Concordia College	1,014.10
1953	Grace, Crescent City	575.51
	Our Savior, Livermore	575.51
	Hawthorne-Babbitt, Nev., Mission	575.51
	California Concordia College	1,051.21
1954	Our Savior, Henderson, Nev.	553.51
	Our Savior, Quincy	553.28
	San Francisco Colored Mission	553.28

	California Concordia College	976.00
1955	Hong Kong	1,675.57
	California Concordia College	981.00
1956	New Guinea School	1,762.00
	California Concordia College	916.44
1957	Pastor and Teacher Scholarships	4,248.06
	California Concordia College	950.63
1958	Philippine Medical Missions	3,488.01
	California Concordia College	954.88
1959—60	Student Room, Davis Church	1,753.59
	Young Sik Chweh, Scholarship	1,500.00
1960—61	Lutheran Braille Workers	4,097.55
1961—62	Mission Worker, Weaverville-Lewiston-Hawford Area	6,070.27
1962—63	Grant-in-Aid Program, California Concordia College	1,200.00
	Chaplain's Assistant, Good Shepherd Home	1,300.00
	Chapel, Good Shepherd Home	3,910.47
1963—64	Worker, San Francisco Chinatown	4,200.00
	District Church Extension Fund	2,756.34
1964—65	Clinical Training for Institutional Chaplain	5,000.00
	Library Fund, Chinatown, San Francisco	1,000.00
	Chapel of the Lambs, Good Shepherd Home	2,614.17
	Scholarship Aid Fund	3,000.00
	Negro Pastor for East Bay	6,573.82
1966—67	Grant-in-Aid, California Concordia College	4,000.00
	Scholarship Aid Fund	3,000.00
	Lutheran Braille Workshop	3,000.00
	Sight Saver Type Literature	500.00

Total   **$86,490.61**

CAROLINA DISTRICT

Formerly Southeastern (Carolinas and Georgia)

1960	Calvary, Charleston, S. C.	$ 1,500.00
	District Scholarships for Girls	500.00
1961	Scholarships — Five at $200 Each	1,000.00
	District Mission Congregations	1,000.00
1962	Scholarships — Five at $200 Each	1,000.00
	St. Luke, High Point, N. C.	1,000.00
1962—64	District Scholarships	2,000.00
	Mission Congregations — Buildings or Equipment	3,000.00
1964—66	District Scholarships	800.00
	Prince of Peace, Charlotte, N. C.	1,000.00
	St. James, Southern Pines, N. C.	2,000.00
1966—68	St. Paul, Gastonia, N. C.	1,000.00
	Lamb of God, Spartanburg, S. C.	1,000.00
1942—66	Annual Preconfirmation Camp at Linn-Haven	14,400.00
1960—66	"Mission of the Quarter" Gifts for Needy Congregations	6,262.81

Total   **$37,462.81**

CENTRAL DISTRICT

1943	Valley, Chagrin Falls, Ohio	$ 5,000.00
	Our Savior, Canton, Ohio	4,000.00

1946	Trinity, Warren, Ohio	5,000.00
	Immanuel, Brunswick, Gary, Ind.	3,500.00
	Redeemer, East Gary, Ind.	3,500.00
1948—49	St. Paul, Parkersburg, W. Va.	5,000.00
	Good Shepherd, Gary, Ind.	4,000.00
	Negro Mission, Louisville, Ky.	5,000.00
	Bethlehem, Parma, Ohio	2,000.00
	Our Savior, St. Matthews (Louisville), Ky.	5,000.00
	Negro Mission, Youngstown, Ohio	2,000.00
	Our Savior, Indianapolis, Ind.	3,500.00
	Emmanuel, Leesville, Ind.	3,000.00
	Peace, Youngstown, Ohio	2,000.00
	St. Luke, Winamac, Ind.	5,000.00
1950	Bethany, Connersville, Ind.	7,000.00
	Redeemer, Youngstown, Ohio (Wickliffe)	3,000.00
1951	Good Shepherd, Brooklyn Village (Cleveland)	5,000.00
	Trinity Memorial, Independence Hill, Ind.	4,000.00
	St. Philip's, Toledo, Ohio	3,000.00
	Worthington, Worthington, Ohio	5,000.00
	Immanuel, Gary, Ind.	3,500.00
1952	Hope, Cedar Lake, Ind.	2,500.00
	Our Savior, Mayfield Heights, Ohio	5,000.00
	Emmanuel, Tell City, Ind.	2,500.00
	Calvary, Bedford, Ind.	2,500.00
	Good Shepherd, Fort Wayne, Ind.	3,500.00
	Gloria Dei, Toledo, Ohio	5,000.00
	Our Savior, Gary, Ind.	5,000.00
	St. James, Marion, Ind.	5,000.00
	Christ, Indianapolis, Ind.	4,000.00
1954	Christ, Mantua, Ohio	5,000.00
	Good Shepherd, Evansville, Ind.	5,000.00
	Our Redeemer, Huntington, W. Va.	7,000.00
	Hope, Akron, Ohio	5,000.00
1955	Zion (Mount Washington), Cincinnati, Ohio	6,000.00
	St. Luke, Rensselaer, Ind.	5,000.00
	Mount Calvary, Dayton, Ohio	5,000.00
1956	Holy Trinity, Greensburg, Ind.	3,000.00
	Redeemer, Highland, Ind.	5,000.00
	Tarrytown Mission, Gary, Ind.	5,000.00
	St. Luke, Plainfield, Ind.	5,000.00
	Redeemer, South Charleston, Ohio	7,000.00
	Faith, Louisville, Ky.	7,000.00
	Grace, Columbus, Ind.	5,000.00
1958	Christ (Groesbeck), Cincinnati, Ohio	5,000.00
	Bethlehem, Fairborn, Ohio	4,000.00
	Concordia, Columbus, Ohio	4,000.00
	Our Savior, Monticello, Ind.	2,000.00
	Trinity, Grafton, Ohio	4,000.00
	Concordia, Greenwood, Ind.	2,000.00
	Emmanuel, Lawrence, Ind.	4,000.00
	Royal Redeemer, North Royalton, Ohio	4,000.00
	Faith, De Motte, Ind.	2,000.00
1959	St. Mark, Brunswick, Ohio	5,000.00
	St. John, Lexington, Ky.	5,000.00

	Faith, Swanton, Ohio	2,000.00
	Redeemer, West Lafayette, Ind.	4,000.00
	Peace, Greencastle, Ind.	2,000.00
1960	Calvary, Jeffersonville, Ind.	5,000.00
	Gethsemane, Fort Wayne, Ind.	5,000.00
	Holy Cross, Crawfordsville, Ind.	6,500.00
	Our Redeemer, Solon, Ohio	6,000.00
	St. Mark, Milford, Ohio	5,000.00
	St. Mark, Shelbyville, Ind.	6,000.00
	Tallmadge, Tallmadge, Ohio	6,000.00
	Victory, Youngstown, Ohio	5,000.00
	Zion, Columbia City, Ind.	5,000.00
1962	Bethany, Columbus, Ohio	4,000.00
	Concordia, Findlay, Ohio	4,000.00
	Concordia, Wooster, Ohio	4,000.00
	Faith, Greenfield, Ind.	3,000.00
	Faith, Madison, Ind.	2,000.00
	Good Shepherd, Mentor, Ohio	3,500.00
	Grace, Dyer, Ind.	4,000.00
	Hilltop, South Bend, Ind.	4,000.00
	Holy Cross, Portage, Ind.	4,000.00
	Student Center Chapel, Bowling Green, Ohio	3,000.00
	Messiah, Cincinnati, Ohio	4,000.00
	Messiah, Indianapolis, Ind.	4,000.00
	Peace, Chardon, Ohio	5,000.00
	Prince of Peace, Oregon, Ohio	4,000.00
1943—62	Ten $500 Gifts to American Bible Society	5,000.00

Total **$354,000.00**

CENTRAL ILLINOIS DISTRICT

1947	Brush College Chapel, Decatur	$ 5,000.00
1948	Our Savior, Lawrenceville	5,000.00
1949	Mount Calvary, Galesburg	500.00
	Christ for Deaf, Jacksonville	10,000.00
1950	Good Shepherd, Hoopeston	6,000.00
1951	Trinity, Casey	6,000.00
1952	Christ for Deaf, Jacksonville	2,000.00
	Holy Cross, Moline	5,000.00
1953	Student Chapel, Champaign	14,155.95
1954	Christ for Deaf, Jacksonville	3,760.47
	Redeemer, Peoria	5,000.00
	Portable Chapel, Urbana	7,000.00
1955	Christ for Deaf, Jacksonville	4,500.00
	Grace, Marquette Heights, Pekin	4,500.00
1956	Concordia, Springfield	6,406.25
	Mount Calvary, Decatur	6,406.25
1957	Immanuel, Macomb	6,047.50
	Trinity, Urbana	6,047.49
1958	Concordia, Marshall	6,190.85
	Christ, Delavan	6,190.85
1959	Christ, Clinton	6,322.16
	Grace, Marquette Heights, Pekin	6,322.17
1960	St. Paul's, Pittsfield	6,673.04

	Immanuel, Charleston	6,673.04
1961	Mount Calvary, Galesburg	6,922.91
1961	Our Savior, Springfield	6,922.91
1962	St. Matthew, Milan	7,100.21
	Immanuel, Peoria	7,100.20
1963	Trinity, Manito	7,228.21
	Addition to Student Chapel, Champaign	7,228.21
1964	Medical Mission Supplies	7,409.90
1964	Good Shepherd, Rochester	7,409.89
1965	Bethesda Home, Watertown, Wis.	7,834.22
1965	District Scholarship Fund	7,834.22
1966	St. John's, Rushville	3,141.45
	First, Mount Sterling	4,712.17
	Medical Mission Scholarship Fund	7,855.61

Total $230,396.13

CHESAPEAKE DISTRICT

1943	Communion Service, Mission in Baltimore, Md.	$ 50.00
1944	Bibles, Service Center, Washington, D. C.	17.50
	Dr. W. A. Maier, 13th Anniversary of Lutheran Hour	100.00
1945	Office Equipment, St. Matthew's Negro Mission, Baltimore, Md.	100.00
	Organ Fund, Redeemer, Portsmouth, Va.	300.00
	Communion Set, Towson Mission, Baltimore	100.00
1946	District Trailer Mission	250.00
	War Relief	644.51
	Lectern, Concordia, Wilmington, Del.	237.50
	School Expansion, Immanuel, Alexandria, Va.	500.00
1947	Altar, First, Towson, Md.	275.00
1948	Chapel, Bethany, Salisbury, Md.	3,000.00
	Southeastern District Church Extension Fund	3,000.00
	Sound Projector, Pilgrim, Westgate, Md.	200.00
1949	Pulpit, Pilgrim, Baltimore, Md.	225.00
1950	Altar, Bethlehem, Washington, D. C.	300.00
1951	Pulpit, Redeemer, Richmond, Va.	250.00
1952	Holy Cross, Baltimore, Md.	1,000.00
	Collins Park Mission, Wilmington, Del.	1,000.00
	St. Andrew, Glenmont, Md.	1,000.00
	Pulpit, Holy Cross, Baltimore, Md.	300.00
	Missions in Japan, Rev. Danker	100.00
	Altar Brasses, District Missions	50.00
	Candlestick and Cross, Greenbelt, Greenbelt, Md.	95.00
1953	Trinity, Chestertown, Md.	1,000.00
	Road Markers — Trinity, Chestertown, Md.; Redeemer, Richmond, Va.; First, Towson, Md.	205.50
	Streufert Memorial Fund, Church Ext. Fund of Synod	250.00
1954	Negro Mission, N. E. Washington, D. C.	1,000.00
	Altar, St. Andrew, Glenmont, Md.	300.00
	Christ, Norfolk, Va.	1,500.00
	Chancel Furnishings, St. Paul, Falls Church, Va.	300.00
1955	Christ, Norfolk, Va.	1,500.00
	Faith, Norfolk, Va.	1,500.00

	St. Paul, Annapolis, Md.	1,500.00
	Pulpit, St. Paul, Falls Church, Va.	300.00
	Chancel Furnishings, Trinity, Chestertown, Md.	300.00
1956	Trinity, Lexington Park, Md.	1,500.00
	Bethany, Groveton, Va.	1,500.00
	Oxon Hill, Oxon Hill, Md.	1,500.00
	Chancel Furnishings, Faith, Collins Park, Del.	300.00
1957	Christ, Seaford, Del.	3,000.00
	Furnishings, Resurrection, Warwick, Va.	300.00
	Furnishings, First, Odenton, Md.	443.79
1958	St. John's, Franconia, Va.	2,500.00
	Trinity, Richmond, Va.	2,500.00
1959	Resurrection, Warwick, Va.	3,500.00
	Resurrection, Baltimore, Md.	1,800.00
1960	Peace, Washington, D. C.	3,000.00
	Holy Cross, Greenbelt, Md.	3,000.00
1961	Cross, Rockville, Md.	2,500.00
	Concordia, Triangle, Va.	2,500.00
	Prince of Peace, London Bridge, Va.	300.00
	Our Savior, Lynchburg, Va.	250.00
1962	Holy Cross, Ashland, Va.	2,500.00
	Grace, Woodbridge, Va.	2,500.00
	Rev. Eissfeldt, Missionary-at-Large, Richmond, Va.	500.00
	Communion Ware to Be Loaned to Missions	500.00
1963	Resurrection, Richmond, Va.	500.00
	Faith, Norfolk, Va.	500.00
	Galilee, Stevensville, Md.	500.00
	Prince of Peace, Springfield, Va.	2,500.00
1964—66	Scholarship Fund	4,000.00
	Young Sik Chweh, Scholarship Fund	300.00
	Inner-City Project, Washington, D. C.	2,000.00
	Mission, Chesapeake, Va.	2,000.00
	Good Shepherd, Sandy Spring, Md.	2,000.00
	Grace, La Plata, Md.	2,000.00
	St. Timothy, Wilmington, Del.	200.00
	Good Shepherd, Roanoke, Va.	140.00
1966—68	Scholarship Fund	4,000.00
	Inner-City Project, Baltimore, Md.	2,000.00
	Inner-City Project, Norfolk, Va.	5,000.00
	Grace, Chester, Va.	3,000.00
	Sue Harris, Wycliffe Translator	500.00
	Peace, King George Courthouse, Va.	500.00

	Total	**$90,783.80**

COLORADO DISTRICT

1944—53	District Mission Congregations	$10,376.48
1952—53	Denver Bible Quiz (Radio Program)	2,367.18
	Silver Anniversary Thankoffering	100.00
	European Relief; Orphans- and Child-Feeding Program	1,750.00
1953—57	District Mission Congregations	11,345.00
1956—57	Dakota Boys Ranch, Minot, N. Dak.	100.00
	Drying Room for Hospital, Nigeria, Africa	1,000.00
1957—59	District Mission Congregations	6,867.78

1958—59	Porto Alegre, Brazil	500.00
	Deaconess Scholarship	500.00
1959—60	District Mission Congregations	3,750.00
	Deaconess Scholarship	175.00
1960—61	Deaconess Scholarship	175.00
	Vacation House, New Guinea	1,145.81
	Student Lounge, Trinity, Alamosa, Colo.	1,000.00
1961—62	U. of Colorado Student Chapel, Boulder, Colo.	1,000.00
	Bethel Chapel for Deaf, Colorado Springs, Colo.	1,300.00
	Deaconess Scholarship Fund	175.00
1962—63	Deaconess Scholarship Fund	300.00
	Mobile Trailer Chapel for District	1,500.00
1963—64	Deaconess Scholarship Fund	300.00
	Mobile Trailer Chapel for District	6,300.00
1964—66	Deaconess Scholarship Fund	600.00
	Well, Eket, Nigeria	1,500.00
	Ambulance, Ambur, India	2,038.00
	Jeep for New Guinea	953.00
	Chapel Fund, Middle America	1,000.00
	Ambassadors for Christ, Colorado District	2,000.00
1966—68	Deaconess Scholarship Fund	600.00
	Ambassadors for Christ, Colorado District	2,000.00
	Mission Work in El Paso-Juarez area	2,400.00
	District Scholarship Fund	2,000.00
	Church Site, Caracas, Venezuela	3,000.00
	Messengers of Christ	600.00
1960—67	District Mission Congregations	18,250.00

Total **$88,968.25**

EASTERN DISTRICT

1946—48	Literature for Trailer Mission	$ 300.00
	Chapel Furnishings, St. John, Emporium, Pa.	1,500.00
1948—50	Chapel Furnishings, Redeemer, Oneida, N. Y.	2,000.00
	Chapel Furnishings, St. Mark, Ridley Park, Pa.	2,000.00
1950—52	School, Faith, Pittsburgh, Pa.	3,000.00
	Visual Aid Equipment for the Deaf	1,000.00
	Deaconess Grant	500.00
1952—54	Chapel Furnishings, Faith, Easton, Pa.	3,500.00
	Chapel Furnishings, Holy Cross, Philadelphia, Pa.	3,500.00
1954—56	Chapel Furnishings, Hope, Levittown, Pa.	5,000.00
	Chapel Furnishings, Ascension, Allison Park, Pa.	4,000.00
1956—58	Chapel Furnishings, Concordia, Jamestown, N. Y.	4,000.00
	Chapel Furnishings, Calvary, Murrysville, Pa.	4,000.00
	Chapel Furnishings, Grace, Vestal, N. Y.	4,000.00
1958—60	Chapel Furnishings, Pinnacle, Rochester, N. Y.	4,000.00
	Chapel Furnishings, Redeemer, Auburn, N. Y	4,000.00
	Lighting Equipment, Alpha (Deaf), Rochester, N. Y.	2,000.00
1960—62	Holy Cross, Clarence, N. Y.	5,000.00
	Christ Memorial, Paoli, Pa.	5,000.00
	Faith, Penfield, N. Y.	5,000.00
1962—64	Mount Olive, Beaver Falls, Pa.	4,000.00
	Zion, Circleville, Pa.	4,000.00

	Trinity, Ithaca, N. Y.		4,000.00
	Trinity Deaf, Pittsburgh, Pa.		4,000.00
1964—66	Hope, Arcade, N. Y.		1,500.00
	Epiphany, Avon, N. Y.		3,000.00
	Good Shepherd, Canandaigua, N. Y.		3,000.00
	Mount Olive, Lockport, N. Y.		3,000.00
	St. Paul's, Somerton, Pa.		3,000.00
1966—68	Our Savior, Mount Pocono, Pa.		3,000.00
	Gloria Dei, Potsdam, N. Y.		4,000.00
	Educational Materials, St. Matthew's, Rochester, N. Y.		500.00
	God's Bank		5,000.00

Total **$105,300.00**

ENGLISH DISTRICT

1946	War Orphans	$	100.00
1947	Grace, Detroit, Mich.		500.00
	Peace, Linda Vista, Calif.		500.00
1948	Dr. Li Yen San (for Visual Education)		500.00
1949	Faith, Mount Vernon, Ill.		500.00
	Ashburn, Chicago, Ill.		500.00
	Grace, Corona, Calif.		500.00
1950	Chapel in Japan and War Orphans		150.00
	Our Savior, Royal Oak, Mich.		500.00
1951	Messiah, Princeton, N. J.		500.00
1954	South Shore, Milwaukee, Wis.		500.00
	St. Michael's, La Grange Park, Ill.		500.00
	Ascension, Birmingham, Mich.		500.00
	St. Stephen, Pittsburgh, Pa.		500.00
	Savior, Paramus, N. J.		500.00
1956	Ascension, Atlanta, Ga.		750.00
	Holy Trinity, Macon, Ga.		750.00
	St. Mark, Port Credit, Ont., Canada		750.00
	St. Matthew, Scarborough, Ont., Canada		750.00
1957	Reformation, Affton, Mo.		750.00
	St. Luke, Willowdale, Ont., Canada		750.00
1958	Fountain of Life, Tucson, Ariz.		750.00
	Mission in Montreal, Que., Canada		750.00
1959	Afton Heights Chapel, St. Paul, Minn.		1,000.00
	Good Shepherd, Toledo, Ohio		500.00
	Faith, Greenfield, Ind.		1,000.00
	Student Work (Concordia Society), Princeton, N. J.		500.00
	Student Work, Mich. St. Univ., East Lansing, Mich.		500.00
1960	Our Saviour, Niagara Falls, Ont., Canada		1,000.00
	Hope, Bridgeville, Pa.		1,000.00
	Grace, San Diego, Calif.		1,000.00
	Christ the King, Warminster, Pa.		1,000.00
	Risen Christ, Plymouth, Mich.		500.00
1962	Ascension, Tucson, Ariz.		1,500.00
	Holy Trinity, Tucson, Ariz.		1,500.00
	Ephphatha, Chicago		1,500.00
	Martin Luther Chapel, Lansing, Mich.		1,500.00
	Holy Spirit, Oakdale Heights, St. Paul, Minn.		500.00
	Prince of Peace, Menomonee Falls, Wis.		500.00

1964	Ephphatha, Chicago	6,000.00
	Scholarship Fund, Philippines	500.00
	Inner-City Missions, Detroit, Brooklyn	3,000.00
	Martin Luther Chapel, Lansing, Mich.	2,500.00
1966	French Lutheran Centre, Montreal, Que., Canada	4,000.00
	Libraries, Overseas Seminaries (5)	5,000.00
	Retreat House, Japan	3,000.00
	Student House, University of Chicago (St. Gregory of Nyssa)	3,000.00

Total   **$54,750.00**

FLORIDA-GEORGIA DISTRICT

1945	European Relief	$ 1,000.00
1946—48	Furnishings, Student Center, Tallahassee, Fla.	1,000.00
1948—50	District Student Aid Fund	500.00
	Student Center, Tallahassee, Fla.	2,500.00
1950—52	Student Center, Gainesville, Fla.	3,500.00
1952—54	Havana, Cuba — Isle of Pines Missions	5,000.00
1954—56	Furnishing Student Center, Athens, Ga.	4,000.00
1956—58	Scholarship Fund	4,000.00
	Chancel-Furnishing Fund	2,000.00
1958—59	Scholarship Fund	3,000.00
	Chancel-Furnishing Fund	1,998.68
	District Student Aid and Recruitment (Offering)	320.54
1959—60	Scholarship Fund	7,750.00
	Chancel-Furnishing Fund	3,600.00
1960—62	Scholarship Fund	9,000.00
	Chancel-Furnishing Fund	3,000.00
1962—64	Scholarship Fund	9,750.00
	Chancel-Furnishing Fund	2,200.00
	Student Center, U. of South Florida, Tampa	2,809.59
1964—66	Scholarship Fund	11,500.00
	Chancel-Furnishing Fund	1,800.00
1966—68	Scholarship Fund	14,000.00
	Chancel-Furnishing Fund	400.00
	Ambassadors for Christ	3,000.00

Total   **$97,628.81**

GULF STATES DISTRICT

1944—49	Trinity, Auburn, Ala.	$ 3,093.70
1949—50	University, Tuscaloosa, Ala.	1,696.71
1950—52	Trinity, Panama City, Fla.	1,595.90
1953—54	Trinity, Dothan, Ala.	2,107.47
1955—56	Christ, Meridian, Miss.	2,455.66
1957—59	St. John, Selma, Ala.	4,178.86
1960—62	Christ the King, Enterprise, Ala.	4,465.49
1962—64	Scholarships, District Students	2,000.00
	Christ the King, Muscle Shoals, Ala.	2,000.00
	Ascension, Marianna, Fla.	500.00
1964—66	Scholarships (Two at $500 each year)	2,000.00
	First, Florala, Ala.	500.00

U. of Ala. Student Center, Tuscaloosa, Ala.	1,500.00
Organ, West Panama Beach, Fla.	500.00
Altar Furnishings, Hymn Books, Sunday School Furniture, Holy Trinity, Mississippi City, Miss.	500.00
1966—68 3-yr. Scholarship ($2,000 and $1,000)	3,000.00
Communion Ware, Scottsboro, Ala.	250.00
Chancel Furnishings, Eternal Trinity, Milton, Fla.	500.00
Church Bus, Bethlehem, Prattville, Ala.	2,000.00
Chancel Furnishings, Grace, Pensacola, Fla.	500.00

Total **$35,343.79**

INDIANA DISTRICT

1964—66	Concordia, Greenwood, Ind.	$ 3,500.00
	Faith, Bloomington, Ind.	4,000.00
	Faith, Columbus, Ind.	4,000.00
	Messiah, Wolcottville, Ind.	4,000.00
	Peace, Indianapolis, Ind.	2,000.00
	St. Paul, East Chicago, Ind.	4,500.00
	Prince of Peace, Martinsville, Ind.	3,500.00
	American Bible Society	500.00
1966—68	Peace, Greencastle, Ind.	5,000.00
	Faith, South Bend, Ind.	6,000.00
	Our Redeemer, Lexington, Ky.	5,000.00
	Faith, Churubusco, Ind.	5,000.00
	Indiana U. Campus Ministries, Bloomington, Ind.	2,500.00
	DePauw U. Campus Ministries, Greencastle, Ind.	3,000.00
	Ball State U. Campus Ministries, Muncie, Ind.	5,000.00
	Indiana State U. Campus Ministries, Terre Haute, Ind.	4,000.00
	American Bible Society	500.00

Total **$62,000.00**

IOWA EAST DISTRICT

1942—44	Chapel, Trinity, Knoxville	$ 6,000.00
1944—50	European Relief and International Projects	
1950—52	Chapel, St. Paul's, Wapello	8,000.00
1952—54	School, St. Paul's, Evansdale	7,500.00
1954—56	Chapel, Calvary, Deep River	5,000.00
	Zion, Hiawatha	2,500.00
1956—58	Medical Mobile Unit, Ambur, India	3,000.00
	Lots, Mount Vernon-Lisbon Parish	6,000.00
	Placement of Lutheran Books in Iowa East Colleges	1,500.00
1958—60	Deaconess Scholarships	1,600.00
	Scholarship Fund for Training Pastors and Teachers in Japan, India, and Philippines	5,000.00
	Scholarship Fund for District Ministerial Students and Teachers at Synodical Schools	5,000.00
1960—62	Scholarships for Foreign Students	5,000.00
	Scholarships for District Students (Ministerial and Teacher) in Synodical Schools	5,000.00
	Deaconess Scholarships	2,400.00
	Home Finding Society, Fort Dodge	600.00

1962—64	Scholarship Training Program for Medical Doctors, Nurses, Technicians	5,000.00
	Training Workers at Eket Hospital, Nigeria, Africa	2,000.00
	Materials, Scholarships, and Salary for Work in Korea, El Salvador, Brazil, Philippines, Hong Kong, Argentina	4,000.00
	Scholarship for District Deaconess	3,000.00
1964—66	Renovation, Tokyo Lutheran Center	5,000.00
	Scholarships for Foreign Students	2,500.00
	Concordia Tract Mission	2,500.00
	Evangelistic Aids, Korea and New Guinea	4,000.00
	Deaconess Student Scholarships	3,200.00
1966—68	Scholarships for District Ministerial and Teacher Students	5,000.00
	Tracts for Missions	3,500.00
	Furnishings for Mission Houses (Furlough Homes for Missionaries), St. Louis	3,500.00
	Student Center, Iowa City	3,500.00
	Student Center, Fayette	2,000.00

	Total	**$112,800.00**

IOWA WEST DISTRICT

1946	Chaplaincy Service in Public Institutions Assistance to Trailer Missions	$ 185.00
1947	Altar for Mission, Castana	100.00
	Lutheran Service Auxiliary, Sioux City	75.00
	Cherokee Mental Institute	50.00
	Clarinda Mental Institute	50.00
	Emergency Planning Council for Orphans	100.00
	Equipment for Recreational Center, Okoboji	100.00
1948	Institutional Work, Sioux City	200.00
	Institutional Work, Cherokee	200.00
	Institutional Work, Clarinda	200.00
	Trinity, Glenwood	300.00
1950	Chapel for Deaf, Des Moines	1,000.00
	Building Fund, Lutheran Deaconess Association	1,000.00
1952	Outdoor Advertising	3,000.00
	Mt. Olive, Des Moines	2,000.00
1954	Calvary Deaf, Des Moines	4,000.00
	School of Nursing, Sioux City Lutheran Hospital	4,000.00
1956	Immanuel, Osceola	3,000.00
	Student Center, Ames	3,000.00
1958	Chancel Furnishings, Immanuel, Guthrie Center	3,000.00
	Chancel Furnishings, Peace, Des Moines	3,000.00
	Lutheran School of Nursing, Sioux City	2,500.00
	Chancel Furnishings, Faith, Sioux City	3,000.00
1960	Hope, Des Moines	5,000.00
	Faith, Early	5,000.00
	Service Project — Combined	2,500.00
	Production of Braille Literature	3,000.00
1962	District Scholarship Fund	6,000.00
	Pilot Project, Southern Iowa	5,000.00
	Clinical Training of Institutional Chaplains	5,000.00
	Home Finding Society	3,500.00

1964	Aid for Young Women Entering Kingdom Work	5,000.00
	Gloria Dei, Urbandale	6,000.00
	Dakota Boys Ranch, Minot, N. Dak.	3,500.00
	Jeeps for Brazil	2,000.00
1966	Aid for Young Men Students	5,000.00
	Bethesda Home, Watertown, Wis.	5,000.00
	Lutheran Home Finding Society	5,325.00
	St. Paul's Youth Center, Iowa City	1,775.00
	Home for Aged, Perry	800.00
	District Workshop in Special Education	700.00
	Mission, West Des Moines	1,600.00

Total **$105,760.00**

KANSAS DISTRICT

1943	Expenses of Missionaries to District Conference	$ 100.00
1944	Pilgrim Deaf, Kansas City, Mo.	260.00
	Pipe Organ Fund, Immanuel, Lawrence	900.00
1945	Church Furnishings, Messiah, Emporia	900.00
	Church Furnishings, Grace, Liberal	900.00
	Church Furnishings, Grace, McPherson	900.00
1946	Church Furnishings, Faith, Ottawa	500.00
	Church Furnishings, Grace, Lyons	500.00
	Church Furnishings, First, Phillipsburg	500.00
1947	Furnishings, Our Redeemer School, Hutchinson	900.00
	Orphans, During War Years	6,360.00
1948	Deaconess Scholarship	500.00
	Church Furnishings, Zion, Chanute	900.00
1949	Organ Fund, Redeemer, Russell	900.00
	Church Furnishings, Hope, Topeka	900.00
	Church Furnishings, Faith, Topeka	900.00
1950	Organ Fund, Our Redeemer, Kinsley	500.00
	Jeep for Japan	1,200.00
1951	Housemother's Room, St. John's College, Winfield	800.00
	Church Furnishings, Christ, Augusta	900.00
	Pews, St. Paul's, Oswego	900.00
1952	Pews, Trinity, Fort Scott	900.00
	Organ Fund, Trinity, Parsons	500.00
	Flood Relief, Grace, Strong City Church	500.00
	Pews, St. Luke's, Manhattan	900.00
1953	Organ Fund, Our Redeemer, Wichita	500.00
	Pews, Immanuel, Norton	**900.00**
	Pews, Immanuel, Oakley	**900.00**
	Organ Fund, Grace, Larned	**500.00**
	Church Furnishings, Zion, Kansas City, Kans.	**900.00**
1954	**Pews, Trinity, Burlington**	**900.00**
	Furnishings, Messiah, Hays	**900.00**
	Pews, Mount Calvary, Wamego	**900.00**
1955	**Pews, Faith, Abilene**	**900.00**
	Pews, First, Sabetha	**900.00**
	Additional Grant for Pews, Faith, Ottawa	400.00
	Pews, Trinity, Girard	900.00
1956	Pews, Grace, Iola	900.00
	Pews, Calvary, Wellington	900.00

	Organ Fund, Zion, Wichita	900.00
	Pews, Faith, Kansas City	900.00
	Organ Fund, Hope, Shawnee	900.00
1957	Organ Fund and Pews, Peace, Greensburg	900.00
	Pews, Grace, Atwood	900.00
	Pews, Bethel, Bethel	900.00
	Pews, Grace, Wichita	900.00
	Building Fund, Grace, Liberal	1,000.00
1958	Pews, Trinity, Leavenworth	900.00
	Chancel Furnishings, Faith, Derby	1,000.00
	Educational Building Fund, Bethany, Wichita	1,000.00
1959	Furnishing Room, Selma, Ala.	820.00
	New Guinea Girls' School (Day of Prayer Offering)	630.61
1961	Church Furnishings, Christ the King, Dighton	1,000.00
	Church Building, Bethel, Columbus	1,000.00
1962	Church Furnishings, Grace, Ulysses	1,000.00
	Chancel Furnishings, Ascension, Wichita	1,000.00
	Pews, Bethany, Overland Park	1,000.00
1963	Church Building, Christ, Elkhart	1,000.00
	Organ Fund, Redeemer, Olathe	1,000.00
1964	Church Building, Christ, Topeka	1,000.00
1965	Organ Fund, Christ the King, Salina	1,000.00
	Church Building, Grace, Hill City	1,000.00
1966	Church Furnishings, University Church, Kansas U.	1,000.00

Scholarships: Ministerial, Teacher, Deaconess

1957	1 Deaconess and 1 Teacher	1,200.00
1958	2 Ministerial, 2 Deaconess	3,200.00
1959	3 Ministerial, 3 Teacher	4,800.00
1960—62	13 granted	5,893.00
1962—64	12 granted	9,311.00
1964—66	16 granted	9,250.00

	Total Regular Mission Grants	**$ 91,524.61**

Day of Prayer Offerings: Allocated by Delegate Vote*

1960	World Relief	$ 710.68
1961	Chapel at Obot Idim, Nigeria	1,748.58
1962	New Guinea Missions	1,000.00
	Chapels for India	1,000.00
	Rev. D. Morthole, Philippines — Books for Training Lay Workers	161.60
1963	Seminario Concordia, Porto Alegre, Brazil	1,000.00
	Seminario Concordia, Buenos Aires, Argentina	1,000.00
	Instituto Concordia, Sao Paulo, Brazil	557.12
1964	Lutheran Social Services, Wichita — Scholarship Fund	1,000.00
	Faith, Kansas City, (Inner City)	500.00
	Synod's Dept. of Social Welfare — Inner City	500.00
	St. John's College, Development Fund	392.62
1965	Concordia Seminary, Taiwan, Student Aid	500.00
	Bible Correspondence Work in S. E. Asia	500.00

	Fukushima Orphanage, Japan	466.55
	Braille Printing Press, Korea	466.54
1966	Scholarship for Theological Student, Brazil	1,100.00
	Portals of Prayer, Sight-saving Edition	1,000.00

	Total Day of Prayer Offerings	**$ 13,603.69**

* Gifts devoted to area for which prayers were offered.

Convention Offerings: Allocated by Delegate Vote

1960	Medical Missions	$ 496.61
1962	Lutheran Social Services	521.66
1964	World Relief for Alaska Earthquake	512.42
1966	25% to International LWML	131.17
	Inner-City Mission, Wichita	393.50

	Total Convention Mission Offerings	**$ 2,055.36**

	Total Regular Mission Project Grants	$ 91,524.61
	Prayer Service Mission Grants	13,603.69
	Convention Offering Mission Grants	2,055.36

	Total	**$107,183.66**

LAURENTIAN DISTRICT

1951	Survey in Western Ottawa	$ 400.00
1952	Our Saviour, Ottawa	800.00
1953	Survey of Cornwall Area	600.00
1954	Survey of St. Lawrence Seaway Area	800.00
1955	Furnishings, St. Paul's, Lively	1,200.00
1956	Student Chapel and Service Centre, Toronto	1,500.00
1957	Elliot Lake Mission	1,000.00
1958	Student Chapel and Service Centre, Toronto	1,200.00
1959	Mount Calvary, Ottawa	1,000.00
	Lutheran Deaconess Association	200.00
1960	Church Extension Fund, Lutheran Church — England	1,000.00
1961	Redeemer, Sudbury	1,132.00
1962	Zion, Wabewawa	1,300.00
1963	Church Extension Fund, Lutheran Church — England	1,300.00
1964	Immanuel, Georgetown	1,000.00
	Motor Bike, Nigeria	300.00
1965	Chapel, St. Mark's, Hanmer	1,000.00
1966	Lutheran Hour, French Language, Quebec, Canada	1,000.00
	Mission for Deaf, Milton and Belleville	400.00

	Total	**$11,400.00**

LOUISIANA DISTRICT

1946	Trailer	$ 3,000.00
1948	Automobile for Trailer	2,250.00
1951	Trinity (Colored), Shreveport	3,000.00
1952	L. S. U. Student Center, Baton Rouge	3,000.00
1953	Gethsemane, Chalmette	2,705.34
1954	Redeemer School, Jackson, Miss.	2,904.06
1955	Trinity, Maplewood	3,100.00

1956	Bethany School, Slidell	3,000.00
1957	St. Mark's, Baton Rouge	2,611.49
1958	Faith School, Harahan	2,594.50
1959	Furnishings, Grace, Houma	1,300.00
	Furnishings, Faith, Greenville, Miss.	1,300.00
1960	Furnishings, Grace, Houma	1,483.10
	Furnishings, Faith, Greenville, Miss.	1,483.10
1961—62	Our Savior, Shreveport	2,856.54
	University Lutheran Chapel, LSU, Baton Rouge	2,856.54
1963—64	Student Center, Lafayette	2,735.91
	Scholarships	2,735.91
1965—66	Student Center, Hammond	2,725.69
	Good Shepherd, Westwego-Marrero	2,725.68
1966—68	First, Natchez, Miss.	*____
	Immanuel, Bossier City	*____

Total   **$50,367.86**

* Amount of grant depends on total received to 1968.

MANITOBA AND SASKATCHEWAN DISTRICT

1954—55	Mount Calvary, Swift Current, Sask.	$1,000.00
	Our Saviour, Saskatoon, Sask.	1,000.00
	Sunday School Leaflets for Indians in W. Manitoba	160.00
1956—57	Our Redeemer, Portage la Prairie, Man.	1,500.00
	Grace, Birch River, Man.	500.00
1958—59	St. James, Carlyle, Sask.	1,000.00
	Good Shepherd, Transcona, Man.	500.00
	Faith, St. James, Man.	500.00
	Hope, Fort Gary, Man.	500.00
1960—62	Grace, Birch River, Man.	500.00
	St. James, Carlyle, Sask.	1,000.00
	Redeemer, Prince Albert, Sask.	2,000.00
	Mount Calvary, Flin Flon, Sask.	1,000.00
1962—64	Good Shepherd, Hudson Bay, Sask.	750.00
	Peace, Kamsack, Sask.	500.00
	Trinity, Moosomin, Sask.	2,000.00
	Holy Cross, Saskatoon, Sask.	1,250.00
1964—66	Kirfield Park Portable for furnishings	700.00
	Victoria Home for Girls, Regina, Sask.	1,350.00
	Glen Elm, Regina, Sask.	1,100.00
	Luther House, U. of Sask., Saskatoon, Sask.	1,350.00
1966—68	Bibles, Provincial Correctional Institute, Regina, Sask.	100.00
	Furnishings for Chapel, The Pas, Man.	1,250.00
	Mission to Deaf, Winnipeg, Man.	2,750.00
	Organ, Our Saviour, Fort Qu'Appelle, Sask.	400.00

Total   **$24,660.00**

MICHIGAN DISTRICT

1946—48	Service Federation	$ 3,225.00
	Braille Hymnal	1,000.00
1948—50	Home for Girls, Detroit (Colored)	1,000.00
	Service Federation	2,000.00

	Home for Aged, Monroe	2,000.00
	Chapel, Ann Arbor	1,200.00
1950—52	Children's Home, Bay City	500.00
	Student Aid for Boys	1,000.00
	Service Federation	3,500.00
	Home for Aged, Monroe	3,500.00
1952—54	Home for Aged, Monroe	5,000.00
	Children's Home, Bay City	1,000.00
	Bible Quiz Program	1,700.00
	District Missions	589.00
1954—56	Home for Girls, Detroit (Colored)	5,000.00
	Student Aid for Girls	4,000.00
	Chapel, East Lansing	2,000.00
	District Missions in Michigan	3,000.00
	Home for Aged, Monroe	1,000.00
	World Relief	1,000.00
1956—58	District Missions in Michigan	5,000.00
	Student Aid for Girls	5,000.00
	World Relief	1,000.00
	Home for Aged, Monroe	4,000.00
	Detroit Lutheran High School	500.00
	Home for Girls, Detroit (Colored)	3,000.00
	Student Center, W. Mich. College, Kalamazoo	2,500.00
	Scholarship, Deaf School, Detroit	2,000.00
	Scholarship, Children's Home, Bay City	1,500.00
1958—60	District Missions in Michigan	11,000.00
	Student Aid for Girls	5,000.00
	Needy Foreign Missions	5,000.00
	Mission Benevolences, Mich.	4,000.00
	World Relief	1,000.00
1960—62	District Missions	8,000.00
	Organ and Library, Concordia College, Ann Arbor	12,000.00
	Foreign Mission	6,000.00
	Student Aid for Girls	6,000.00
1962—64	District Missions	15,000.00
	Foreign Missions	5,000.00
	Student Aid for Girls	10,000.00
1964—66	District Missions	7,000.00
	Inner-City Missions	3,000.00
	Missionary Vacation Home, New Guinea	7,000.00
	Chapel Furnishings, CMU, Mount Pleasant	5,000.00
	Student Aid for Girls	8,000.00
1966—68	District Missions	10,000.00
	Inner-City Missions	5,000.00
	Furnishings, Chapel for Deaf, Flint	5,000.00
	Libraries for Overseas Seminaries	5,000.00
	Student Aid for Girls	8,000.00
	Furnishings, Mission House, St. Louis	3,100.00

Total **$221,814.00**

MINNESOTA DISTRICT

1944—46	Portable Chapel, Duluth	$ 5,000.00
1946—48	Executive Secretary for Institutional Work	5,000.00

	Minor Projects	1,000.00
	European Relief	2,400.00
1948—50	Chancel Furnishings, Chapel for Student Center	5,000.00
	For Completion of Portable Chapel	646.00
	Concordia College	550.00
	Missionary Bertram	150.00
1950—52	Chapel, Battle Lake Island Camp	8,000.00
	Chancel Furnishings, University Chapel	198.50
	Visual Aid Library	1,000.00
	Deaconess Scholarship	300.00
	Quonset Hut for Chapel in Japan	1,500.00
1952—54	Chapel, Zion, Atikokan, Ont., Canada (Minn. Dist.)	8,000.00
	Jeep for New Guinea Mission	3,000.00
	Furnishings, Mission House, St. Louis	2,000.00
	Scholarship, Ministerial	1,000.00
	Scholarship, Deaconess	600.00
	Lutheran Memorial Center Organ Fund	5,000.00
1954—56	Formosa Seminary Facilities	8,000.00
	Sunday School for Twin City Deaf	4,000.00
	University Lutheran Student Center	5,000.00
	Aeroplane for New Guinea	3,500.00
	Clinic, Monterrey, Mexico	2,000.00
	Scholarship, Korean Ministerial Student	1,500.00
	Scholarship, Deaconess	800.00
	St. Phillip's Negro Mission, Chattanooga, Tenn.	800.00
	Portable Parsonage (Trailer)	3,500.00
1956—58	Silver Bay-Beaver Bay Area Missions	16,000.00
	Nigeria, Africa, Hospital	8,000.00
	"Little Mexico" Mission, Los Angeles, Calif.	5,000.00
	Christian Growth Human Relations Institutes	2,000.00
	Scholarships, Deaconess	1,200.00
	Dakota Boys Ranch	1,500.00
	New Guinea, Amplifiers and Typewriters	1,200.00
1958—60	Deaf Chapel, Twin Cities	20,000.00
	Concordia College Dormitory Furnishings	19,000.00
	New Guinea Hospital	1,000.00
	Korea Seminary Library	5,000.00
	Scholarships, Deaconess	1,600.00
	Clinical Training for Chaplain Bert Streufert	1,600.00
	Chaplaincy Training Program	4,500.00
1960—62	Minnesota District Mission Expansion	10,000.00
	Dakota Boys Ranch, Two Buses	9,000.00
	District Missions	8,000.00
	Indian Missions in Minnesota	12,000.00
	Deaconess Scholarships	1,600.00
	Jeep for Dr. Ji, Korea	3,000.00
	Appreciation Gifts for Missionaries	2,000.00
	Scholarships, Students Preparing for Full-time Church Work	3,000.00
1962—64	Aid to Schools in Nigeria	15,000.00
	Aid to Missions to Blind	3,000.00
	Dormitory Furnishings, Concordia College, St. Paul	20,000.00
	Indian Missions in Minnesota	12,000.00

	Scholarships, Minnesota Students Preparing for Full-time Church Work	6,000.00
	Philippines, Training National Pastors	6,000.00
	Taiwan, Seminary Buildings	5,000.00
	Total	**$282,644.50**

MINNESOTA NORTH

1964—66	Scholarships, Minn. North Students for Ministry	$ 3,000.00
	Sunday School Picture Leaflets for Foreign Fields	500.00
	Equipment for Chaplain, Cambridge, Minn.	1,000.00
	Motor Scooter for Foreign Missionary	500.00
	Furnishings, Gloria Dei, Cold Spring	2,500.00
	Taiwan Seminary Classrooms	2,500.00
	Educational Wing, Bethlehem, Baudette	10,000.00
	Purchase Church Site, Manitouwadge, Ont.	2,000.00
1966—68	Share Cost of Site, El Salvador Mission, Caracas, Venezuela	8,000.00
	New Guinea, Toward Purchase of Airplane	5,000.00
	Philippines, Training of National Workers	3,000.00
	Scholarships, District Full-time Church Work	6,000.00
	Equipment for Braille Transcription Program	3,000.00
	Total	**$47,000.00**

MINNESOTA SOUTH

1964—66	Primary School for Orphanage, Moreira, Brazil	$ 1,000.00
	Classroom Expansion, Mission for Deaf, Minneapolis	20,000.00
	Motor Boat, Zacapa, Guatemala	500.00
	Chapel Furnishings, Mankato State College, Mankato	9,000.00
	District Mission Expansion	10,000.00
	Scholarships, District Students Preparing for Church Vocation	4,000.00
	Scholarships, Chaplaincy Clinical Training	500.00
1966—68	Two Jeep Pickups, Argentina	5,000.00
	Korea Lutheran Mission	12,000.00
	Tractor, New Guinea	6,800.00
	Chaplaincy Service, Mankato-St. Peter Area	5,000.00
	Scholarships, District Students Preparing for Church Vocation	5,000.00
	Concordia Tract Mission	700.00
	Deaf Mission	5,000.00
	Total	**$84,500.00**

MONTANA DISTRICT

1942—44	Movie Projector for Montana-Dakota District	$ 100.00
	Trailer Missions (4-Year Project)	400.00
1944—46	Trailer Missions	364.64
1946—48	Visual Aids for the Deaf	617.00
1948—50	Christian Day School (4-Year Project)	811.38
	Visual Aids for the Deaf (4-Year Project)	65.70
1950—52	Christian Day School	1,048.56
	Visual Aids for the Deaf	75.05

1952—54	Student Room at Missoula	1,446.92
	Literature Project	105.37
1954—56	Mission Assistance in Montana	1,495.52
	Altar Furnishings for Parks	56.49
1956—58	Kalispell Camp Project	1,390.81
	Books for University Libraries	95.60
1958—60	Student Aid Recruitment Fund	1,694.07
	Education Materials for Deaf	161.69
1960—62	Equipment, Glasgow and Superior Missions	1400.00
	Song Books in Braille for Blind	75.00
1962—64	Yellowtail Dam Mission (Fort Smith) Reallocated to Boulder Mission	1,999.61
	Snowy Mountain Campsite — Reallocated to Tract Missions	181.80
1964—66	Scholarships, Students Preparing for Church Vocations	2,170.08
	Christian Literature, Montana State Prison	325.08
1966—68	Building Fund, Chapel for Deaf, Great Falls	2,145.00
	Christian Literature, Montana State Prison	325.00

| | Total | **$18,550.37** |

NORTH DAKOTA DISTRICT

1942	North Dakota Missions	$ 171.16
1943	Christmas Cheer for War Prisoners	10.00
1944	Trailer Mission Camera	100.00
	Medical Endowment Fund, India	62.04
	"Lutheraner"	9.64
1945	Mission Talkie	248.43
	Mission Movie	25.00
	Mission Film	7.20
	Mission Survey	100.00
	Communion Set and Educational Materials for Deaf	100.00
1946	Medical Kits	1,084.00
	Postwar Religious Literature	74.00
	European Orphanages	590.00
1947	European Orphanages	560.00
	Refugee Clothing and Religious Literature	39.29
	Deaf Mission	100.00
	Garrison Dam Mission Project	1,750.00
	Fargo Office	120.00
1948	Books for School at Garrison Dam Mission	50.00
	LLL Camp Site	500.00
	Seminar for Gamma Delta	40.00
	Deaf Mission	150.00
	Building Fund for Japanese Missions	300.00
1949	Deaf Mission	130.00
	School Expenses for Displaced Person	150.00
	LLL Camp Site	400.00
	Deaconess Scholarship	125.00
	Student Centers	450.00
1950	Building Fund (Bismarck), Altar (Zion)	1,000.00
	Displaced Person	165.00
	Boys Ranch, Mapleton	100.00
	Visual Aids at Grafton School for Feeble-Minded	100.00

	Student Center	200.00
	LLL Camp Site	1,000.00
	Deaconess Scholarship	175.00
	Lutheran Welfare, Fargo	1,839.37
1951	Deaconess Scholarship	150.00
	Deaf Chapel, Devils Lake	97.65
	Gamma Delta	178.00
1952	Gamma Delta Club Room, Fargo	3,000.00
1953	Deaf Chapel, Devils Lake	1,350.00
	Convention Offering (Deaf Chapel)	384.36
	Deaf Chapel, Devils Lake	71.25
1954	Furnishings, Gamma Delta House, Grand Forks	3,000.00
1955	Furnishings, Boys Ranch	3,000.00
1956	Deaconess Worker at Grafton State School for	
	Mentally Retarded	3,000.00
1957	St. Mark's, Minot	1,500.00
	Messiah, Mandan	1,500.00
	Deaconess Scholarship	150.00
1958	Furnishings for New Unit of Boys Ranch	3,000.00
1959	Religious Teacher at Grafton State School	3,000.00
	Student Scholarship Fund	837.50
	Ministry to Migrants of Red River Valley	837.50
1960—62	Immanuel, Lynch	3,000.00
	House of Mercy, Fargo	3,000.00
	District Scholarship Fund	1,350.00
1962—64	Wittenberg Student Chapel, Grand Forks	3,000.00
	House of Mercy, Fargo	3,000.00
	Dakota Boys Ranch, Minot	1,375.00
	Deaconess Scholarship Fund	350.00
1964—66	Ambassadors for Christ	3,000.00
	Dakota Boys Ranch	1,800.00
	Deaconess Scholarship Fund	1,500.00
	St. Andrew's, West Fargo	1,150.00
	Student Chapel, Grand Forks	300.00
1966—68	Chapel, Valparaiso, Chile	3,000.00
	Mill Neck Manor School for Deaf, Mill Neck, N. Y.	3,000.00
	Chapel for Deaf, Devils Lake	1,500.00
	Scholarship, Springfield Seminary Student	1,500.00
	Messengers of Christ	460.00

Total	**$69,366.39**

NORTH WISCONSIN DISTRICT

1944—46	Literature for Blind	$ 1,000.00
1946—48	Mohammedan Missions	5,000.00
1948—50	Camp Luther (District Camp)	3,500.00
	Lutheran Deaconess Association	2,000.00
1950—52	Lutheran Hour Broadcast, Luxemburg, Germany	4,000.00
	Parsonage, Puerto Barrios, Guatemala	1,600.00
1952—54	Equipment for Bush Hospital, New Guinea	8,000.00
	Lutheran Braille Workers (Printing Presses)	3,000.00
1954—56	Bethesda Lutheran Home, Watertown	15,000.00
	Equipment for Hospital, Ambur, India	5,000.00

1956—58	Chapel & Student Center, State Coll., River Falls	16,000.00
	Japanese Missions	1,000.00
1958—60	Chapel and Education Unit, State School for Deaf, Delavan	15,000.00
	Dakota Boys Ranch, Minot, N. Dak.	500.00
1949—59	Additional Gifts to Camp Luther	1,805.28
	Additional Gifts to Home Missions	6,100.00
1960—62	Hong Kong Scholarship Fund	8,000.00
	University Chapel Expansion, Madison	10,000.00
	District Church Extension Fund	1,500.00
1962—64	Caribbean Area, Training Program for Pastors	8,000.00
	Bethesda Lutheran Home, Watertown	6,000.00
	Lutheran Children's Friend Society, Wauwatosa	6,000.00
	Language Laboratory, Concordia, Milwaukee	4,000.00
1964—66	Lutheran Braille Workers, Inc.	5,000.00
	John of Beverley Workbooks for Deaf	2,000.00
	Clinical Training of Pastors for Institutional Missions	5,000.00
	Salvation by Publication, South America	6,000.00
	Equipment, District Missions	7,000.00
1960—65	Deaconess Scholarship Fund	600.00
1960—67	Additional Gifts to District Missions	7,000.00
1966—68	Perkins Braillewriters for Transcribers of N. and S. Wis. Districts	2,500.00
	Site Purchase, Campus Ministry, Stevens Point	10,000.00
	Total	**$177,105.28**

NORTHERN ILLINOIS DISTRICT

1942—43	District Mission Churches	$10,000.00
1944	Equipment for District Missions	5,000.00
1945—47	Typewriters for Missionaries, South America	400.00
	Child Rehabilitation in Europe	20,000.00
	Library for the Blind	1,000.00
1948	Negro Missions, Chicago South Side	10,000.00
1949	Missionary's Home, Japan	10,000.00
1950—51	Portable Chapel for District	10,000.00
1952	Retreat for Missionaries in Philippines	5,000.00
1953	Equipment for District Missions	15,000.00
1954	Missionaries' Residence, Chia-yi, Formosa	3,500.00
	Student Residence, Bible Institute, Monterrey, Mexico	9,000.00
1955	Parsonage for District Institutional Missionary	15,000.00
1956	District Mission Equipment Fund	15,000.00
1957	Expansion of Seminary in India	15,000.00
1958	Missionary Residence, Korea	15,000.00
1959	Zion, Fairbanks, Alaska	15,000.00
1960	Grace, Streamwood	15,000.00
1961	Meadowdale Mission, No. Illinois	15,000.00
1962	Chicago Inner-City Missions	17,500.00
1963	Printshop and Equipment, New Guinea	17,500.00
1964	Town-Gown Facility, De Kalb	20,000.00
1965	Capital Fund for Robert Taylor Homes-Altgelt Gardens — Christ the King — No. Illinois	20,000.00
1966	Redeemer, Hampton Park	10,000.00
	Messengers of Christ	10,000.00

1967	Chapel Site, Caracas, Venezuela	10,000.00
	Duplex Residence, First Immanuel, Chicago	10,000.00
	Total	**$318,900.00**

NORTHERN NEBRASKA DISTRICT

1942	Institutional Mission Work, Omaha	$ 250.00
1944	City Missions, Omaha	1,500.00
1946	Postwar European Project of LWML	1,785.00
1947	Chapel, Faith, Omaha	2,500.00
1948	Chapel, St. Paul's, Thermopolis, Wyo.	5,200.00
1950	Chapel, Trinity, Casper Wyo.	6,150.00
1952	Chapel, Hope, South Sioux City	9,600.00
1954	Chapel, Bethel, Lander, Wyo.	10,500.00
1956	Chapel, Zion, Douglas, Wyo.	11,500.00
1958—60	Good Shepherd, Fremont	12,150.00
1960—62	Christ the King, Cody, Wyo.	13,607.06
1962—64	Faith, Gering	15,500.00
1964—66	First, Plattsmouth	15,500.00
	Total	**$105,742.06**

OHIO DISTRICT

1964	Faith, Avon	$ 4,000.00
	Holy Cross for Deaf, Columbus	4,000.00
	Our Savior, Newark	4,000.00
	Pilgrim, Granville	4,000.00
	St. Mark, Chesterland	4,000.00
	St. Matthew, Huber Heights	4,000.00
	Hough Avenue Mission Project, Cleveland	3,000.00
	American Bible Society	500.00
1966	Mount Calvary, Antwerp	2,900.00
	Trinity, Tiffin	2,800.00
	Faith, Mansfield	2,900.00
	Holy Cross, Madison	2,800.00
	Our Savior, Chillicothe	2,800.00
	Redeemer, Sidney	2,800.00
	Mission Project (M.O.U.L.D.), Cincinnati	1,000.00
	American Bible Society	300.00
	Total	**$45,800.00**

OKLAHOMA DISTRICT

1942	Children's Friend Society	$ 34.66
	Parish Center, Muskogee	186.99
	Parish Center, Oklahoma City	60.00
	Lutheran Children's Home	131.34
1943	Children's Friend Society	41.01
	Hope School, Muskogee	25.00
	Parish Center, Oklahoma City	60.00
	Parish Center, Muskogee	113.01
1944	Parish Center, Muskogee	228.95
	Parish Center, Oklahoma City	120.00

	Children's Friend Society	47.00
1945	Children's Friend Society	38.00
	Service Center, Lawton	360.00
	Service Center, Oklahoma City	120.00
	Parish Center, Muskogee	144.41
1946	Children's Friend Society	225.70
	Medical Kits and Supplies	156.31
	Furnishings, Trinity, Norman	1,000.00
1947	Children's Friend Society	148.00
	European Orphanage	128.00
	Furnishings, Zion, Stillwater	1,000.00
	American Bible Society	67.33
	Trailer House	1,000.00
1948	Chancel, Hope, Muskogee	1,000.00
1949	Chancel, Mount Calvary, Watonga	500.00
	Chancel, St. Paul's, Texhoma	500.00
1950	Chancel, Good Shepherd, Midwest City	500.00
	Chancel, Our Savior, Tulsa	500.00
1951	Deaconess Scholarship	250.00
1952	Redeemer, Claremore	500.00
	Deaconess Scholarships	500.00
	Chancel, Christ, Oklahoma City	500.00
	Chancel, Mount Olive, Miami	500.00
	Chancel, Christ, Shattuck	500.00
	Chancel, First, Ada	500.00
	Camp Lutherhoma	500.00
1953	Deaconess Scholarships	500.00
	Chancel, Redeemer, Oklahoma City	500.00
1954	Deaconess Scholarships	500.00
	Chancel, Prince of Peace, Tulsa	500.00
	Chancel, Christ the Redeemer, Tulsa	500.00
	Zion, Stillwater	1,000.00
1955	Lutherhoma	500.00
	Student Center, Norman	1,000.00
	Deaconess Scholarship	125.00
	Chancel, Messiah, Oklahoma City	500.00
1956	Deaconess Scholarship	125.00
	Chancel, St. John's, Pryor	500.00
	Lutherhoma	500.00
	Student Center, Norman	1,000.00
1958	Student Center, Norman	1,500.00
	Deaconess Scholarship	500.00
	Chancel, Christ, Elk City	500.00
	Chancel, Our Savior, Altus	500.00
1959	Student Center, Norman	1,000.00
	Ministerial Scholarships	600.00
	Church Extension Fund	1,000.00
1960—62	Scholarships, Ministers and Teachers	1,200.00
	Scholarships, Girl Churchworkers	2,000.00
	Chancel Furnishings, Our Savior, Oklahoma City	500.00
	Senior Citizens, Inc., Oklahoma City	1,500.00
	Concordia Tract Mission	1,500.00
1962—64	Scholarships, Ministers and Teachers	1,200.00
	Scholarships, Girl Churchworkers	2,000.00

	District Church Extension Fund	1,500.00
1964—66	Scholarships, Ministers and Teachers	1,800.00
	Scholarships, Girl Churchworkers	2,500.00
	University Church and Student Center, Norman	2,000.00
	Chancel Furnishings, University Church, Norman	500.00
	Chancel, Holy Cross, Lawton	500.00
	Chancel, Peace, Edmond	500.00
	Lutheran Deaconess Association	500.00
	Lutheran Social Services	500.00
1966—68	District Student Aid Fund	4,000.00
	Chancel Furnishings, Subsidized Congregations	1,000.00
	Group Foster Home, Tulsa	500.00
	Ambassadors for Christ Program	500.00

| | Total | **$51,735.71** |

ONTARIO DISTRICT

1949—52	Trinity, Toronto	$ 3,000.00
	Scholarship, Lutheran Deaconess Association	300.00
1952—54	Bethel (German), Kitchener	4,000.00
	Sunday School Material for Two Missions	25.00
1954—56	Our Saviour, Ottawa	1,000.00
	Parsonage, St. Paul's, Kirkland Lake	1,000.00
	Chapel-Parsonage, Grace, St. Catharines	1,000.00
	Grace, West Lorne	1,000.00
1956—58	Mount Calvary, Ottawa	1,000.00
	St. Luke's, Tillsonburg	1,000.00
	University Lutheran Chapel, Toronto	1,500.00
	Our Saviour, Thistletown	1,000.00
1958—60	Our Saviour, London	2,000.00
	Sunday School Equipment, Grace, Elliott Lake	500.00
	Rev. E. Hahn, Muslim Mission, India (Special)	500.00
	Medical Missions — Shipping of Medical Samples	500.00
	Orphanage, Moreira, Brazil	200.00
1960—62	Building, Our Saviour, London	1,500.00
	Prince of Peace, Burlington	1,500.00
	Church Furnishings, Redeemer, St. Thomas	1,000.00
	St. John's, Mount Forest	1,000.00
1962—64	Messiah, Stony Creek	1,750.00
	Gethsemane, Windsor	1,750.00
	Redeemer, Sudbury	1,750.00
	Faith, Kitchener	250.00
1964—66	Motorcycles, New Guinea Workers	2,000.00
	Scholarship, National Student, Brazil	1,500.00
	Scholarship, Medical Mission National Student, Nigeria	500.00
	Braillewriters for Workers in Ontario	500.00
	Immanuel, Georgetown	1,750.00
	School Equipment, School for Missionaries' Children, Japan	500.00
	Communion Sets for New Missions, Ontario	750.00
	Christ Our King, Erindale	1,500.00
1966—67	Equipment, Schools for Deaf, Belleville and Milton	500.00
	Audiovisual Equipment, Peace, Exeter	200.00
	Scooter, Missionary in India	950.00

Mission Churches — London, St. Catharines,		
Hamilton, and Kitchener ($1,000 each)		4,000.00
St. Matthew's, Stratford		850.00

Total	**$45,525.00**

OREGON-WASHINGTON-IDAHO DISTRICT (1942)

1943	Furnishing of Lutheran Office, Portland, Oreg.	$ ——
1944	Circuit Rider	2,000.00
1946	Deaconess Scholarships	800.00

OREGON-WASHINGTON DISTRICT (1948)

1948—50	Support of Four Parish Workers	8,000.00
1952	Parish Workers	5,000.00

NORTHWEST DISTRICT (1952)

1952—54	Church Extension Fund	4,000.00
1954	Orphanage in Brazil	5,000.00

Total	**$24,800.00**

(Projects Continued in Reports of Oregon District and Washington District)

OREGON DISTRICT

1956—58	Parish Worker	$ 2,500.00
	Chapel in Southern Oregon	2,500.00
1958—60	Parish Worker	2,500.00
	Chapel and Parsonage, Philippines	2,500.00
	Reimbursement to Northwest District Church Extension	
	for Furnishings in Student Center, Eugene	875.00
1960—62	Children's Wing, Hospital, Eket, Nigeria	3,000.00
	Good Shepherd Lutheran Home, Terra Bella, Calif.	3,000.00
1962—64	Church Extension Fund for Chapel, First,	
	Lakeview, Oreg.	3,000.00
	Furnishings, Boarding School for Missionaries'	
	Children, Nigeria	1,500.00
	Campus Program, U. of Oregon, Eugene	1,500.00
	District Church Extension Fund	1,500.00
1964—66	Chapel, Faith, Monmouth, Oreg.	3,500.00
	Chapels, Juneau and Chugiak, Alaska	3,500.00
1966—68	Scholarships, Student Aid	2,500.00
	District Campus Work, Promotion	1,500.00
	Furnishings, Six New Chapels ($500 each)	3,000.00
	Clinical Training for District Chaplains	1,000.00

Total	**$39,375.00**

SOUTH DAKOTA DISTRICT

1944	Organ, Memorial, Sioux Falls	$ 250.00
1945	Gas Furnace, St. Paul, Spearfish	450.00
	European Relief (Clothing and Food)	——
1946—50	Trinity Deaf Chapel, Sioux Falls	10,000.00
1950—51	Deaconess Scholarships	300.00

1951—52	Organ, Student Chapel, Concordia, Vermillion	3,000.00
	Deaconess Scholarship	150.00
1952—53	Student Center, Mount Calvary, Brookings	3,000.00
	Family Worship Hour	125.00
	Deaconess Scholarship	175.00
1953—54	St. Luke, Rapid City	3,000.00
	Deaconess Scholarship	175.00
	Family Worship Hour	125.00
1954—55	South Dakota Children's Benevolent Association	3,000.00
1955—56	Indian Missions in South Dakota	3,000.00
	Deaconess Scholarship	125.00
1956—57	Trinity, Edgemont	3,000.00
	Deaconess Scholarship	125.00
1957—58	Indian Missions in South Dakota	3,000.00
	Deaconess Scholarship	175.00
	Trinity Deaf, Sioux Falls	125.00
1958—59	Furnishings, Christ, Winner	3,000.00
	Deaconess Scholarship	175.00
1959—60	Chapel Furnishings, Mount Calvary, Brookings	3,500.00
	Deaconess Scholarship	175.00
1960—61	Scholarship for Training Institutional Chaplains	3,500.00
1961—62	Furnishings, Ascension, Rapid City	3,500.00
1962—63	Hospital at Eket; Books and Supplies for Seminary	
	at Obot Idim, Nigeria	3,500.00
1963—64	Ambassadors for Christ	4,000.00
1964—65	Remodel and Refurnish Student Center,	
	U. of S. Dak., Vermillion	4,000.00
	Memorial for Missionary Olive Gruen,	
	Educational Materials, Taiwan	500.00
1965—66	Trailer Chapel, Northwest Mission, Arpan	4,500.00
1966—67	Furnishings, Hospice House, Southern State	
	College, Springfield	4,500.00
1960—67	Seven Deaconess Scholarships at $225	1,575.00

Total	**$69,725.00**

SOUTH WISCONSIN DISTRICT

1948	Four District Missions, $500 Each	$ 2,000.00
	Organ for a District Mission	300.00
1949	Four District Missions, $500 Each	2,000.00
	Classroom Furnishings for a District Mission	400.00
1950	Three District Missions, $1,000 Each	3,000.00
1951	Three District Missions, $500 Each	1,500.00
	Two District Missions, $250 Each	500.00
1952	One District Mission	1,000.00
	Organ for a District Mission	100.00
	Missions in Nigeria, Africa	302.00
1952—54	Two Students at St. Louis Seminary, $250 Each	500.00
	Organ for a District Mission	150.00
	Chapel for Deaf, Delavan	500.00
	Six District Missions, $800 Each	4,800.00
1954—56	Missions in India	370.00
	Pastor Hubert Brueggemann Memorial,	
	"This Is the Life"	100.00

	Chapel for Deaf, Delavan	4,787.62
	Four Students at Formosa Seminary, $300 Each	1,200.00
	Electric Organ, St. Luke's, Richland Center	1,100.00
	Concordia College, Milwaukee	500.00
	Miss Lydia Schultz Memorial — Deaconess Assn.	25.00
	Pastor Edward Schmidt Memorial, District Church Extension Fund	100.00
	Missions in Japan	345.72
1956—58	Agricultural Missions Among Lepers, Philippines	3,000.00
	Medical Missions in Philippines	3,000.00
	New District Missions	4,000.00
	District Church Extension Fund	3,869.40
	Mrs. Otto Hein Memorial — Concordia College, Milwaukee	100.00
	Missions in Philippines	278.72
1958—60	Silent Church, Madison	2,000.00
	Bethesda Home, Watertown	2,000.00
	Four Scholarships for Students (Teacher)	4,000.00
	Missions in Korea	2,000.00
	Medical Missions in New Guinea	2,000.00
	Silent Church, Madison	2,000.00
	District Church Extension Fund	691.42
1961	Retreat Offering: Concordia Tract Mission	1,200.00
1960—62	District Camp	8,000.00
	Scholarships:	
	Deaconess Students	2,000.00
	Women (Teacher Training)	3,000.00
	Men (Ministerial or Teacher Training)	3,000.00
	Educational Grants:	
	Visual Aid Equipment, Korea	2,500.00
	Books for Seminary Libraries, Formosa (Taiwan) and Hong Kong	3,000.00
	Student Emergency Fund, Springfield Seminary	2,500.00
1962	Retreat Offering: Evangelism Film for District and John of Beverley Workbooks for Deaf	1,076.00
1962—64	Rooftop Schools, Hong Kong	2,500.00
	Medical Scholarships	2,000.00
	Training Program, Guatemala	6,000.00
	District Scholarships	7,000.00
	Chapel and Rooms, U. of Wis.	5,000.00
	Sol-Fa Hymnal, Nigeria	1,500.00
	District Camp	5,000.00
	Obera, Misiones, Argentina	5,000.00
	Dakota Boys Ranch, Minot, N. Dak.	1,000.00
1964—66	District Scholarships	5,000.00
	Furnishings for Campus Houses, Milwaukee Oshkosh, Whitewater, Madison	11,000.00
	Clinical Training for Two Pastors, — Institutional Chaplaincy	5,000.00
	Ministry to Latin Americans in Milwaukee	3,000.00
	Chancel Furnishings, Mission Churches	6,000.00
	Lutheran Servicemen's Library, Korea	5,000.00
1966—68	Christian Conference Grounds, Korea	5,000.00
	Clinics for Medical Missionaries in New Guinea	500.00

District Scholarships	4,000.00
Parochial School, First Lutheran, San Salvador, El Salvador	3,000.00
Furlough to Brazil for Missionary Pacheco, Missionary to Spanish-Americans, Milwaukee	1,000.00
Church, Caracas, Venezuela	2,000.00
Clinical Education, for Chaplaincy Pastors	5,000.00
Ministry to Seamen	3,000.00
Chancel Furnishings, Mission Churches	6,000.00
Prince of Peace Volunteers	500.00

Total   **$180,795.88**

SOUTHEASTERN DISTRICT

(Since 1959 Carolina)

1948	Our Savior, Raleigh, N. C.	$ 3,000.00
1950	St. John's, Winston-Salem, N. C.	2,000.00
1952	Bethlehem, Aiken, S. C.	3,000.00
1954	Faith, Kinston, N. C.	3,500.00
	Good Shepherd, Greenville, S. C.	2,500.00
1956	Holy Trinity, Columbia, S. C.	2,500.00
1958	Holy Trinity, Statesville, N. C.	3,000.00
	Reformation, Charlotte, N. C.	2,000.00
	Scholarships for Ministerial, Teacher, Deaconess Students	1,000.00

Total   **$22,500.00**

SOUTHERN CALIFORNIA DISTRICT

1946—48	Trinity, Indio, Calif.	$ 6,000.00
1948—50	Zion, Blythe, Calif.	6,000.00
1950—52	Zion, Victorville, Calif.	5,000.00
1952—54	Grace, Bishop, Calif.	6,000.00
1954—56	Immanuel, Chino, Calif.	3,500.00
	Calexico Mission	5,000.00
1956—58	Immanuel, Twenty-Nine Palms	5,000.00
1958—60	Church Extension Grant for Perris, Calif.	5,500.00
	Church Extension Grant for Santa Paula, Ojai, Calif.	5,500.00
	Deaconess Scholarship	800.00
1960—61	Dr. Walter A. Maier High School, Los Angeles	4,720.00
	Pilgrim Deaf, Los Angeles	4,720.00
	Scholarship, Mexican Ministerial Student	1,180.00
	District Institutional Chaplaincy Training	1,180.00
1962—64	UCLA Student Chapel	6,366.00
	Arrowhead Lutheran Camp	6,366.00
	Ministry to Deaf, Southern California	1,592.00
	Concordia Tract Mission	1,592.00
1964—66	USC Student Chapel	5,383.23
	Lutheran Braille Workers, Inc.	5,383.23
	Building Fund for Mexicali, Mexico	5,383.23
	District Student Aid Fund	897.24
	Scholarships, Selma, Ala., Academy	897.24

1966—67	Mission, Mexicali, Mexico	* 2,788.00
	Good Shepherd Home of the West and Arizona State	* 2,763.00
	Pastoral Clinical Training and Student Aid	* 460.53

| | Total | **$99,971.70** |

* To March 1967

SOUTHERN ILLINOIS DISTRICT

1943—44	Furnishings for Mission Stations	$ 1,045.00
1944—46	Furnishings for Mission Stations	2,375.00
1946—48	Furnishings for Mission Stations	2,375.00
	Trailer Mission	500.00
	European Relief	500.00
1948—50	Chapel, Our Savior, Carbondale	10,000.00
	Furnishings for Mission Stations	2,421.76
	Negro Mission Properties	4,600.00
	Lutheran Deaconess Association	250.00
1950—52	St. John's, East St. Louis	10,000.00
	Physical Needs of Mission Stations	1,682.50
1952—54	Chapels at Highland and Fairfield	11,583.12
	Physical Needs of Mission Stations	1,947.40
	Lutheran Deaconess Association	300.00
1954—56	Chapels at Carmi and Hillsboro	10,679.24
	Physical Needs of Mission Stations	3,789.45
	Lutheran Deaconess Association	300.00
1956—58	Chapels at Godfrey and McLeansboro	12,758.88
	Physical Needs of Mission Stations	2,241.49
	Lutheran Deaconess Association	300.00
1960—62	Grants to Nine District Missions	2,700.00
	Deaconess Scholarship Fund	300.00
	Student Emergency Fund, Springfield Seminary	2,000.00
	Hope, Mount Carmel	12,000.00
1962—64	St. Paul's, Hardin	15,000.00
	Grants to Eight Mission Stations	2,214.90
	Lutheran Deaconess Scholarship Fund	350.00
1964—66	S. I. U. Chapel, Carbondale	15,000.00
	Ambassadors for Christ	3,000.00
	Grants to Four Mission Stations	1,066.75
	Foreign Missions (Offering, Day of Prayer)	413.06
	Lutheran Deaconess Scholarship Fund	350.00
1966—68	Building Project, Our Savior, Carmi	15,000.00
	Lutheran Deaconess Scholarship Fund	350.00

| | Total | **$149,393.55** |

SOUTHERN NEBRASKA DISTRICT

1943—44	Literature, Institutional Mission Work	
	Furnishings, Wyoming and Nebraska	
	Mission Chapels	
	Furnishings, Nebraska U. Chapel	$ 1,200.00
1945—46	Furnishings, Mission Chapels	
	European Relief	3,000.00
1947—48	Organ, Nebraska U. Chapel	5,000.00

1949—50	Equipment, Student Center, U. of Wyoming	
	Furnishings, for Mission Chapels	5,000.00
1951—52	Chapel Furnishings, C. T. C., Seward	
	Furnishings for Mission Chapels	5,000.00
1953—54	Assistance in Erection of Two Chapels	5,000.00
1955—56	Radio Mission Program	
	Furnishings for Mission Chapels	
	Educational Scholarships	
	Assistance in Erection of Two Chapels	8,000.00
1957—58	Educational Scholarships	
	Laundry Equipment, Nigerian Mission	
	Grant to Church Extension Fund	
	Assistance in Renovation of One Mission	
	Chapel and Furnishings for One Mission	10,000.00
1959—60	Furniture for Children's Service Society Office	2,000.00
	Minor Grants, Miscellaneous Equipment,	
	Institutional Missions	2,108.45
	Pews, Christ, St. Paul	2,000.00
	Scholarships: District Students — Four at $250,	
	Two at $500	2,000.00
	District Church Extension Fund	2,000.00
	Royal Gorge Dam Mission near Dutch John, Utah	2,000.00
1961—62	Printing Press, Nigeria	3,000.00
	Scholarships:	
	Eight at $200, Concordia Teachers College, Seward	
	Four at $100, St. John's College, Winfield, Kans.	
	One of $200, Concordia Senior College,	
	Fort Wayne, Ind.	
	Four at $50 and One of $200, Concordia	
	Seminary, St. Louis	
	Two at $200, Concordia Seminary, Springfield	3,000.00
	Furnishings, Student Center, Kearney	1,500.00
	Chancel and Worship Center, Student Center,	
	Laramie, Wyo.	1,500.00
	Redeemer, Jackson, Wyo.	3,000.00
	90 subscriptions to *Lutheran Witness* and *Concordia*	
	Theological Monthly for Pastors in South America	824.42
1963—64	Educational Scholarships, 22 District Students	4,000.00
	Special Needs, New Guinea	1,500.00
	Program for Mentally Retarded and Handicapped	
	Children of District	1,500.00
	Chapel Furnishings, Saratoga, Wyo.	1,500.00
	Dakota Boys Ranch, Minot, N. Dak.	1,500.00
	Student Center, U. of Nebr., Lincoln	1,500.00
	Three Motor Scooters, Pastors in India	1,500.00
	96 2-yr. Subscriptions to *Lutheran Witness* and	
	Concordia Theological Monthly, Missionaries in	
	South America	919.56
1965—66	Educational Scholarships, 17 District Students	2,000.00
	Diagnostic Equipment, Wandoor, India, Hospital,	
	and 80 Subscriptions to *Lutheran Witness* or *Der*	
	Lutheraner, Missionaries in South America	1,500.00
	Bethesda Lutheran Home, Watertown, Wis.	1,500.00
	Korean Missions	1,500.00

	Campus Ministry	1,500.00
	Institutional Chaplains Fund	1,500.00
	Emmanuel, Green River, Wyo.	1,500.00
	Ambassadors for Christ, Recruitment Training Seminars	1,500.00
	Mission Furnishings Fund	1,500.00
1966—68	Scholarships, District Students	4,000.00
	Scholarships, South America Students	1,500.00
	Institutional Ministries	2,000.00
	Mission Selected from Projects Catalog	1,500.00
	Campus Ministries	2,000.00
	American Bible Society	2,000.00
	Concordia Tract Mission	2,000.00

	Total	**$110,052.43**

TEXAS DISTRICT

1942—44	Beautification, Concordia College Chapel, Austin	$ 1,000.00
1944—46	District Auto Fund	1,000.00
	Chapel Organ, Concordia College, Austin	500.00
1946—48	Walther League Camp, La Grange	2,000.00
	Mexican Missions of Texas	2,000.00
	Concordia College Chapel, Austin	500.00
	European Relief	500.00
1948—50	Negro Mission, Dallas, Tex.	2,000.00
	Walther League Camp, La Grange	2,000.00
	Work Among Deaf of Texas	500.00
	Institutional Missionary, Houston	250.00
	Lutheran Deaconess Scholarship	250.00
1950—52	Student Activity Building, Denton	5,000.00
	Walther League Camp, La Grange	100.00
1952—54	Spanish Mission, Harlingen	10,000.00
	Walther League Camp, La Grange	500.00
	Student Activity Building, Denton	500.00
1954—56	Girls Dormitory, Concordia College, Austin	10,000.00
1956—58	Texas Home for Aged Work	5,000.00
	Spanish Mission, Laredo	3,000.00
	Deaf Work in Texas	2,000.00
1958—60	Texas Tech Student Center, Lubbock	6,000.00
	Student Activity Building, Texas A & M College, College Station	6,000.00
1960—62	Chapel, U. of Texas, Austin	7,000.00
	Redeemer, Nacogdoches, and Student Chapel, Austin College, Nacogdoches	7,000.00
1962—64	Tarleton State College Chapel and Student Center, Stephenville	9,000.00
	Matamoros Mission, Matamoros, Mexico	9,000.00
1964—66	Land Purchase for Chapel and Student Center, U. of West Texas, Canyon	10,000.00
	Chapel and Student Center, Texas A & M, College Station	10,000.00
	District Church Extension Fund	1,000.00
	Church Furnishings, Faith, Post	1,000.00
	Woman Counselor for Two State Colleges, Denton	2,250.00
	Vicar for Hospital Work, Galveston	1,600.00

1966—68	Faith, Ozona	10,000.00
	Negro Mission, Port Arthur	20,000.00
	Inner City Mission Work, Houston	5,000.00
	Total	**$152,850.00**

UTAH-IDAHO DISTRICT

1948—50	Chancel Furniture, St. Paul's, Boise, Idaho	$ 1,000.00
1950—52	Altar Furniture and Linens, Good Shepherd, Arco, Idaho	30.00
	Slide Projector and Screen, Zion, Burley, Idaho	30.00
	Building Program, Redeemer, Salt Lake City, Utah	550.00
	Chairs, Concordia, Weiser, Idaho	200.00
	Paint, Calvary, Gooding, Idaho	42.00
	Chancel Furnishings, Christ, Wendell, Idaho	200.00
	Chairs, First, Tooele, Utah	100.00
1952—54	Chairs, Good Shepherd, Boise, Idaho	360.00
	Building Program, Zion, Burley, Idaho	300.00
	Chairs, Concordia, Weiser, Idaho	75.00
	Chairs, First, Tooele, Utah	200.00
	1954 Scholarship for Girl	100.00
1954—56	1955 Scholarship for Boy	100.00
	1956 Scholarship for Girl	100.00
	1956 Scholarship for Boy	100.00
	Hymnbooks, Faith, Mountain Home, Idaho	100.00
	Chancel Furnishings, Trinity, Layton, Utah	300.00
	School Furnishings, Christ, Murray, Utah	400.00
	Church Furnishings, Zion, Burley, Idaho	200.00
1956—58	Faith, Pocatello, Idaho	700.00
	Building Program, Zion, Burley, Idaho	250.00
	Pews and Floor Covering, Calvary, Gooding, Idaho	700.00
	1957 Scholarships for Boys at $100	200.00
1958—59	Walther League Convention Grant	100.00
	Four Scholarships at $250	1,000.00
	Chairs, Zion, Burley, Idaho	200.00
	Pews, Hope, Idaho Falls, Idaho	500.00
	Organ, Good Shepherd, Boise, Idaho	250.00
	Hymnals, Calvary, Salt Lake City, Utah	112.50
1960—62	Four Scholarships, District Students for Church Professions	1,600.00
	Organ, Faith, Mountain Home, Idaho	600.00
	Advertising, Montpelier, Idaho	25.00
	Altar Books, Redeemer, Kimberly, Idaho	60.00
1962—64	Scholarships for Full-Time Church Work	1,600.00
	Chancel Furnishings, Holy Trinity, Logan, Utah	1,200.00
1964—66	Scholarships, District Students for Church Professions	1,600.00
	Organ, St. Paul's, Aberdeen, Idaho	250.00
	Church Sign, First, Tooele, Utah	125.00
1966—68	Scholarships, District Students	1,600.00
	Visual Aids for Deaf	300.00
	Summer Worker at McCall, Idaho	1,000.00
	Hymnals, Bibles, Communion Ware, Richfield, Utah	100.00
	Totals	**$18,564.50**

WASHINGTON DISTRICT
(Former Oregon-Washington)

1956—58	Furnishings for Chapel-Student Center, Pullman	$ 2,500.00
	Support of Parish Workers	2,500.00
1958—60	Furnishings for Mission Stations in Washington	3,000.00
	Campus Ministry	2,500.00
1960—62	Student Grants-in-Aid	3,000.00
	Campus Mission, U. of Wash., Seattle	3,000.00
1962—64	Student Grants-in-Aid	3,000.00
	Training Program, Pastors and Lay Workers in Caribbean Area	3,500.00
1964—66	Student Grants-in-Aid	3,500.00
	Enlarged Literature Program	3,500.00
	Chapel, Katherine Luther Home for Girls, Seattle	1,000.00
1966—68	Furnishings, U. of Wash., Campus Chapel and Student Center, Seattle	2,000.00
	Subsidy for Lutheran Chaplain Service in Walla Walla Area	3,500.00
	Student Grants-in-Aid	3,500.00
	Visual Aids, Faith Deaf, Spokane	500.00
	Total	**$40,500.00**

WESTERN DISTRICT

1944	St. John's, Chillicothe, Mo.	$ 1,500.00
1945	Redeemer, Elizabethton, Tenn.	2,500.00
1946	St. John's, Fayetteville, Ark.	2,500.00
	Faith, Kirksville, Mo.	3,000.00
	Bethany, Erwin, Tenn.	2,000.00
1947	Bethany, Erwin, Tenn. (Second Grant)	3,000.00
	Hope, Mary Ridge, Overland, Mo.	2,000.00
1948	St. Michael's (Negro), Kinloch, Mo.	500.00
	Our Savior, Eldorado, Ark.	4,000.00
	First, Blytheville, Ark.	2,500.00
1949	First, Blytheville, Ark. (Second Grant)	1,500.00
1950	Bethlehem, Johnson City, Tenn.	5,000.00
	Bethany, Eldon, Mo.	2,000.00
	Christ Memorial, Affton, Mo.	5,000.00
1951	Faith, Oak Ridge, Tenn.	6,000.00
	St. John's, Fayetteville, Ark. (Second Grant)	1,000.00
	Our Master, Ferguson, Mo.	3,000.00
	Webster Gardens, Webster Groves, Mo.	3,000.00
	St. John's, Russellville, Ark.	2,500.00
1952	Conquest for Christ	1,000.00
	First, Neosho, Mo.	3,000.00
	Trinity, Clinton, Mo.	4,000.00
	First, Hot Springs, Ark.	2,500.00
	St. Philip's (Negro), Chattanooga, Tenn.	2,500.00
1953	Concordia, Sikeston, Mo.	3,000.00
	Atonement, Florissant, Mo.	3,000.00
	Holy Cross, Kansas City, Mo.	5,000.00
1954	Zion School, Poplar Bluff, Mo.	5,000.00
	St. Philip's (Negro), Chattanooga, Tenn. (Second Grant)	1,000.00
	St. Michael's (Negro), Kinloch, Mo. (Second Grant)	1,000.00

1955	Bethlehem, Warrensburg, Mo.	4,000.00
	Trinity, North Little Rock, Ark.	5,000.00
	Hope, Maryville, Mo.	5,000.00
	Trinity, Nevada, Mo.	6,000.00
1956	Grace, Versailles, Mo.	5,000.00
	Mount Calvary, Excelsior Springs, Mo.	5,000.00
1957	St. John's, Russellville, Ark. (Second Grant)	9,500.00
	First, Cleveland, Tenn.	9,500.00
	Trinity, Bristol, Tenn.	9,500.00
1958	Immanuel, Rolla, Mo.	9,500.00
	St. John's, Kansas City, Mo.	9,000.00
	Grace, Lamar, Mo.	9,000.00
1959	Ascension, Madison, Tenn.	9,000.00
	Transfiguration, St. Louis, Mo.	9,000.00
1960—62	Redeemer, Paragould, Ark.	3,250.00
	St. Paul's, Branson, Mo.	3,250.00
	St. Matthew's, Sullivan, Mo.	3,250.00
	Faith, Tullahoma, Tenn.	9,000.00
	St. Paul's, Fulton, Mo.	9,000.00
	Concordia, Kingsport, Tenn.	9,000.00
	Trinity, Louisiana, Mo.	3,250.00
1962—64	Holy Trinity, Bowling Green, Ky.	10,000.00
	Grace, Murfreesboro, Tenn.	10,000.00
	Trinity, Louisiana, Mo. (Second Grant)	5,000.00
	Holy Trinity, Rogers, Ark.	10,000.00
	Faith, Dexter, Mo.	10,000.00
	Hope, Maryville, Mo. (Second Grant)	5,000.00
1964—66	Faith, Magnolia, Ark.	5,000.00
	Mission Service Volunteer Program	5,000.00
	Faith, Hopkinsville, Ky.	10,000.00
	Timothy, Blue Springs, Mo.	10,000.00
	Faith, Waynesville, Mo.	10,000.00
	Transfiguration, St. Louis, Mo. (Second Grant)	10,000.00
	Campus, U. of Mo., Columbia	10,000.00
1966—68	Trinity, Columbia, Tenn.	10,000.00
	St. Paul's, West Memphis, Ark.	10,000.00
	Immanuel, Murray, Ky.	10,000.00
	Grants-in-Aid	5,000.00
	Good Shepherd, Memphis (Frayser), Tenn.	10,000.00
	Grace, Clarksville, Ark.	5,000.00
	Faith, Kirksville, Mo. (Second Grant)	10,000.00
	Special Gift for Furnishing St. Louis Missionaries' Furlough Home (Shower Gifts)	3,748.27
	Total	**$401,248.27**
	Total District Grants	**$4,699,262.15**
	Total International Grants	**$1,863,262.33**
		$6,562,524.48

Index

DATE DUE

MAY 15 72			
FEB 15 76			
FEB 15 78			
5/5/89			
MAR 14 94			
GAYLORD			PRINTED IN U.S.A